DISCURSIVE PSYCHOLOGY IN PRACTICE

D1414665

DISCURSIVE PSYCHOLOGY IN PRACTICE

Edited by
Rom Harré
and Peter Stearns

SAGE Publications
London • Thousand Oaks • New Delhi

Editorial arrangement and Introduction © Rom Harré and
Peter Stearns 1995
Chapter 1 © John Wiley & Sons Ltd. 1992
Chapter 2 © P. Stearns 1995
Chapter 3 © N.C. Much and M. Mahapatra 1995
Chapter 4 © The American Psychological Association 1993
Chapter 5 © R. Harré 1995
Chapter 6 © D. Carbaugh 1995
Chapter 7 © C. Erneling 1995
Chapter 8 © M. Egerton 1995
Chapter 9 © S. Calvert 1995

First published 1995

 SAGE Publications Ltd
6 Bonhill Street
London EC2A 4PU

SAGE Publications Inc
2455 Teller Road
Thousand Oaks, California 91320

SAGE Publications India Pvt Ltd
32, M-Block Market
Greater Kailash – I
New Delhi 110 048

British Library Cataloguing in Publication data

A catalogue record for this book is
available from the British Library.

ISBN 0 8039 7736 0
ISBN 0 8039 7737 9 pbk

Library of Congress catalog card number 95–070196

Typeset by Mayhew Typesetting, Rhayader, Powys
Printed in Great Britain by The Cromwell Press Ltd,
Broughton Gifford, Melksham, Wiltshire

Contents

Notes on Contributors

Sandra L. Calvert is an Associate Professor of Psychology at Georgetown University. She has a PhD in developmental and child psychology from the University of Kansas. Her research activities involve the impact of information technologies such as television, computer and virtual reality on children's attention, memory and social behaviour.

Donal Carbaugh is Professor of Communication and Faculty Affiliate in American Studies and American Indian Studies at the University of Massachusetts, Amherst. His most recent book is *Situating Selves: the Communication of Social Identities in American Scenes.*

Derek Edwards is Reader in Discursive Psychology in the Department of Social Sciences, Loughborough University, where he is a member of the Discourse and Rhetoric Group. He has been an active advocate and developer of a discourse-based perspective on psychological topics such as memory, causal reasoning, categorizing, learning, scripted actions and descriptions of personal dispositions and mental states. His books include *Common Knowledge* (with Neil Mercer) and *Discursive Psychology* (with Jonathan Potter). He is associate editor of the *British Journal of Social Psychology.*

Muriel Egerton was a senior community worker in Belfast in the 1970s. She then studied psychology, doing a doctorate on the social construction of emotions at Oxford University. She now holds an ESRC fellowship at Manchester University, researching outcomes for mature students in terms of occupation, income, health and family relations, so combining interests in social policy and psychology.

Christina Erneling is an Associate Professor in the Department of Psychology at Umeå University, Sweden, and has been teaching philosophy and psychology at York University, Toronto, Canada. She has published *Understanding Language Acquisition: the Framework of Learning* and is the co-editor (with David Johnson) of *Reassessing the Cognitive Revolution: Alternative Futures.*

Rom Harré is a Fellow of Linacre College, Oxford, and Professor of Psychology, Georgetown University, Washington DC. His publications include *Varieties of Realism, Pronouns and People* (with P. Muhlhäusler), and most recently *Physical Being*, a study of the role of the body in human life.

Manamohan Mahapatra is Reader and Head of the Department of Anthropology, The Government College, Phulbani, Orissa. He holds a PhD in anthropology from Utkal University and has served on the Faculty of Anthropology at Utkal University and BJB College, in Bhubaneswar, Orissa. He has held several other posts with the Orissa State Government Education Service. He was research scholar under Professor Cora Dubois on the Harvard Bhubaneswar Project, and a Visiting Research Associate at the University of Chicago, the Committee on Human Development. Dr Mahapatra has expertise in the traditional temple culture and folk religion of coastal Orissa, and in culture and social welfare issues of tribal and scheduled caste populations of Orissa, and has published numerous articles on traditional Hindu culture, tribal culture and change in Orissa. His books in English include *The Bauri of Bhubaneswar, Traditional Structure and Change in an Orissan Temple*, and *A Textbook of Social Anthropology*.

Nancy Carol Much holds a PhD in human development from the University of Chicago. From 1990–94, she was Assistant Professor of Psychology at Georgetown University. She has been a postdoctoral fellow at Michigan State University, a Research Associate at the University of Chicago, and has conducted long-term field research in Orissa, India. She has published in the areas of discourse analysis, socialization, and social cognition, comparative ethics and moral development, ethnopsychologies, and semiotics of visual imagery in psychotherapy; she has done applied work in the ethnography of educational evaluation. Dr Much is currently working as an independent scholar and a consultant in educational research.

Jonathan Potter is Reader in Discourse Analysis in the Department of Social Sciences, Loughborough University, where he is a member of the Discourse and Rhetoric Group. He has been researching fact construction in various realms, including 'riot speak', scientific discourse, political disputes and everyday conversation. He is the co-author of various books, including *Discourse and Social Psychology* and *Discursive Psychology* (with Derek Edwards). He is completing a book on fact construction and is co-editor of *Theory and Psychology*.

Peter Stearns is Heinz Professor of History and the Dean of the College of Humanities and Social Sciences at Carnegie Mellon University. He is also founder and editor-in-chief of the *Journal of Social History* and editor of a monograph series on the history of emotion. His most recent book is *American Cool: Constructing a Twentieth Century Emotional Style*.

Introduction: Psychology as Discourse Analysis

Rom Harré and Peter Stearns

Our choice of exemplary cases of empirical research

This book illustrates the use of some new methods that are animated by one of the major contemporary theories of human action. This is the point of view that highlights discourse as the characteristic feature of human life. Our aim in choosing the illustrative cases of research to be displayed in this volume was to provide the reader with sufficient detail and depth to show what the discursive approach could accomplish. In choosing to illustrate only one of the variety of analytic, non-experimental methodologies we knowingly sacrificed breadth to depth. However, there is much published material available, and illustrations of the use of other methods in research are referred to throughout *Rethinking Psychology* and *Rethinking Methods in Psychology*. In both these books several non-experimental but empirically based approaches to the problems traditionally taken as the subject matter of psychology were explained. Each was developed as a well-tried methodology based on a carefully constructed theory. In one way or another each opened up an aspect of the general conception of human beings as active, symbol-using creatures intentionally engaged in joint projects. Since our plan was to make available a wide variety of 'new' approaches we aimed at a fairly comprehensive spectrum of styles and methods.

We could sum up the position of the new cognitivism by stressing its contrast with conventional cognitivist beliefs as described by Shweder:

Ontologically speaking, knowledge in general psychology is the attempt to imagine and characterize the form or shape of an inherent central processing mechanism for psychological functions (discrimination, categorization, memory, learning, motivation, inference and so on). Epistemologically speaking, knowledge seeking in general psychology is the attempt to get a look at the central processing mechanism untainted by content and context, and so on.

The main force in general psychology is the idea of that central processing device. The processor, it is imagined, stands over and above, or transcends, all the stuff upon which it operates. It engages all the stuff of culture, context, task, and stimulus material as its content.

Given that image the central processor itself must be context and content independent. That means, in effect, that the processor must be describable in terms of properties that are either free of context/content (abstract, formal, structural properties) or general to all contexts/contents (invariant, universal properties). (1991: 80)

According to the new cognitivism there is no such processing mechanism. So the task of psychology cannot be to test hypotheses about the existence, nature or workings of hidden cognitive mechanisms. Rather it must be to try to reveal the structure of those discursive productions in which psychological phenomena are immanent and to discover how the various cognitive skills required to accomplish the tasks that psychology studies are acquired, developed, integrated and employed. Language use, the most characteristic human symbolic activity, not only is a main object of study for discursive psychologists, but also serves as a model or analogue for the study of other non-linguistic phenomena. For example the new psychology of the emotions is built upon the idea that emotion displays and feelings are functionally equivalent to those linguistic performances we call 'speech acts': that is they express judgements, for instance moral judgements, and are used to perform social acts, for instance protesting. In contrast with conventional cognitive approaches which seek emotional uniformities, the new psychology emphasizes not only the wide expressive functions of emotions but also their dependence on specific functional and cultural contexts. In addition to the psychology of the emotions we have chosen a wide range of examples of new-style research into topics which have been tackled by older methods with less than satisfactory results.

Discursive psychology is allied with but not reducible to any of the neurosciences. There is nothing in the human universe except active brains and symbolic manipulations. Brains, like hands, tennis rackets and pens, are among the instruments people use for bringing off their everyday intentions and projects. However a complete account of the *game* of tennis is possible without our knowing anything at all about that part of the explanation of why the racket behaves as it does: that belongs to physics. All we need to know is what a player can do with it, what a player should do with it (the rules of this particular context) and what a player does do with it. The complex physics of networks of elastic strings responding to the impact of a moving elastic sphere is irrelevant to the study of tennis as a human practice. As John Gardner once remarked, the clowns would be just as sadly funny if we found that their heads were full of sawdust. To be sadly funny cannot be defined with respect to any brain process, however highly correlated with clowning. An exposé of neural architecture could never have them rolling in the aisles.

In this volume we complete the exposition of the new cognitivism as a scientific paradigm. A scientific paradigm includes a general metaphysical theory, often implicit, which serves to specify the ontology of the 'universe' to which our scientific efforts will be applied. The Newtonian universe is a shifting pattern of atoms, in absolute space and time. The psychological universe is a continuously modulating public and private discourse, in a complex and changing pattern of moral orders. With each ontology there is an associated methodology, and some copy-book examples are usually offered in which the ontology and methodology can be seen at work. Here we present some examples of discursive methods in action. In presenting these illustrative researches we have in mind older studies of the same or similar topics, with which our case studies are meant to be compared with advantage. We claim to have achieved both a deeper understanding of the phenomena and a clearer view of their nature. Instead of rushing into research with some preconceived idea as to what the nature of our subject matter might be, we have taken Wittgenstein's advice and paused to look closely at what it is we are interested in trying to understand. While no doubt there is much that we have failed to see, we are confident that our notions of remembering, being angry, having divine powers and so on are more adequate to the subject matter than those embedded in the cognitive psychology of the recent past.

But there is another aspect to the new cognitivism. 'Psychology' is itself a discursive enterprise, appearing concretely in books and papers, and in the 'instruments', such as questionnaires, rating scales, repertory grids and so on, through which most empirical studies are carried on. Discursive psychology is reflexive, taking itself and its older cousins as part of its subject matter. The contrast drawn in some of the chapters which follow between the old and the new psychology is itself laid out in terms of the discursive properties of psychological enquiry and its standardized products and methods. The need for a psychology of psychology is now very adequately met.

Part One
Dismantling the inner/outer distinction: the psychology of emotion, memory and exotic cognitive states

Perhaps the sharpest contrast between the old and the new cognitive psychology shows up in the case of memory and the emotions. In both fields the orthodox view involves the idea that the displays of emotion and declarations or claims to remember are mere consequences or effects of some 'inner' process or state which is the real phenomenon.

There has been a shift away from conceiving remembering as an inner process representative of the past. A clear Wittgensteinian look at remembering as it occurs in everyday life has led to the realization that memories are constituted in public and private negotiations between potentially rival claimants as to what the past has been. In looking at declarations of rememberings as discursive acts, Edwards and Potter draw our attention to the inadequacy of accounts of the presentation of 'memories' in which veridicality, the 'real past', that which distinguishes an accurate recollection from one which is flawed, is taken as if it were somehow outside the frame of discursive constructions. The 'construction of facticity' is itself a rhetorical project having a place in the unfolding of this or that conversation. The very idea that telling a memory is reporting a subjective recollection is itself a 'version of the mental life', part of a discursive presentation of how things were. In this chapter we can see how the discursive approach can be turned back upon psychology itself. Laboratory studies of memory simply take for granted an unexamined construction of the past as a real resource, when it is created for experimental purposes by the experimenter himself or herself.

From a discursive point of view there are two classes of phenomena that are equally part of the total complex that is comprehended under the term 'emotion'. There are feelings and displays conceived as expressing a wide range of judgements and social acts. But there are also vocabularies in use through which we track, correct, comment upon and manage our emotional feelings and displays. These are as much part of the total complex that adds up to the 'psychology' of emotion as the expressions and feelings, and more so than the reactions of the limbic system! The psychology of the emotions has been the greatest beneficiary so far of the new discursive methods, and this part continues with some further work in the emotionology of the English language pioneered by Peter Stearns. Emotions are often studied as constants in the human repertoire, varying only by virtue of differences in personality. Sometimes viewed as precognitive impulses, emotions can also be examined from a cognitive standpoint. Some psychologists hope to develop cognitive maps of emotion that can then be applied to computation, giving artificial intelligence an emotional dimension and range. On the other hand a growing body of research focuses on an emotion repertoire as a product of culture and discourse. Not necessarily denying the availability of basic impulses and cognitions, the constructionist research argues that the principal content of emotion, as it is experienced individually and as it is shared with others, is shaped by potentially varied cultural standards. This is why emotional range and use differ considerably from one culture to another, and also why emotional experience changes over time. Grief, for example, is handled quite variably in different cultural contexts. It has also changed in modern Western history. Nineteenth-century Victorian culture expanded the indulgence of grief, seeing it as an important and highly functional expression. In contrast, cultural standards began to turn against grief in the 1920s, as the functions of the emotions shifted and became more negatively evaluated. The shift affected public rituals and private experiences alike, creating an important case study in the potential, though also the limitations, of emotional change.

The third study in this part, in which the picture of an inner reality is brought into question, examines the discursive production of a seemingly exotic social categorization based upon a special cognitive state, the routine divine possession of a Brahmin healer in Orissa. During the 'possession' a *Kalasi*, a man or a woman who is recognized as possessed by the Goddess, has the appearance and apparently the experience of a 'personality' quite different from their ordinary one. The *Kalasi* creates the public illusion of *darshan*, possession by a divinity. At the same time the role of *Kalasi* is a category of social identity, of considerable local power and significance. Much and Mahapatra show in detail how the categorization and cognitive display appear through integrated features of conversational interactions among the healer and her clients. The experience of *darshan* is created by the *Kalasi*'s semiotic, ritual and discursive acts, which are effective only in relation to specific cultural-symbolic and social-structural contexts. This, again, is in sharp contrast to psychodynamic and other accounts, which typically cite exotic or pathological states of mind in the person possessed by the god, in the participants in the activities of the cult, or in both.

Part Two
Cognition in public: the psychology of decision and action

Because discursive psychology approaches seemingly 'individual' psychological phenomena such as memory as part of a larger cultural production, it automatically redefines the relationship between individual psychology and social behaviours. Through language and culture society defines the individual's memory, emotion and religious possession – and this list may grow, perhaps even to include aspects of intelligence itself. The same attention to psychology in context, rather than abstracted towards a single mental mechanism, permits new understanding of how people move to action and decision in public forums.

In this part we turn to the task of illustrating the new methodology at work in research into some central topics of cognitive psychology. In the first contribution, by Edwards and Potter, the traditional field of study called 'attribution theory' is transformed – from the attempt to investigate the structure of a cognitive mechanism generating differential lay explanations of the causes of actions, to an investigation of the forms of attributive talk and their place in conversation. Edwards and Potter inaugurate our investigation of the cognitive aspects of action by displaying the discursive conventions at work in explanatory talk. They take as their focus of study some everyday accounts of the way people attribute responsibility for actions and other phenomena. A simple linguistic study of what is said is not enough. While something is to be learned from the study of decontextualized verb choices, and from the study of idealized conversation, both take for granted a certain 'program' for an attributional conversation, in which causes are assigned. It seems as if it is a question about how one describes *what is there*. But what is there is itself a discursive production, just as what *was* there is a discursive production put to use in memory studies.

The problem of how we choose among alternatives and execute courses of action once a choice has been made is investigated by Carbaugh and by

Harré. Carbaugh shows how the processes of deciding are located in the complex conversations of a community, and how certain key expressions function in carrying the theoretical weight of a point of view. Harré's study of the 'grammar' of the ways we take on and shed personal responsibility discursively shifts the psychology of action away from the vain attempt to give substance to the myth of the 'will', and yet preserves the idea of irreducible human agency.

In Harré's chapter two main schemata are presented. They have been widely used in the physical sciences for explaining how naturally occurring events are produced, but they can also be found in the explanatory formats of the human sciences, and in the discursive practices of everyday life. The 'Humean' schema assumes a passive being, whose behaviour is wholly accounted for by the state of the environment and the external impulses to which that being is subjected. The 'agentive' schema assumes an active being with productive powers, the exercise or frustration of which may or may not be found to have its source in environmental conditions. Human agency seems for the most part to be pictured well by the agentive schema, but care is needed in its interpretation. In so-called 'cognitive science' the schema or something very similar is presented as a sketch of the structure of a mental mechanism, perhaps one which processes information. According to the discursive point of view the schema rather represents the grammar of discursive presentations of oneself to oneself or to others as an agent. We act to fulfil what we say.

Carbaugh presents a dispute about the fate of a parcel of land in terms of discourses of opposing parties to the argument. Each party shapes its discourse around a certain key term. For the 'developers' the disputed territory is 'up there', which, as Carbaugh shows, serves to position the piece of ground as 'part of the town'. For the environmentalists it is 'down there', which claims it for the park reserve. Decisions are reached not by individual cognitive processing of information, but in the gradual domination of one discourse by the other in the conversations of the citizens. The dispute between the parties, argues Carbaugh, is better seen as a drama than as a debate, as one way of describing the situation begins to dominate the other and a discursive consensus begins to emerge. The psychological phenomena are fully visible in the discourse of the participants. It is there that consensus is reached, that decisions are seen to be made and that 'minds' are changed.

In the course of these three chapters we demonstrate how the analysis of what is public and open to view, namely the discursive procedures by which explanations are given, decisions come to be formulated and responsibilities are assigned, offers complete examples of psychological research. There are no hidden *psychological* processes of which the discursive activities are outward manifestations. But these investigations pose a special kind of question to developmental psychologists: namely, how are the relevant skills acquired?

Part Three
The language game of language acquisition

The examples in this volume are meant to illustrate the power of the idea that cognition is a discursive process, and so to be found quite as much in public-collective activities as in derivative privatized and individualized versions of the basic 'outer' forms. What of the processes by which the basic skills of cognition, the basic linguistic and other symbol-using capabilities, are acquired? Erneling shows how the very point of view that pays off so handsomely when we are tackling the substantive problems of cognitive psychology is equally fruitful when it serves as the basis of a theory of language acquisition.

Erneling argues that the classical problems of the psychology of language acquisition are solved neither by the idea that children learn a language by making and testing semantic, syntactic and pragmatic hypotheses, nor by the idea that experience activates an in-built grammatical or even semantic system, or that there exists in each of us a cognitive system primed to search out 'language' from the blooming, buzzing environment. The existing data point to a Wittgensteinian explanation, in which the properties of the jointly produced discourse of the infant and the child carer are enough to explain how language is learned. Rather than solving the classical problems of how a child could learn language from the paucity of the examples it can experience, the Wittgensteinian orientation displays them as artefacts of a certain point of view. A picture of natural and trained regularities in behaviour serving to make possible rule-governed 'language games' of endlessly sophisticated developmental potential is shown to be the only account that is commensurate with current empirical research into the way that language skills are acquired within a linguistic environment. Language is a tool for action, not an abstract calculus fleshed out in sound.

Part Four
Some uses of traditional methods

The turn to discourse as a main focus of psychological research carries with it certain revisions of empirical methodology. New methods of research have been highlighted in the contents of this and the two previous volumes. However, there is a place for more traditional methods in psychologically relevant discourse analysis. In this final part we offer two examples of how, on the margins, so to say, the statistically analysed 'experiment' has a place.

Egerton uses quite standard factor analysis methods to extract certain discursive norms which constrained how people talked about public violence and angry incidents (represented by how they answered a questionnaire) and so, as seen from the discursive point of view, how they thought about these issues. In both the studies described in this chapter the incidents which participants were asked to describe were fictional. This use of made-up vignettes parallels in an interesting way the use of thought experiments in the natural sciences, a parallel which deserves further consideration.

Discourse, in particular that kind of discourse in which stories are presented, need not always make use of words. Children (and for that matter adults) are accustomed to another medium for story telling: namely, sequences of pictures. In studying how pictures facilitate learning, Calvert makes use of a pictorial discourse medium. By setting up a simple sorting task she explores the development of capacities to understand a narrative presented visually.

Conclusion

Rather than looking for the subject matter of psychology behind the judgements that are displayed in the public interactions between people and that we each experience privately, the new cognitivism finds the major topics of psychology to be exemplified in those very experiences and displays themselves. Since these are one and all skilled actions of various kinds, the task of psychology is to identify these skills, and to try to give explicit expression to the norms, rules and conventions that are immanent in their use. The intuition that much of psychology is concerned with symbolic interactions does not collapse it into a department of micro-sociology, since the skills and intentions of individual people are central to the explanation of what happens, and the private realm of symbol manipulation is as much a topic for discursive psychology as the public arena. Nor does the grounding of skills in bodily states and processes collapse psychology into a branch of the neurosciences, since the bodily organs with which we think and act are to be interpreted as among the tools we put to use in realizing our plans and intentions.

PART I
DISMANTLING THE INNER/ OUTER DISTINCTION:
the Psychology of Emotion, Memory and Exotic Cognitive States

1 Remembering

Derek Edwards and Jonathan Potter

Ulric Neisser's (1981) 'ecological' analysis of the memory of John Dean was in three ways a welcome departure from much previous memory research. First, it attempted to examine remembering in a natural context: specifically through a comparison between John Dean's testimony to the Watergate hearings, and the published transcripts of some of the original conversations between Dean, Nixon and others. As Neisser (1982) has argued, the study of remembering in natural contexts holds the promise of studying non-trivial and non-artificial behaviours, and of revealing the functionality of ordinary remembering – why people remember what they do, when, in what context and with what significance. These are not merely 'contextual' issues for a psychology of remembering, but promise to inform our understanding of the nature of the process itself. Second, in adopting a functional view of remembering, the study of Dean's testimony attempted to make sense of the pattern of his rememberings by reference to personal goals such as his perceived need to tell the truth and a desire to display himself in a favourable light. Third, and crucially, it stressed the importance and novelty of studying memory for its accuracy rather than for its inadequacies – a move heavily influenced by the 'ecological optics' of J.J. Gibson (1966). It is this latter issue, of veridicality and how this is assessed, that we wish to examine here. Our argument is that Neisser's approach to discursive remembering fails to take proper account of the nature of discourse itself, and specifically, its pragmatic organization.

With Neisser and others (for example, Costall and Still, 1987), we shall argue that memory and indeed other 'cognitive processes' can be fruitfully examined as they occur in natural settings; however, we shall emphasize the need to pay full attention to the social and discursive issues raised by such a study. We shall also adopt a form of functional analysis. However, we shall follow the implications of such an analysis much further than Neisser has done, employing methods and insights derived from the social psychology of discourse and rhetoric (Billig, 1987; Potter and Wetherell, 1987), from ethnomethodologically influenced approaches to conversational data in general (e.g. Atkinson and Heritage, 1984; Levinson, 1983), and from critical approaches to the theoretical formulations of cognitive science (e.g. Suchman, 1987).

Specifically, we suggest that in any account of conversational remembering, what is required is not merely an extension of traditional cognitive concerns into real-world settings, but a refocusing of attention upon the dynamics of social action, and in particular of discourse. There has as yet been little attempt to deal either with naturally occurring conversational discourse or with the issues of truth construction and the experimenter's own role in that process, which we shall deal with here.

Studies of memory have invariably begun from some unquestioned notion of what really happened – an undisputed record or version of original events that can be taken to represent the original experience (for the subjects) and also (for the psychologist) the essential criterion of what is remembered, forgotten, inferred, distorted and so on. Without this prior knowledge of the 'truth', the traditional psychology of memory cannot proceed. Indeed, the starting point for the John Dean study was precisely the availability of tape transcripts of meetings in the Oval Office, which enabled the accuracy of Dean's testimony, taken as evidence of his memory, to be examined. It is the task of this chapter to criticize the assumption that the truth of events can, and must, be pre-established in this way as a necessary condition for the study of remembering. We offer an alternative approach both to remembering and to the establishment of true versions, which examines those things as discursive activities and as participants' concerns.

In the first section of our chapter we focus on Neisser's conceptualization and operationalization of the ideas of accurate remembering, truth and truthfulness. That involves an examination of the adequacy of his conceptual division of three kinds of truth (or of memory, since, as we have argued, the one depends upon the other); and an examination of problems with the criteria used to show Dean's truthfulness. In the second section we illustrate these points by examining 'remembering' in a natural context – a dispute over what was said at a press briefing given by the then UK Chancellor of the Exchequer (the senior minister responsible for major economic policy), Nigel Lawson. This material has the advantage of being similar in many crucial ways to the John Dean/Watergate material (disputations about what was really said at a politically sensitive meeting, about the adequacy and accuracy of various versions of those events, about the status of various 'objective' records, and so on), but at the same time it provides additional elements which were missing from the restricted data source that Neisser concentrated on. In particular, it provides for an analysis of the rhetorical context of the event, as well as an opportunity to study processes of event reconstruction occurring over time, which Neisser (as Bartlett before him) also recognizes as an important feature of real-world studies.

It is important at the outset that we make clear the basis upon which we are subjecting Neisser's paper to close scrutiny. It is not out of any disregard either for Neisser's work in general, or for the Dean paper in particular. On the contrary, we perceive this work to represent a significant and welcome departure from earlier laboratory-based and information-processing orientations, and to have mapped out many of the important issues that confront the relocation of cognitive studies in the context of real-world activities. It is precisely because of the significance and value of Neisser's work that it merits close attention. Moreover, in pursuing the discourse-analytic perspective, and in addressing notions of truth, veridicality, accuracy of accounts, and how these things are analysable as discursive accomplishments, we inevitably raise issues of how cognitive psychology, or any other study of remembering, constructs truths of its own. Psychology's construction of truths (evidence, models, theory) about remembering are intimately involved in how truth and memory are defined operationally in the analysis of subjects' rememberings. So Neisser's paper itself becomes a proper subject for study just as, in other spheres, analysts of discourse and social action have studied the construction of scientific knowledge (Woolgar, 1988). It is one of the most significant features of the discourse-analytic approach that the same methodology that reveals how ordinary persons construct versions of reality can be turned upon science itself.

Re-examining John Dean's testimony

John Dean was the key witness in the Watergate hearings. Dean had provided in his opening written statement, and again under cross-examination, detailed accounts of conversations in the Oval Office of the White House, between himself, President Nixon, and various high-ranking White House officials. The subsequent publication of selected transcripts of some of those conversations was seen as providing an opportunity to examine the accuracy of Dean's testimony. Neisser's concern was with what an analysis of Dean's testimony could tell us about the workings of his memory, and about memory in general. In particular, he set out to show that there was a sense in which Dean could be accurate, while apparently misremembering virtually all of the important details.

In Neisser's analysis, not only did Dean misremember the details of time, place and conversation, he also frequently misremembered even the *gist* of what happened and what was said. Despite this, there is usually a deeper level at which he is right. He gave an accurate portrayal of the real situation, of the actual characters and commitments of the people he knew, and of the events that lay behind the conversations he was trying to remember. (1981: 4)

Neisser's 'deeper level' of accuracy is the third of a three-part distinction that he draws between kinds of accurate recall. These are: (1) 'verbatim recall' or 'literal memory'; (2) 'gist'; and (3) 'repisodic memory', in which Dean 'extracted the common themes that remained invariant across many conversations and many experiences, and then incorporated those themes in his testimony' (1981: 20). Unlike Bartlett's (1932) story reconstruction, confabulated and altered across many retellings, 'repisodic' memory is recall distilled from many different but related experiences, in which some significant essence of the truth of things remains, despite all sorts of inaccuracies of detail and circumstance. Notably, 'repisodic memory' has not been taken up with enthusiasm in laboratory-based studies of memory, probably because it does not fit easily into the usual methodological constraints. It involves persons having to go through a long series of personally significant experiences, and without the knowledge that they will be called upon to construct a painstaking account of it all later.

Neisser's concern with delineating various 'levels' of accurate recall is part of a broader attempt to establish a Gibsonian 'ecological psychology of memory'. While the constructivist, information-processing approach has emphasized forgetting – the distortions, confabulations, and general un-reliability which result when memories are schematically assembled in some kind of cognitive processor – the ecological perspective seeks to emphasize memory's veridicality: true remembering is something like abstracting the nature of the world from invariances in the flow of the subject's visual field. Neisser's point is that if we look at 'gist' and 'repisodic' remembering in context they can be seen as ways of getting it right about the past.

Three kinds of truth

Let us begin with Neisser's three-part distinction: (1) verbatim recall; (2) gist; and (3) repisodic memory. Each can be considered as a kind of text.

Verbatim recall   This is the kind of recall that is conventionally taken as unproblematically accurate and without distortion, the successful achievement of rote memorization. Rote learning has found itself out of favour in psychological laboratories during the reign of distortion-oriented information-processing and schema approaches. Neisser points out (1982: 17) that, in spite of this neglect, verbatim recall plays an important part in many people's everyday lives, in so far as people might rehearse and remember the Lord's prayer, the national anthem, songs and poetry, and so on.

However, these sorts of achievements are notable for the special nature of the social-discursive contexts deemed appropriate for their production. The repeated performance of a prayer or a poem is just that: the speaker reproduces her own performance on each occasion. The distinctive feature of these materials is that they are designed for repetition such that, in each case, there is some normatively agreed standard with which any particular rendition can be compared. The situation is quite different with natural dialogue such as that occurring between Nixon and Dean in the Oval Office. It is tempting to imagine that such a dialogue could be rendered to look like the script of a play, such that this could provide a neutral criterion for assessing the accuracy of Dean's version. However, a brief examination of the debate among linguists and conversation analysts about the transcription of talk would quickly show the weakness of that idea. Transcriptions are always highly conventionalized versions of talk, in which the level and content of the encoding of speech depend crucially upon, and develop alongside, the analytical insights that are revealed by it (e.g. Cook, 1990). The general point is that our familiarity with standard orthography gives the idea of assessing verbatim recall a deceptive simplicity which is misleading in practice, where our criteria will be contingent upon the context and purpose of our study.

In addition, pragmatic analyses of speakers' reportings of verbatim versus gist versions of other people's speech (i.e. direct and indirect quotation) point to an interesting patterning of everyday talk that is not reflected in analyses that restrict themselves to considerations of recall accuracy. Speakers may choose to quote speech indirectly *as* gist, or directly *as* verbatim recall, according to such considerations as 'footing' (Goffman, 1979; Levinson, 1988). That is, whatever they may otherwise imply about memory, verbatim and gist reportings afford options for speakers to associate themselves more or less directly with the reported speaker, offering opportunities for acting as intermediary or spokesperson, and for constructive formulations of what was said, or indeed for displaying oneself as possessing a rather acute and veridical recall of otherwise doubtful or questioned events (Wooffitt, 1990). While such studies may not tell us what speakers are *able* to remember, their relevance to the study of memory increases as our interest shifts to ecological settings in which remembering is studied as an actual and contextualized activity.

Recall of gist One of the central difficulties with the idea of assessing the accuracy of gist is that, in ordinary conversation, what may be taken as an adequate or accurate gist is, on any particular occasion, and for the participants involved, a disputable matter. Its adequacy will depend upon the communicative context in which the speaker is called upon to produce it. In the context of psychological experiment this contingency of gist upon communicative considerations is usually amongst those features of everyday talk that find themselves controlled out of the study. What counts as gist is resolved by fiat, by the experimenter, as part of the methodology. A piece of text is analysed for its case-grammatical event structure, story or script structure (Rumelhart, 1975; Thorndyke, 1977; Schank and Abelson, 1977), or is subdivided in advance into a set of 'idea units' (Bransford and Johnson, 1972) or of 'propositions' (Kintsch and Van Dijk, 1978), and the experimenter then counts up how many of these units a subject manages to recall. The social-discursive process of defining gist is expropriated by the analyst, who also has to judge whatever alterations and rewordings subjects produce as legitimate paraphrases or as illegitimate distortions or omissions.

In ordinary conversation, what counts as adequate or accurate gists and summaries is a matter for the participants themselves to resolve. And the criteria for doing so will themselves be occasioned and disputable, according to the pragmatic work that the summary is supposed to achieve. For example, we can compare the cognitive psychological notion of gist with the conversation-analytic notion of 'formulations', which are conversational events where the nature of an earlier sequence of talk is formulated (Heritage and Watson, 1979; Schegloff, 1972). Typically, such formulations are not neutral summaries but are designed for specific upshots relevant to future actions (Greatbatch, 1986). This is equally true of institutional contexts. For example, Edwards and Mercer (1989) have analysed the way that summaries of classroom lessons, of activities, findings and conclusions, are used by teachers to reformulate capricious and problematical classroom events according to their originally planned outcomes – in effect, articulating classroom events in terms of what 'ought' to have happened. Others have examined the role of formulations in legal and scientific contexts (Atkinson and Drew, 1979; Yearley, 1986).

Clearly, then, it makes no sense to talk about accurate gist in any decontextualized way, abstracted from conversational pragmatics. We shall demonstrate that Dean's testimony needs to be understood in terms of the pragmatic constraints and objectives of legal discourse.

Repisodic memory   Neisser defines this as a cognitive phenomenon, the process of '[extracting] the common themes that remained invariant' – a very familiar sort of cognitive-perceptual process, often favoured in accounts of perceptual learning, pattern recognition, language and concept acquisition, and so on (see, for example, Nelson's 1981 discussion of the acquisition of 'script' knowledge). Our aim is to question the status of 'repisodic memory' as a cognitive process, as an aspect of Dean's thought, and to relocate it as an artefactual category fashioned through a 'cognitivizing' of Dean's discourse, based on a *prior commitment* to Dean's basic truthfulness. The notion of an accurate 'repisodic' memory which is independent of gist and verbatim recall is the outcome of a carefully constructed argument. Neisser's very recognition of the phenomenon relies crucially upon his possessing a knowledge of the truth of what 'really happened' in the White House, which is independent of, but comparable with, Dean's testimony. This is not merely a matter of comparing the tape transcripts with Dean's accounts. It is not verbatim recall, or even gist, that is at stake here. What Dean's 'repisodic' memory is claimed to have got right is the general nature of Nixon's involvement and culpability in the cover-up of the Watergate conspiracy.

That the tape transcripts afford such an interpretation is not at all as straightforwardly obvious as it might appear. Indeed, in his foreword to the published transcripts, Nixon himself is quoted as claiming that they clearly *contradict* Dean's testimony (Neisser, 1981; 1982). Neisser himself relies upon other sorts of evidence:

> the outcome of those trials vindicated him . . . If history has ever proven anything, it surely proves that Dean remembered those conversations and told the truth about them. (1981: 3)

Neisser can assert in advance of analysing his testimony that Dean was right: the historical outcome is taken not only as self-evident, but as proving Dean's mnemonic correctness. However, this seems to be a rather circular way of demonstrating truthfulness. In so far as Dean was a crucial prosecution witness, the outcome of the trial merely corresponds with the general upshot of Dean's testimony. The verdict is of Nixon's guilt, not of Dean's truth, whether verbatim, gist or repisodic; and it is based on legal criteria, not scientific.

Neisser's presentation of Dean's testimony

Dean's testimony is presented as representing, with minor reservations, the best efforts of a man with a good memory at accurately recalling the reported events:

> The impression Dean made when he testified – that he had a good memory and was determined to tell the truth, even if only because truth-telling would best serve his own interests – was essentially correct. (1985: 24)

Moreover, the correctness of Dean's account is warranted in a very direct fashion by the transcripts: '*The transcript makes it quite clear* that Nixon is fully aware of the coverup' (1981: 9). Note how the transcript itself is presented as the agent of its own interpretation (cf. Latour, 1987), disguising Neisser's own interpretative work in coming to that conclusion. Rather than taking Dean's testimony as a (fairly direct) window upon his memory, we propose that it may be taken instead as a pragmatically designed piece of discourse. It is a series of accounts, occasioned by cross-examination, and oriented towards the avoidance and assigning of blame and mitigation. Seen in this light, features of Dean's testimony are open to new readings. Features that are ostensibly signals of truthfulness and accuracy, the outcome of mnemonic cognitive processes, are revealed as communicative devices that Dean uses for warranting his *claims* to truthfulness and accuracy.

Neisser notes some inaccuracies in Dean's testimony about the meeting with Nixon and Haldeman on 15 September 1972. His examination of the transcript reveals that:

Nixon did not say any of the things attributed to him here: he didn't ask Dean to sit down, he didn't say Haldeman had kept him posted, he didn't say Dean had done a good job . . . he didn't say anything about Liddy or the indictments. Nor had Dean himself said the things he later describes himself as saying: that he couldn't take credit, that the matter might unravel some day, etc. (1981: 9)

Neisser's principal concern appears to be the extent of Dean's accuracy – how little detail or even gist is correct, while he manages nevertheless to convey the correct impression, that Nixon was engaged in, or at least party to, a cover-up operation. But the pragmatically situated nature of Dean's account is ignored. Both Dean's testimony and the transcript itself were 'just as incriminating' (1981: 9). This word 'incriminating' calls out for further attention, in that it implies a discourse-functional context of Dean's story. For example, Dean presents himself in the following ways:

1   As scrupulously modest and honest, not taking credit for the work of others: 'I responded that I could not take credit because others had done much more difficult things than I had done' (quoted by Neisser, 1981: 9).
2   As having a particularly good memory. He makes direct claims to this effect: 'anyone who recalls my student years knew that I was very fast at recalling information' (1981: 5). He also supports it indirectly via the use of vivid descriptive and narrative detail and supposedly direct quotation, all of which serve to bolster his appearance as someone with a virtually direct perceptual access to the original events: 'you know the way there are two chairs at the side of the President's desk . . . on the left-hand chair Mr Haldeman was sitting' (1981: 11); 'I can very vividly recall the way he sort of rolled his chair back from his desk and leaned over to Mr Haldeman and said, "A million dollars is no problem"' (1981: 18).
3   As being under the awesome influence and direction of the highest authority in the land (the President of the United States) – as being, therefore, less culpable himself for his own involvement. Dean rhetorically reiterates Nixon's title, rather than calling him Nixon: 'When you meet with the President of the United States it is a very momentous occasion, and you tend to remember what the President of the United States says when you have a conversation with him (1981: 6).

On this analysis, Dean's testimony can be seen as a pragmatically oriented phenomenon and certainly not merely a straightforward window upon the workings of his memory. It is contextually occasioned both in terms of conversational turn-taking (as responses to questions, accusations, etc.), and also more broadly in terms of the business of the hearings – as relevant to determining the extent of various people's complicity and guilt, including his own, as well as his own credibility as a witness. It is similarly a part of Dean's display of 'truthfulness' that he expressed metacognitive disclaimers about accuracy: he was careful to deny verbatim recall, but claimed to remember the gist (1981: 3).

Our argument is that Dean's *truth* is indistinguishable from his mode of *accounting*. His version of his 'memory' is operationally an account, rhetorically couched, in which the accuracy of his detailed evidence is warranted with further accounts of his mnemonic methods, the fact of his self-attributed 'good memory', and the metacognitive claim that people do recall important events, such as a conversation with the President of the United States. Where we would disagree with Neisser is in his reading of these pragmatically oriented claims as if they were literal renderings of the nature of Dean's memory.

The pragmatically formulated nature of Dean's rememberings is clearly displayed when we examine a different study of Dean's testimony carried out by Molotch and Boden (1985). Their concern was entirely different from Neisser's, in that they focused upon the exercise of power in Dean's cross-examination. Further, their choice of data was also different: whereas Neisser concentrated almost exclusively on Dean's testimony to Senator Inouye, Molotch and Boden's topic was Dean's testimony to Senator Gurney. The difference between the two kinds of testimony is startling. Inouye asked Dean relatively open-ended questions and allowed him to give long and elaborate answers without interruption. He also provided the opportunity for Dean to warrant his credibility by providing the extensive account of his own special memory skills which is discussed by Neisser. Gurney, in contrast, asked many questions which required simple yes/no answers and at times cut Dean off when he tried to elaborate beyond these. His questioning was also noted as being 'hostile', peppered with disagreements and admonishments.

This difference, of course, is not merely incidental. Molotch and Boden chose to focus on Gurney's examination because he was 'Nixon's man' on the committee which examined Dean (Molotch and Boden, 1985: 275). As such, an adversarial relationship was established, with Gurney attempting to discredit Dean's testimony. For others on the Ervin Committee which examined Dean, particularly Democratic senators such as Inouye, this adversarial relationship did not obtain. Moreover, Molotch and Boden stress that Dean's actions made him a tempting 'scapegoat' and thus he had considerable personal investment in showing that responsibility lay further up in the White House hierarchy.

The point, then, is that these differences in Dean's testimony need to be understood as an occasioned discursive product oriented to issues of blame (for Nixon) and mitigation (for himself). In Gurney's hostile examination we see Dean's versions criticized, cut off and variously undermined; while in Inouye's sympathetic questioning Dean is given free rein to organize blamings and mitigations. The difference is graphically illustrated by interchanges specifically on the topic of Dean's memory. As indicated above, Neisser makes much use of Dean's elaborate account to Inouye of his own memory skills and he takes this account to be essentially correct. However, Dean also refers to his memory skills in the course of Gurney's questioning:

> *Dean*: . . . I've told you I'm trying to re*call*. My mind is not a *tape* recorder. It *does* recall (0.3) im*press*ions of conversations *very* well, and the impression *I* had was that he told- the- he told *me* that Bob had reported to *him* what I had been doing. That was th- the impression that very // clearly came out.
>
> *Gurney*: In other words, your- your *whole* thesis on saying that the President of the United States knew about Watergate on September 15 is *purely* an *impression*, there isn't a *single shred* of evidence that came out of this meeting.

(Slightly simplified from Molotch and Boden, 1985: // indicates overlap, where Gurney interrupts Dean; italicization indicates emphasis in delivery; (0.3) indicates a pause of 0.3 seconds; a hyphen- indicates a cut-off in mid utterance.)

Two things are striking about this passage. First, in this account, which follows a series of turns where he had found difficulty in answering questions and was 'in a bit of trouble' (1985: 281), Dean finds it useful to emphasize the shortcomings of his memory as well as its virtues. The disclaimer about being a tape recorder allows Dean to account for various inadequacies in his answers, while the emphasis on the 'gist' quality of remembered impressions allows Dean nevertheless to warrant his essential accuracy. Second, while Neisser and more tacitly Inouye (who does not disagree with Dean's assessments) accept Dean's version, Gurney provides an opposing view. So, rather than displaying a remarkable abstraction of repisodic truth, a capturing of underlying themes and experiences, in Gurney's formulation Dean has provided '*purely* an *impression*' and not 'a *single shred* of evidence'. We can start to see, then, the way that Dean's memory accounts are carefully designed to fit the functional-discursive context, and that Neisser's reading of them, as revealing the natural workings of memory, is just one of a variety of interpretative possibilities – indeed, the one offered by Dean himself.

The substantiation of Dean as essentially (repisodically) a truth-teller requires an account of how he nevertheless got things variably right or wrong. Repisodic memory is defined by Neisser as a characteristic of individual, cognitive processing, and correspondingly the account of Dean's truth and error is also framed in terms of individual psychological processes. Neisser notes that Dean's apparently superior (more accurate) recall on 21 March 1973 is something that requires an explanation. It was supposedly a set-piece script that Dean had rehearsed, and it had for Dean a basis in his psychological aspirations, in his hopes and fears, and in his efforts at self-presentation: it 'fulfilled Dean's hopes' of giving 'a personal lecture to the President . . . It became John Dean's own story' (1981: 16). Neisser seems close here to providing what we have been arguing for, an account of Dean's conversational rememberings as pragmatically occasioned, but opts instead for a personality-oriented, dispositional account (Wetherell and Potter, 1989).

Amongst all of Dean's repisodic correctness in assigning blame and duplicity, the one area in which Neisser has it that Dean got things noticeably wrong was in claiming a special role for himself:

Dean's errors . . . follow, I believe, from Dean's own character and especially from his self-centred assessment of events at the White House. What his testimony really describes is not the September 15 meeting itself but his fantasy of it: the meeting as it should have been, so to speak. (1981: 10)

His ego got in the way again. (1981: 18)

His ambition reorganized his recollections . . . A different man in the same position might have observed more dispassionately, reflected on his experiences more thoughtfully, and reported them more accurately. Unfortunately, such traits of character are rare. (1981: 19)

Thus, Dean's account is explicated by Neisser in terms of truth and error, where errors are due to personal biases, which might be eliminated in a more perfect person.

Neisser's form of accounting here is a familiar one. Numerous studies of the argumentation of lay people (Pollner, 1987; Yearley, 1987), of legal personnel (Atkinson, 1978; Yearley, 1985) and in particular of scientists (Gilbert and Mulkay, 1984; Potter, 1984) show that people tend to attribute deviation from what they *perceive* to be the truth to distorting factors such as personality, lack of competence, and a variety of social-psychological and sociological factors. Put another way, there is seen to be nothing to explain in the case of 'factual' accounts because they simply reflect the way things are; it is only when distortions arise that there is something to explain. This idea is reflected in Neisser's treatment of Dean. Dean is presented as functionally distorting the truth in favour of his own 'ego', while with regard to the character of Nixon and others he merely tells the (repisodic) truth. It is this straightforward acceptance of the truth of things, we suggest, that stops Neisser from coming to grips with the functional orientation of what he takes to be factual accounts (cf. Potter and Edwards, 1990; Smith, 1990). Indeed, Neisser's whole argument is based on the premise that memory can be understood as essentially veridical in a Gibsonian fashion and thus he is forced, by his own rhetoric, into having to discount error in this way, as basically not to do with memory *per se*, but nevertheless produced via the distorting prism of another individual factor such as personality. This is unfortunate for an ecologically situated approach to remembering, since one of its most important points of departure from conventional laboratory studies is precisely that the latter seek to exclude all sorts of interesting and essential features of everyday accounts of past events, as not really 'memory' as such, but extraneous to the intrinsic workings of that faculty. The study of remembering as an everyday practice does not have to adopt the psychology of individuals as its explanatory basis (Edwards and Middleton, 1987).

Our argument, then, is that to study conversational remembering we have to study how recollections are governed by conversational contingencies – the pragmatics of speaking – rather than by appealing to the traditional apparatus of mentalistic, dispositional psychology, and the truth–error distinction. Dean's presentation of himself as having a good memory, as being unwilling to take credit that belongs to others, as only following the authority of others, as telling the truth, all serve to enhance his reliability as a prosecution witness, to bolster his own disputed version of things, and to mitigate his own culpability under cross-examination.

Lawsongate: function and construction in remembering

Having established the importance of a pragmatic approach to discursive remembering, we turn now to the task of elaborating our theoretical position, and then to demonstrating how it can be applied.

Discourse analysis

The most economical way of introducing discourse analysis is to highlight the interrelated concepts of function, variation and construction. This will allow us to start to indicate how discourse analysis can provide a very different perspective on traditionally 'cognitive' phenomena, such as memory.

Function A number of disparate traditions of language research have stressed its functional nature, most obviously speech-act theory and linguistic philosophy more generally (e.g. Austin, 1962; Wittgenstein, 1953) and ethnomethodology and conversation analysis (e.g. Garfinkel, 1967; Sacks, 1992). Workers in these traditions stress that people do things with their discourse – they make accusations, ask questions, justify their behaviour and so on – and therefore their discourse will be designed accordingly.

These examples should not be taken to imply that the kinds of phenomena we are concerned with can simply be subsumed under the reasons–intentions–goals logic of ordinary reasoning (Yearley, 1988). Our concern is the organization of discourse rather than the mentation of speakers. Indeed, we take issue with the kinds of speech-act approaches which depend on specification of intentions (see Levinson, 1983; and Schegloff, 1988; for critiques). Take, for example, the classic study of the way speakers 'open up' the closings of telephone conversations (Schegloff and Sacks, 1973). It is possible to examine the workings of this discursive practice without having to decide in each case whether a speaker was artfully and thoughtfully using this technique to get someone off the phone, or whether they were simply finishing their telephone call in a 'natural' and unselfconscious manner. Likewise, we can be interested in the way particular kinds of descriptive vocabularies afford specific kinds of evaluations without making the assumption that the speakers intend those evaluations, or even that intentions are a viable analytic resource.

Of particular analytic consequence is the fact that the functional or interpretative work done by a stretch of discourse may be inexplicit or hidden. Rather than the specific activity type being formulated in the manner of an Austinian formal speech act ('I name this ship the *Titanic*'), in many cases activity is embedded, kept tacit or concealed (see, for example, Drew, 1984 on requests; and Pomerantz, 1980 on eliciting invitations). Because the action orientation of discourse is often disguised in this way, one of the aims of discourse analysis is to reveal its working; one important way of achieving this is through an analysis of variation.

Variation   The action orientation of discourse makes for variability: what people say will differ according to what they are doing with their words. An event will be described in different ways as the function changes from excusing, for example, to blaming. Variability of this kind has been repeatedly identified in a wide variety of discursive contexts (see Potter and Wetherell, 1987). This variability is central for analysis because of its close connection to function. Because function leads to variation, so variation can be used as an analytic clue to work back to function. We can predict that function will lead to certain kinds of variation and look for the presence of those variations (Gilbert and Mulkay, 1984; Potter and Mulkay, 1985; Wetherell and Potter, 1992).

Construction   This perspective on discourse, which sees discourse as put together for purposes and to achieve particular consequences, is a constructivist one (cf. Gergen, 1985; Potter and Wetherell, 1987; Potter et al., 1990; Woolgar, 1988). The metaphor of construction highlights three things: that discourse is manufactured out of pre-existing linguistic resources; that active selection is involved; and that much of the time we understand the world in terms of specific linguistic versions.

Neisser has been moving from his early cognitive constructivist position (Neisser, 1967) increasingly towards a position where memories are organized as reflections of the true facts, albeit after a process of repisodic synthesis. The constructivism we are concerned to develop here, however, is of a different kind. Whereas in the cognitive constructivism characteristic of Neisser's early work a person's reality is created through the operation of a variety of mental schemata, analysis and synthesis processes and such, in the discursive constructivism we are recommending the constructive processes are to be found in the organization of talk, and in the situated ordinary reasoning it embodies. Earlier studies have begun to examine the empirical and theoretical bases for studying remembering as a discursive practice (see Middleton and Edwards, 1990 for a summary). The present study seeks to develop a discourse-analytic basis for such work, to investigate how far the phenomena which have traditionally been understood as cognitive or mental can be differently understood not only as real-world activities (as Neisser proposes) but more specifically as features of everyday discursive practices.

It is important to emphasize that for this kind of naturalistic discourse-analytic inquiry we shall need to take a more circumspect position on 'truth' than either the information-processing or the ecological approaches have done. Given our constructivist theoretical position it would be quite inappropriate for us to legislate as to the truth of the matter; for this is exactly one of the central concerns of the participants' ordinary reasoning. Indeed, as work in the sociology of scientific knowledge has shown, it is vital to maintain a neutral position with respect to what the participants treat as facts, or else their own interests and purposes begin to contaminate the analytic conclusions (see Woolgar, 1988 on symmetry). As we have argued, this is precisely the issue raised by Neisser's (1981) study, and it is the reason that article has been given the close critical scrutiny usually reserved for textual 'data'; it is not that it represents a form of psychologizing that is especially worthy of criticism.

Thus in the analysis that follows 'the truth of what really happened' will not be the starting point for analysis, as it was for Neisser; nor will it be the end goal of the analysis. Rather, our concern will be with the discursive practices of reasoning which the participants bring to bear on this concern. In effect, we are moving from a view of people struggling to remember with the aid of their mental faculties to a view of people struggling with one another in their talk and texts over the real nature of events. It will be our aim to show the essentially contingent and functionally oriented nature of any construction of factuality, or 'true versions of events'. That is, just as we have suggested with respect to John Dean, accounts of 'what happened' occur within and as part of communicative activities such as assigning blame, denying responsibility and justifying interpretations, and are therefore variable in a systematic way that is subject to the requirements of those rhetorical activities.

We turn now to the second body of data, the press reports concerning 'Lawsongate'. While a comparison of a scientific report with a set of newspaper reportings may at first seem inappropriate, we intend to show that very similar issues are raised, and are problematical, in both. These issues include: the ways in which contentious versions of 'what really happened' are constructed, the way appeals are made to ostensibly objective criteria for warranting such claims, the use of rhetorical devices in the establishment of claims to accuracy, and the deployment of explanatory devices for accounting for errors in other people's accounts. After a preliminary summary of the dispute between Chancellor Lawson and the journalists, we shall divide our analysis of the press accounts into three main sections, each of which concerns a major issue in the psychology of remembering, as in the case of John Dean's testimony:

1 dispute over *where* the truth lies
2 dispute over the *nature* of the truth
3 dispute over the nature of the *error*.

Lawsongate: a gist

During November 1988, over several weeks, the British press carried a series of reports and discussions of the content of a disputed conversation which had taken place on the evening of Friday 4 November between Nigel Lawson, then Chancellor of the Exchequer, and 10 journalists from the Sunday newspapers. This meeting was universally characterized as a regular event, one of a series of 'off-the-record' briefings, in which senior politicians are able to 'float ideas in the press' – forthcoming policies, plans and so forth – to which they do not yet want publicly to commit themselves. It was one of a series of 'unattributable' briefings called 'lobby journalism', the 'lobby' being the group of journalists (note that 'lobby' does not carry here its usual connotation of partisan political pressure groups). Controversy, allegations and counter-allegations, between journalists and Lawson, centred around several key issues. The most contentious of these issues concerned what Lawson had said about plans to alter benefits payable to old-age pensioners. The Sunday papers reported that a major and controversial alteration was looming, in which benefits, currently payable universally to all pensioners, would in future be 'targeted' upon the more needy, through a process of 'means testing' (income assessment), such that some would receive reduced allowances or none at all, while others might receive increases. Lawson subsequently (on Monday, on radio, television and in Parliament) denied that he had said any such thing, claiming at one point that the journalists had got together and their 'fevered imagination' had produced 'a farrago of invention', 'inaccurate, half-baked' accounts which 'bear no relation whatever to what I said' (*The Times, The Guardian*, Tuesday 8 November). The existence of a tape recording of the meeting, itself the subject of later claims and denials, led to whimsical comparisons with Watergate, dubbed 'Lawson-gate' (*The Observer*, 13 November), and 'a fish and chips version of Nixon's White House Tapes. Expletive deleted' (*The Guardian*, 9 November).

The analytic materials we used were derived exclusively from five newspapers: *The Guardian, The Times, The Observer*, the *Sunday Mirror* and *The Sunday Times*. These particular papers were chosen because they are for the most part considered to be 'quality' papers (the exception, the *Sunday Mirror*, had its own journalist present at the briefing) and they cover a range of political opinion, with *The Guardian*, the *Sunday Mirror* and *The Observer* usually being thought of as rather less right-wing or conservative than *The Times* and *The Sunday Times*. The papers were collected each day for a fortnight after the controversial briefing and every article referring to it was collected and photocopied. These articles were coded into a series of topics to allow for a qualitative yet systematic analysis. The total archive runs to 53 articles.

Where the truth lies   In this first analytic section our goal is to show that the issue of *where* the truth lies, or what *counts* as the factual record, is a live one for participants. Different participants on different occasions made different suggestions as to how the facts could be checked. Moreover, we suggest that it would be wrong to take these suggestions as neutral descriptions of attempts to comprehend, because the descriptions can themselves be understood as embedded features of the rhetorical conflicts being played out between the newspapers and the government representatives.

The tape recording   All parties to the dispute made frequent recourse to the existence of some objective record which might reveal the unequivocal truth about the original events. The most obvious of these was a tape recording of the meeting, made by a government official who was also present. Neither the tape recording, nor a transcription of it, have to date materialized in public:

> when Sunday newspaper journalists challenged him [Lawson] to justify his claims by producing a transcript of the interview a further Treasury embarrassment was revealed. The tape recorder used by an official to record the meeting had failed to work properly. (*The Times*, 8 November)

The failure or otherwise of the tape recording was a recurring source of controversy. The papers suggested that this recording would vindicate their version of what went on, just as Neisser took the 'Presidential transcripts' to vindicate Dean, and they offered motivated accounts for its non-appearance; the absent tape 'inevitably . . . fuelled suspicions of a cover-up' (*The Observer*, 13 November). Press reports detailed several contradictory Treasury statements to the effect that the tape recorder had malfunctioned so that the tape was blank, that there was a transcript of the recording but it would not be released, that the pause button had been accidentally pressed so that the spools did not turn, that the original tape had been lost, and so on.

Treasury officials and journalists alike offered detailed descriptions to warrant their own versions of what happened. Thus:

> A Treasury spokesman told *The Guardian* on Wednesday that the tape recorder was a fairly sophisticated machine . . . the light was on but it did not work . . . The tape was blank, according to the Treasury. The machine was a voice-activated recorder. It did not work properly. (*The Guardian*, 11 November)

The machine's sophistication appears here not as a warrant for how good it was, but on the contrary, as a reasonable basis offered by the Treasury for its unreliability or difficulty of operation.

As counter-evidence that the recorder *was* working, and that the spools were turning, the journalists offered graphic, contextually rich descriptions of the sort that, to Neisser, lent such credibility to John Dean:

> At one point I heard a click, and assumed the tape had run out. It was directly in front of me. When I looked to check, the spools were still spinning. The clicking I heard turned out to be Don Macintyre of the *Sunday Telegraph*, seated to my right, chewing a pen top. (*Sunday Mirror*, 13 November)

Conflicting claims to the existence, or non-existence, of the tape recording thus varied according to the claimant's pragmatic situation. More interestingly, so also varied the ostensibly objective grounds upon which those claims were made. It seems that we can best make sense of these accounts by viewing them as summoning up details of description and of context not according to some abstract overall criterion of truth or accuracy, but because of the specific rhetorical work they could sustain.

Thus far, the reader might be forgiven for thinking that this dispute only exists because the full verbatim record is missing. Indeed, the logic of the journalists' suspicion about the missing tape seemed to be based on its potential for resolving the dispute. However, when we come to examine the dispute about the adequacy of the journalists' notes this assessment seems much less plausible.

The journalists' notes Despite the absence of the tape recording, even Lawson appeared willing to grant the existence and reliability of the journalists' detailed shorthand notes. Here *The Guardian* quotes his words in Parliament:

> The journalists concerned know very well and if they *look in their notebooks* they will see that the stories that appeared in Sunday's newspapers bear *no relation whatever* to what I said. (*The Guardian*, 8 November)

Lawson here remarkably claims the journalists' own records as evidence against their accounts, a rhetorical device that is consistent with his claim that they had 'concocted' their stories for lack of anything more exciting to report, but which runs the obvious risk of being directly contradicted by the journalists themselves. *The Guardian* (a daily paper not represented at the lobby briefing) offers its own rationale for Lawson's challenge. The fact that the meeting was to be 'off the record' allowed Lawson room for rhetorical manoeuvre:

> So the hacks' notebooks contain only a sketchy summary, not a verbatim note. Mr Lawson was thus on safe ground when he challenged them to back their stories with quotes (*The Guardian*, 9 November)

According to *The Guardian*, then, the notion that there existed 10 careful and independent sets of detailed shorthand notes was unfounded.

Now, the variable status of these shorthand notes, as possibly precise records of what really happened, is particularly interesting. In the other newspapers, and in *The Guardian* itself, we are informed that there existed 'verbatim notes of the Chancellor's words' (*The Sunday Times*, 13 November) taken by '10 fully trained shorthand-writing journalists' (*The Guardian*, 9 November). Yet elsewhere, and sometimes in the same article, *The Guardian* casts serious doubts upon the existence and reliability of those detailed records. Rather than trying to sort out a factual from a false version, we can make sense of this variability by considering the pragmatic contexts in which the two accounts occur (cf. Potter and Wetherell, 1987).

The functional orientation of claims for the detailed accuracy of the journalists' notes is straightforward enough. They operate, in the context of criticism of Lawson, as parts of arguments that support the journalists' versions of events against Lawson's claims for what he said. However, the functional orientation of *The Guardian*'s claim that the journalists had only a sketchy summary is slightly more complex. It becomes clear when we note that this claim is part of a broader critique of the lobby system, with its practice of unattributable press 'leakings' – 'a system from which, chiefly because of the scope which it offers for tendentious manipulations, *The Guardian* unilaterally withdrew two years ago' (*The Guardian*, 11 November). In this version the very unanimity of the Sunday press reports, which in other contexts was used as a warrant for their truth and accuracy, merely shows up their inadequacy:

> With that perfectly drilled unanimity which the lobby system shares with the Brigade of Guards . . . Two of the so-called heavies [i.e. the 'quality press'] actually gave the story an identical headline . . . the stories underneath were equally similar in content. (*The Guardian*, 7 November)

Similarly, and in a clear rhetorical context:

> Because they assumed that the comments were unattributable, the correspondents present did not attempt their usual assiduous verbatim note. Instead they gathered afterwards to ask each other the traditional lobby question: 'What's the story?' . . . The stories duly appeared, with that impressive unanimity which is the dangerous fruit of mass lobby briefings, on Sunday morning. (*The Guardian*, 11 November)

So, in one discursive context (criticizing Lawson), we are told about a detailed set of notes carefully taken by 10 independent senior journalists, each offering in its record of events a basis of truth sufficiently independent of the journalists' own press stories that they could serve as benchmarks for the accuracy of those same stories. In another discursive context (criticizing the system of lobby journalism), the same notes are characterized as sketchy and incomplete, and in any case, the product of collusion and post-event reconstruction by the journalists concerned. Accounts of whether the notes contained sufficient records of the event clearly vary according to rhetorical context.

Similar variability is observable in Lawson's discourse, at least as this is reported in the press. Having at first made strong claims that the journalists' reports were fabricated inventions, he subsequently declared 'that the unsourced quotations that had appeared were "absolutely accurate"' (*The Guardian*, 11 November). Again, we have what appear to be contradictory versions of events in the discourse of one of its major participants. And again, rather than concerning ourselves with what the absolute truth might be, we can analyse Lawson's variability in terms of the pragmatics and sequencing of his different accounts.

Lawson's second version, in which the journalists' quotations were accepted as accurate, followed the appearance in the press of detailed narratives of what 'actually' happened in the briefing, rich in description of surroundings and sequence, of dialogue and context. These narratives were themselves framed as responses to Lawson's earlier accusations of wild journalistic inaccuracies, 'described . . . as "the most inaccurate, half-baked and irresponsible" he had seen in 10 years' (*The Sunday Times*, 13 November). The pragmatic work done by Lawson's apparent volte-face was to maintain his disagreement with the journalists, while conceding the accuracy of their reports. This was achieved by his switching the issue from what he actually said to the claim that what he had said had been misunderstood:

> Treasury officials later said that Mr Lawson regarded all the accounts of the briefing given by journalists during the last few days as broadly accurate, though he strongly contested the interpretation given to them. (*The Times*, 10 November)

The upshot of Lawson's new statement was of vital importance to the issue of defining what really happened. It now hardly mattered whether there was a direct record of the meeting or not, since the dispute concerned not what was said, but what was meant. That is, despite the dispute about the tape recording which presupposed that it would decide the facts of the matter, here we see the parties agreeing about the words – the 'verbatim truth' – but disagreeing over their interpretation.

The role of constructive work in defining the original event, rather than merely the remembering of it, was now clearly established. But note that even this appears as a pragmatic, discursive resource. It is Lawson, not the journalists (who still claimed to have a clear record which supported their version), who points up the constructive nature of versions. The point is that participants themselves can do what psychologists do, offering either objective or constructive notions of reality, but here we see these theoretical positions deployed flexibly as options, with participants moving from one version to the other, as context and pragmatics require (cf. Woolgar, 1988). The reality–construction dichotomy, upon which axis the constructivists and the Gibsonians dispute the real nature of mind, appears here as an everyday rhetorical resource for bolstering different sorts of pragmatic work. 'Realist' common sense is useful when you have a stake in claiming knowledge of the unambiguous truth. Constructivism comes into its own as a device for discounting that claim in others.

What the truth is   The notion that the epistemological status of 'original events' is problematic is, of course, nothing new to cognitive psychology, at least when it is concerned not with memory but with comprehension. It has been commonplace at least since Bartlett (1932) that comprehension and memory are closely linked. Memory is understood to be a function of the comprehensibility of the original experience, and indeed has even been described as a sort of reiteration of the process of comprehension itself (Schank, 1982). Similarly, models of the comprehension of textual materials are understood to require detailed and well-organized memory components – models of the world, of events and of how inferences can be made through consultation with those components – in order to enable sense to be made of the text itself (Winograd, 1980).

However, the dependence of memory upon comprehension is generally framed as a problem concerning what goes on in the minds of the cognizers – whether experimental subjects or simulations. Psychologists themselves appear to be immune from the problem. They have direct access to the experimental 'input', have often invented it themselves, having built into it its level of comprehensibility, its degrees of ambiguity and so on, and can plainly see its meaning.

> In a psychological experiment, it is relatively easy to determine whether what the subject says is true. The experimenter knows what really happened because she staged it in the first place, or because she kept a record with which the subject's report can be compared. (Neisser, 1981: 2)

But in everyday conversational remembering, and in the Lawsongate data, it is precisely the status of the original events that is at issue. By removing that controversy from their study, by expropriating the 'input' as the psychologist's privileged knowledge, a major problematic to which ordinary rememberers address themselves is systematically excluded. The outcome is that the constructive, to-be-achieved nature of that 'original event' cannot be studied. We shall examine now some of the interpretative work that was done in the 'Lawsongate' reports, and then discuss the implications of our analysis for the psychology of memory.

The journalists' presentations of what happened at the meeting went through three distinct phases. In the first Sunday reports, which prompted all the controversy and denials, the story was simply one of what an anonymous government minister had revealed about plans to 'target' welfare benefits for the elderly upon the less well-off:

> Means test threat to pensioners . . . 'Targeting' would entail switching resources from benefits currently paid to all pensioners . . . and concentrating instead on helping the poorest. (*The Observer*, 6 November)

This and similar versions of what was said were picked up in the Monday dailies, when Lawson's counter-claims were first being voiced:

> The plan is to divert more resources to the genuinely needy by removing the rights of better-off pensioners to receive such universal benefits as [listed]. (*The Times*, 7 November)

The second phase came after Lawson's 'farrago of invention' speech, whereupon the journalists produced detailed narrative accounts of the meeting. It was in these accounts that the journalists first oriented themselves to the fact–interpretation distinction, and the constructive task of justifying the meanings that they had assigned to what the Chancellor had actually said:

> *The Times* contacted several of the journalists present at the meeting and all were adamant that while the Chancellor did not specifically mention the removal of the £10 Christmas bonus, the loss of free prescriptions for pensioners and the introduction of means testing for old people, the meaning was clear. (*The Times*, 7 November)

The major issue for interpretation centred upon the word 'targeting'. Lawson claimed that it was not meant to imply redistribution of resources, but rather the much less controversial offering of *extra* resources to the poor. The journalists were later united in their claim that Lawson had been forced into this offering of extra cash in order to extricate himself from the embarrassment caused by the original leak:

> Extra benefits for 2.6 million pensioners rushed through to cover Lawson's means test gaffe. (*The Guardian*, 25 November)

The very notion of a distinction between fact and interpretation, between what was precisely said and what was obviously meant, was originally introduced by Lawson when faced with the detailed rebuffs of his claim that the journalists had misrepresented him: the journalists had got the quotes right, but had placed the wrong interpretations upon his words. In the third phase the journalists' interpretative work in phase two has become a taken-for-granted background for reverting to a factual account, of what we all know Lawson really said. Let us look at phases two and three.

The journalists happily operated with the distinction Lawson had offered, between what was said and what was meant:

> Heading: '*Guardian* political reporters sift through the facts, fancies and furore surrounding the Chancellor's briefing on pensions'. (*The Guardian*, 11 November)

In this metaphor, facts pre-exist like little objects, which can be sifted through and separated, like wheat from chaff, from those other little objects, the 'fancies' of interpretation. However, the facts in question are not merely the words said, but their meanings. Interpretations have to be made into facts. The journalists' interpretations are presented as what any rational person would be forced to acknowledge, given such powerful warrants as accurate records, independent accounts, vivid memories, contextual plausibility ('logic') and common knowledge (what everyone knows). And thus the interpretations become indistinguishable from the facts of what was actually said.

Common knowledge

> The [press] interpretations of what the Chancellor told the lobby correspondents on Friday *chime in completely with other government moves* (*The Times*, 8 November)

> Any 'practising politician' will tell you never, ever speak of means testing when a euphemism can be used . . . Instead, *1988 Tories speak* of 'accurately targeting need'.

> The meaning of targeting under this government *has never been in any doubt.* (*The Sunday Times*, 13 November)

Context and logic

> The main message [that imputed by the journalists], in fact, was in line with earlier ministerial statements on targeting. It was a logical next step. (*The Guardian*, 8 November)

Discourse context

> With his words about child benefit *still ringing in our ears*, Mr Lawson *turned immediately* to the pensioners . . . *As with child benefit*, it sounded as though what he had in mind was . . . switching resources from universal benefits . . . and putting money instead into means-tested payments, targeted on the poorest. Indeed, *the very next question* [on the need to 'educate' his back benchers] reflected that conviction. (*The Observer*, 13 November)

> *Given his previous remarks* about child benefit and his observation that most pensioners were now well-off enough to afford the new, means-tested charges for health check-ups, that sentence could only mean one thing. (*The Sunday Times*, 13 November)

> I said I was going to write about the changes in pensioners' benefits. I recall using the word 'cuts'. It was another chance for the Treasury to inform me that Lawson had been talking about a new and extra benefit. He [Gieve] didn't do so. (*Sunday Mirror*, 13 November)

The other sorts of warrants – appeals to accurate records, independent sources and vivid memories (graphic descriptions of the scene) – have already been discussed as not at all self-evident, but accomplishments in the rhetoric of truth-telling. What we have in total, then, is a series of discursive devices through which the journalists were able to justify their claims to having provided true and accurate versions of events, such that the upshot of all of their interpretative work is to formulate it as hardly necessary. The conclusions are obvious, the only ones permissible, inherent in the facts, so that the fact–interpretation distinction is once again pragmatically closed down, with the journalists' account the only one remaining:

> Targeting (the polite word for means testing). (*The Sunday Times*, 13 November)

> It is entirely right that he should not get away with denying what he said, or with calling a dozen journalists liars. (*The Guardian*, 15 November)

In the *Sunday Times* formulation, 'targeting' is given simply as a direct translation of the term 'means testing' – terms differing only in their politeness conditions. This effectively short-circuits the fact–interpretation dichotomy altogether, in favour of the journalists' version. The *Guardian* quotation similarly reifies as simple fact what once had to be carefully established and argued. What Lawson might have meant is now what Lawson actually said. In addition, Lawson's inaccuracy appears here presuppositionally, as given information; it is multiply embedded in layers of presupposition:

1   Interpretation is gone: what he said and meant are the same.
2   x (to deny what he said) presupposes y (that he said it).

3   That he should get away with x (denying what he said) presupposes x
    and therefore y.
4   'It is entirely right that' further embeds the other already nested
    propositions.

Clearly, we are now a long way from the difficult business of textual
interpretation, where the issue of what Lawson may have said and might
have meant was at stake.

What the error is   One of the features that we noted in Neisser's study is
that to accomplish his account of Dean's truthfulness he also has to deal
with error. Basically, error posed him an interpretative problem, for it was
not encompassed by his 'repisodic' account of Dean's remembering (Gilbert
and Mulkay, 1984). To maintain the coherence of his account some
other principle needs to be invoked, and the distorting prism of Dean's
personality, his vanity, serves this purpose. While Dean's account of Nixon
is offered as repisodically correct, his own role in events is distorted.

In a similar fashion, the journalists sought to provide a dispositional
account of Lawson's behaviour:

> Yet Mr Lawson, though perhaps a trifle insensitive, is a highly intelligent man.
> So is there something which might account for the timing of the leak? (*The
> Guardian*, 7 November)

> But while he is clever, he is sometimes too clever by half. He doesn't suffer fools
> gladly . . . His super-confidence verging on super-arrogance has too often stirred
> up trouble . . . It was hubris, many [Conservatives] will suspect, which got him
> (and them) into needless trouble this week (*The Guardian*, 9 November)

> . . . an object lesson for *the cavalier Chancellor* to choose his words more
> carefully. (*Sunday Mirror*, 13 November)

For both Neisser and the journalists, truthful accounts need no such
explanation. There may indeed be an explanation for why somebody
chooses to tell the truth: it may be in one's interests to do so (Neisser on
Dean); one may be forced to admit certain things when presented with
overwhelming evidence and argument (the journalists on Lawson). But the
nature of the account itself is straightforward: it is the truth. Falsity, on
the other hand, calls for a different *kind* of explanation. An infinity of
falsities are possible, so we need to account for why particular ones are
produced. Dean's vanity led to his presenting himself favourably;
Lawson's cavalier self-confidence and arrogance led him to think he could
contradict blatant truths, and escape the consequences.

This problem is faced just as much by Lawson as by the journalists.
That is, he has to account for why the journalists got it wrong about the
content of the briefing. Lawson offers an error account in the course of the
parliamentary debate on 7 November. However, it is perhaps significant
that the newspapers we studied chose not to quote this passage, which we
have taken from the official *Hansard* record and which has a rather
different structure to those accounts quoted:

Mr Lawson: . . . the statements that appeared in the press on Sunday bore no relation whatever to what I in fact said. What I have said to them is that, while we were absolutely, totally committed to maintaining –

Ms Clare Short [Birmingham, Ladywood]: They will have their shorthand notes.

Mr Lawson: Oh yes, they will have their shorthand notes and they will know it, and they will know they went behind afterwards and *they thought there was not a good enough story and so they produced that*. (*Hansard*, 7 November)

Rather than give an account of the error in terms of psychological dispositions, which anyway would be rather more difficult to accomplish for 10 individuals simultaneously, Lawson provides an account stressing the institutional pressures on reporters to provide good stories. Lawson's version here attends both to the unanimity of the reporters' accounts (they were the same because they were contrived together) and the difference from what he was intending (because that was not a good enough story).

We have argued against the notion of a singular, objective truth that is independent of any particular version of it, or of the constructive work necessary in formulating it. Neisser, Dean, Lawson and the journalists all take pains to establish the credibility of their versions of truth against possible refutation. In doing so they each present the truth of what happened as what should be obvious to any rational person who is apprised of the evidence, while presenting dispositional accounts of the other participants' errors. As we noted earlier, this is a classic move made in the practice and rhetoric of science, where true knowledge requires no contingent explanation, since it is the outcome of the objective scientific method. In contrast, 'false' knowledge is accounted for as being due to some other process – some personal quirk or bias, social influence, false reasoning or whatever.

The problem with these speculative dispositional accounts of error is not so much with their own intrinsic validity, but rather with the obverse upon which they depend for contrast: the notion of a singular, objective truth, independent of guile or rhetoric, of construction and justification, or of any alternative construction. In the case of cognitive studies of memory, truth is equivalent to the psychologist's direct access to the input. But we have argued that this notion of direct, unconstructive access to a singularly meaningful input is illusory, an artefact of experimental design that avoids rather than usefully pins down the epistemological issues of everyday remembering.

Discussion: Neisser, truth and discourse analysis

Let us start by summarizing the principal points we have made. In the first section we argued that Neisser's three kinds of truthful remembering – verbatim, gist and repisodic – are each problematical: there can be no neutral, interpretation-free record against which to check claims; what counts as gist is an occasioned phenomenon closely related to the specific concerns and interests of the participants; the overall themes and patterns that are taken to exist are not separable from the rhetorical orientation of the different participants. Second, we suggested that Dean's accounts of his memory and his displays of memory could themselves be understood as occasioned productions oriented to the assignment of guilt to the President and towards preventing his own 'scapegoating'. Indeed, Neisser's own version of Dean's performance was seen selectively to reify (read as literal) or ironize (read as functional) Dean's discourse in such a way that the theoretically important notion of repisodic abstraction of real features of the world could be sustained, while certain systematic errors were accounted for as due to flaws in Dean's personality.

In the second section we explored this critique further by taking a situation which was comparable to Watergate, but where details of disputation were still readily available. We showed, first, that formulations of where the truth lies are not merely the academic concern of psychologists, but of practical interest to different parties engaged in a dispute about what went on. Our key point was that these different versions need to be understood as organized rhetorically. Participants' versions of events, and their selection of criteria for truth, could not be disentangled from the pragmatic deployment of these formulations. Second, we showed the way that reasoning about the true nature of the disputed briefing was carried out in a public, accountable manner, and, furthermore, that this reasoning was at its most elaborate when the dispute was at its most acute. Prior to this overt disputation, and again subsequent to it, versions of what happened were treated as straightforward or even self-evident. Finally, we showed the way that both 'sides' in the dispute maintained the coherence of their positions by the use of error accounting, and we pointed out the parallel with the similar form of accounting engaged in by Neisser with respect to Dean's purported errors.

What we have argued, therefore, is that if we are to properly comprehend what Dean, Lawson and the journalists were doing we need to understand the way notions of accuracy, veridicality, truth and so on occur in discourse as pragmatically occasioned accomplishments. Neisser's interest in Dean is consistent with his reading of Gibson: perception is to be treated as essentially veridical, and memory is to be studied for how accurate it is. Verbatim recall, gist and 'repisodic memory' are different sorts of accuracy. But when it comes to contentious claims to knowledge the psychologist is in deep epistemological water. How do *we* (as psychologists) know the truth of what is out there, as distinct from, and as a criterion for measuring, how our subjects know it?

All three of Neisser's types of truth, or of accurate recall, featured problematically as to-be-constructed outcomes of the journalists' discourse. The possibility of an objective, *verbatim* record which would solve all problems of what really happened was addressed, but lost itself in the disputation about the tape recording, about the journalists' notes, and about the independence of other sources of information. It is clear that even the existence of a 'verbatim transcript' would not have changed things because both Lawson and the journalists concentrated their efforts not upon what was actually said, which was soon conceded, but upon what it was reasonable to interpret was meant (cf. Emmison, 1989). The *gist* of what was said turns out to be precisely the contentious matter to be resolved concerning what was 'meant', the object of all the journalists' work on contextual situational descriptions, discourse context, common knowledge (what 'we all know' the British government to mean by 'targeting') and the appeal to plausible inference ('logic'). The *repisodic* truth was equivalent to the consensual upshot: like Nixon, Lawson was finally represented as having 'said it', and as having plainly tried to 'cover up' what he said.

'What really happened', the truth of the matter, is intrinsically a major issue to be dealt with in any study of remembering, whether it be grounded in everyday accounts or laboratory based. The adoption of experimental controls, through which the nature of the 'input' is rendered relatively certain and unambiguous, only serves to disguise or side-step the importance within everyday remembering of the interpretative and constructive work that has to be done with regard to that original truth. Indeed, we might say that everyday conversational remembering often has this as its primary concern: the attempt to construct an acceptable, agreed or communicatively successful version of what really happened (Edwards and Middleton, 1986 refer to this as the 'validation function'). Laboratory studies of individual memory neither resolve nor shed light upon the process; they merely remove the issue from the agenda. The psychologist acts authoritatively as validator, knows absolutely what really happened, and arbitrates accordingly after the results are gathered in. The subjects' rememberings are allowed no part in that process, of arbitrating on what the 'real truth' was, and so they are debarred from what is often, in everyday remembering, their major concern. (In fact, Edwards and Middleton, 1986, 1987, and also Neisser, 1985, point out that rememberers may frequently have other communicative goals, more important to them than strict accuracy.)

It is not merely that controlled experiments have the advantage, offering us the luxury of keeping records of the 'input' that in ordinary life we do not have. It is that experiments allow us to design (1) what that input should be (often very simple materials for which the subjects have no responsibility, and no stake in their significance), and (2) what the criteria for accurate remembering should be. The ordinarily problematical, and pragmatically occasioned, nature of factual constructions of the 'input' are simply not allowed to rise.

It is important to note that, on this argument, both the 'information-processing' and the 'ecological' approaches to mind are subject to the same problematic with regard to what 'really happened'. Both require that the objective world is unproblematically known *by the psychologist*, in some way not open to the subjects, in order for the psychologist to know to what extent the subject, whether perceiving, comprehending or remembering, got it right or not. Both perspectives ask the same question of Dean: what did he get right, and what wrong, measured against the psychologist's privileged access to the truth?

The difference between the information-processing approach to reported memories, and that of discourse analysis, is that the former takes reports as evidence for an essentially perceptual process, which is conceived as a kind of distorted re-experiencing, overlaid or altered by subsequent experience and by the machinations of inner cognitive structures and processes, with the report serving merely (and directly) as evidence of those underlying processes. In fact, Neisser (1976) and other theorists such as Barsalou (1988), who offers an AI-oriented cognitive-structural model of autobiographical memory, are also critical of the particular notion of fixed mental representations. However, they do not promote the sort of pragmatic-discursive critique offered here, which would apply equally forcibly to those alternative cognitive perspectives. For discourse analysis, as we have demonstrated, remembering is studied as action, with the report itself taken as the act of remembering, and studiable as a constructed, occasioned version of events. It is analysed directly as discourse, rather than taken as a window upon something else that is supposed to be going on inside the reporter's mind. In examining remembering as a discursive activity we pursue not only a real-world or everyday process, as Neisser recommends, but also a richly symbolic and communicative activity, as Bartlett urged in criticizing Ebbinghaus's pursuit of the putatively unadulterated mental faculty of memory.

In ordinary conversation, versions of past events are constructed as part of the pragmatics of speaking. There is no one version that can be taken in abstraction as the person's 'memory'. This implies some grounds for a radical departure not only for traditional information-processing approaches to textual memory, but also for ecological studies of discursive remembering. It seems reasonable to abandon the simplistic version of ecology – minds in context, in situational surroundings – and to pursue a more constitutive study of ecology. Mind can be studied as intrinsically social and contextualized; it makes sense to begin with no *a priori* separation of person/mind from its embodiment in communicative practices (cf. Billig, 1987; Edwards and Mercer, 1987; Edwards and Middleton, 1986; 1987; Potter and Wetherell, 1987; Potter and Edwards, 1990; Sampson, 1988). It is both possible and fruitful to pursue the study of action itself – accounts, versions, constructions – that is, discursive activity. Rather than offering us a window upon the workings of something else called 'mind', discourse can be examined for how speakers orient themselves to notions of mind, using these as resources in conversation (such as in framing accounts of truth and falsity, accomplishing blamings and excuses, mitigations and accusations, explanations of why people do what they do, and so on). Our recommendation is to let go of a commitment to mind as a pre-existing, independently knowable explanation of talk and action (much as Suchman, 1987 argues with regard to cognitive 'plans'). Like the 'truth', the cognitions that are thought to apprehend and distort it are also researchable as discursive formulations, as *versions* of mental life, framed in talk and text, and oriented to the pragmatics of communication. The study of how conceptualizations of cognitive processes are deployed in everyday and scientific discourses will be a major focus of further work.

Note

This chapter was originally published as 'The Chancellor's Memory: Rhetoric and Truth in Discursive Remembering', *Applied Cognitive Psychology* (1992) 6: 187–215. © 1992 John Wiley & Sons Ltd (abridged).

2 Emotion

Peter Stearns

Emotion is a human reaction to some stimulus, a reaction that involves both physiology and cognition. Many emotions generate changes in the body, like the faster heartbeat of fear or anger, or the blushing attached to embarrassment; and many generate clear physical expressions, like the tears of sadness, grief or (for some) anger. Emotions are not however merely physical reactions. They also have an inherent cognitive component that involves judgements about what reactions are appropriate to the stimulus, about the acceptability or unacceptability of the emotional expression, and about the extent to which it can be indulged. Thus people to an extent select how angry they will become, and certainly how much anger they will display, not just in spontaneous response to the magnitude of the stimulus but in keeping with the social setting. A given incident will provoke different levels of anger depending on whether the provoker is one's superior or subordinate. Physical expressions themselves may be to some extent chosen, depending on values internalized in cognition. Thus whether people cry when angry depends at least in part on cultural factors, which in turn lead to decisions about whether anger can be expressed directly or whether a kind of frustrating shame is best articulated through tears (Whiting and Child, 1953; Miller, 1983). Emotions, discursive psychology argues, generate symbols that convey judgements; both the judgements (is this something that warrants jealousy?) and the symbols, including bodily display, are selected in part according to quite diverse cultural cues. Finally, in adults some emotions can be experienced almost entirely cognitively. People, recalling physical sensations of anger, can talk about how a situation makes them angry – without necessarily exhibiting or experiencing physical symptoms. Some entire emotions, like sadness, may not have physical stimulus, though they may yield physical symptoms. Emotion, in sum, is a complex human package different from action and from thought but related to both.

Emotion's complexity has generated study from a variety of angles. Physiologists and many psychologists have examined the physical side, looking for example at signs of emotion in early infancy or examining facial expressions as indices of spontaneous emotional response. Social psychologists have been more concerned with emotions' role in interactions among individuals, trying to define functions in these terms. Sociologists have worked on definitions of basic emotion, but have also studied the generation of emotion in particular settings such as the workplace.

Anthropologists, concerned with cultural variations in emotion, and more recently historians and historical sociologists, dealing with changes in emotional standards and experience, have focused on variations in emotional life and the results of different kinds of emotional formulations. Philosophers, finally, have considered issues of fundamental definition.

Overall, research on emotion has taken a decided upswing in recent years. New academic organizations and new journals reflect growing interest. Formal emotions study goes back to the nineteenth century, after a long tradition of philosophical speculation on the nature and qualities of discrete emotions. Evolutionary theory helped organize a surge of psychological research, designed to discuss emotions' evolutionary function and their links to animal behaviour. A functionalist approach to emotion based on assumption of evolutionary utility continues to define a major thrust in this research field. Other theoretical paradigms developed later, including a belief that emotions should be seen as pre-verbal communication devices for the human species, serving social more than purely individual functions on this base. Interest in emotion, however, has fluctuated among scholars during the twentieth century, with the recent crest resulting from a concern for aspects of the human experience that are not simply computer-like, from a sense that emotional rules may be changing in our society, and from a new set of theoretical assumptions. The array of disciplines now involved in emotions research sets up creative challenges for the interpretation of emotion. It also reflects profound disagreements about what emotions are and, even more important, whether they should be approached primarily in terms of the experience and behaviour of individuals or in a more social context, in which wider interactions receive greatest attention. Important recent advances in understanding emotion march in step with heated debates.

Nature versus nurture

The most belligerent camps in the emotions field involve naturalists or universalists on the one hand, and constructionists on the other. The definition of emotion offered at the outset had to ignore the leading fault lines, in arguing for an amalgam of innate and socially constructed features in any realistic definition of the phenomenon. In fact, many scholars reject compromise, insisting on all-or-nothing commitments to one of the two leading camps.

Naturalists, often building from Darwinian beliefs about emotions' role in human survival, tend to argue for a series of innate emotions, essentially uniform (at least from one group of people to the next) and often, as with anger or fear, biologically grounded (Kemper, 1981; 1987; Ratner, 1989). Many naturalists devote great effort to definitions in principle, worrying about how many basic emotions there are and trying to assign species-enhancing functions to each one. Other approaches to naturalism are possible that move away from fixed emotion lists while preserving the importance of an innate, physiological component. Psychoanalyst Daniel Stern (1985), utilizing studies of infants, has posited a set of 'vitality affects', defined as very general surges of emotional energy in infants that are then shaped by contacts with adult care-givers into discrete emotions. Possibly some combination approach will turn out to work well, with a few basic emotions (like fear) combined with the more general vitalities that can be moulded into a more variable array including such possibilities as jealousy (found in many cultures but not all, and probably involving a blend of several distinct emotions including grief, anger and fear) or guilt.

Constructionists argue, in contrast, that emotions are culture-specific. They vary with the culture: some emotions crucial in one culture simply cannot be found elsewhere, and some common emotions are quite differently defined and expressed, again depending on the specific context. Some constructionists reject or ignore naturalist arguments altogether: emotions are variables, their functions depending on cultural definition, and nothing more. Others may accept a vague idea of certain basic impulses, but they are not very interested in this aspect as they go on to study more specific formulations. Constructionism is the great new theoretical paradigm of the late twentieth century in emotions research, unifying diverse empirical efforts in various disciplines including branches of psychology. Like naturalism, constructionism has generated a good deal of theoretical assertion, bent on staking out the general claims of society- or culture-specific causation and attacking real or imagined fallacies in the naturalist approach. But along with some bombast has come a growing array of challenging empirical findings.

The naturalist–constructionist dispute, applying to emotions research the old nature–nurture controversy, cuts across disciplines to a degree. No historian or anthropologist interested in emotion can fail to be some variety of constructionist. But both sociologists and psychologists can be found in either camp, with sociologists however increasingly tending towards constructionism and psychologists on balance more interested in naturalism because of its compatibility with scientific assumptions of uniformity and ready replicability. No major research projects have yet blended the two approaches, though some possibilities exist, for example in the area of socialization. Child rearing in two emotionally different cultures could be carefully compared, to see what combination of innate impulse and social norms determines how children are emotionally shaped. To some extent, the naturalist and constructionist approaches bear on different aspects of emotion. Naturalists focus on the functions that emotions offer individuals, though they may assume some societal response to uniform signals. Constructionists focus more clearly on connections between social needs that cause a particular kind of emotional display, and the social results that same display generates. They deal less with emotion in the individual, often assuming without really testing a correspondence between individual expression and group norms. Both camps agree that emotions are vital aspects of personal experience and vital bridges between one individual and the next. They have not generated any synthesis of their separate approaches or even much interest in the prospect of such synthesis.

Naturalism and science

A central attraction of the naturalistic approach to emotion is its apparent link to scientific concern for uniformities and laboratory replicability. If emotions and their functions can be uniformly defined, then psychologists who study them can easily assume the mantle of science, looking for standard patterns that can be verified through repeated observation or repeated questionnaires administered to subjects in laboratories. Invocations of science may be particularly important to a branch of psychology which, in examining a topic as potentially subjective as emotion, might seem to lack essential rigour. While outright physiological studies of emotion − examining changes in hormonal levels, for example, under the impact of emotion − have not in fact drawn great interest recently, other scientific modes retain great popularity. Some attention is given to animal and infant responses that indicate emotion, to bolster the argument that emotions are manifested before significant cultural intervention. Even more research has been devoted to facial expressions. Pictures of emotional expressions are modelled by members of other cultures, and subjects are asked to identify the emotion involved. The results demonstrate some impressive consistency. Most people regardless of culture agree on the faces that show sorrow, or surprise, or rage. There are some interesting anomalies: Argentinians do badly on emotion identification from pictures, and the Japanese do not identify anger well. Nevertheless, the facial expression results unquestionably further the idea of emotions as a preverbal communication device, instinctual and therefore invariant in the human experience (Malatesta and Izard, 1984; LaBarre, 1987).

The implications of the expressions work cannot be pressed too far, as we shall see. But the bigger problem with the work is that it explains so little of real emotional life. Knowing what face shows anger does not greatly advance an understanding of what anger is or what results it brings. Implicitly recognizing these limitations, many naturalists counter with a return to definitional efforts that maintain a scientific aura and that certainly rely on assumptions of emotional uniformities, but that may have surprisingly little empirical base. The definitional efforts often focus on relating one emotion to another. Recent work on jealousy, for example, worries about whether this emotion is itself basic or (in the more common view) is a 'blended' emotion with ingredients of grief, sadness, anger and fear. Or the definitions may spin out emotional subcategories. Jealousy here may be 'reactive' to actual threats to the object of a person's love, or it may be 'suspicious', deriving from some inner insecurity and having little to do with external reality. Finally, definitional psychologists spend a great deal of time hypothesizing the functions an emotion has. Recent students of romantic jealousy, for example, have moved away from an earlier generation that stressed jealousy's potential for causing violence or emotional collapse (though these are still acknowledged) to its uses in helping to anchor or recement romantic relationships (Salovey, 1991). Sadness is seen as an unpleasant emotion (despite cross-cultural evidence that shows societies in which people rather enjoy sadness), with the function of turning a person inward towards self-examination, conserving energy that will ultimately improve capacity to address problems when the sad mood passes (Stearns, 1993). A few add that sadness may also serve to elicit help from others. Guilt fulfils the function of indicating profound apology for wrongdoing and so opening the way for an individual's reintegration in a circle of friends or loved ones.

These definitional efforts clearly have merit. They can generate questionnaire experiments that ask subjects what they do when sad, or how they respond to another person's expression of guilt. Some of these experiments, for example in asking how people seek to relieve feelings of jealousy, produce apparently replicable results, at least within a single culture such as that of American college students. But most of the definitions share naturalist assumptions about uniform emotional essentials. A given emotion has a set of functions, and different contexts matter little in this formulation. The way jealousy should be defined and its variants categorized applies to people generally, though it can be readily recognized (a point to which we will return) that individuals vary in the extent and type of jealousy they experience. The quest for understanding emotion remains, fundamentally, a quest for universals.

The constructionist case

Against the emotional universals argument and its apparent scientism, social or cultural constructionists argue that context and function determine emotional life and that these vary: basic ingredients, emphasizing uniform instincts, functions and physiology, simply mislead. To advance their case, the constructionists offer three characteristic approaches. First, they argue a lot, raising a host of good questions about the hard science line. This is the constructionist equivalent to naturalist definitions and theorizing. Constructionists thus point out the statistical problems in the facial expressions work. They distinguish between infancy and adulthood, arguing that emotional impulses seen in infants are not in fact equivalent to adult emotional experience. They offer alternative definitions of emotion itself that move away from fixed categories like anger and fear as 'basics' and emphasize emotions less as visceral reactions than as cognitive appraisals. Thus some Eskimos, with a culture that views sharing a spouse as normal, will not have the same gut-wrenching jealous reaction to this phenomenon as will a male Arab. Dangerous situations must be appraised as such for us to feel fear, and this will vary culturally. In many societies, social inferiors will react to someone else's anger very differently from social superiors, for the key ingredient is the cultural code. Emotions as responses to cultural standards and, through them, to varied functional requirements sit at the base of the in-principle constructionist response to naturalist arguments (Averill, 1985; 1980; Harré, 1986b).

The second, and more empirical, ingredient of the constructionist path involves repeated demonstrations of the tremendous variety in emotional characteristics from one culture to the next. This comparative observation, in turn, has two facets: first, cases in which a society offers an emotion which contemporary Americans, for example, simply do not have, at least in any definable version; and second, cases in which a similar emotion is handled in radically different ways. In the first instance, where anthropologists most gleefully display their wares, we learn of responses to death (by the Ilongot) involving head-hunting raids, rather than anything we would connect with grief. Japanese *amae*, for which there is no equivalent English term, seems to encompass a feeling of sweet dependence on another person. Tahitians use the term *mehameha* to describe a special kind of fear reaction associated with the perception of the uncanny or supernatural – again an emotion that contemporary Americans do not exactly have or at least cannot put a precise name to. The Ifaluk, a Pacific island group, use a concept called *fago* to denote the emotion felt in the face of another person's distress, best translated as a mixture of compassion, love and sadness; interestingly, the Ifaluk have no emotion exactly corresponding to sadness itself. *Fago* can be painful, but the Ifaluk take pride in their capacity to feel *fago*, which implies that they are gentle, mature and generous. Examples could multiply, for it is clear that distinct emotions or emotional combinations are invented by various societies without full counterparts in other settings. Their displays, in turn, involve different kinds of judgements and different ways of explaining to others how it is with oneself (Levy, 1973; Lutz, 1988; Morsbach and Tyler, 1986; Rosaldo, 1980).

The second anthropological point is equally compelling: treatment and expression of recognizable emotions vary a great deal from one culture to the next. In the urban slums of Brazil, amid great hardship and frequent infant death, maternal attachment to babies is extremely limited when compared with the standards of many other societies. Significant love of children is hard to identify in this instance, despite a common assumption that it must be a natural condition. Tahitians do not clearly recognize grief at the death of a loved one. Anger is an unexpected variable. Of course, cultures differ in what it is permissible to be angry about: in one Pacific island case, for example, failure of a smoker to share his smoke is a legitimate cause rather the reverse of angry sentiments in the contemporary United States. But the variance goes beyond this. The Utku Inuit group simply does not seem to become angry, after early infancy. The Utku do not display hostile responses in what most Westerners would clearly identify as anger-producing situations, rather describing such situations as funny or 'too bad' in an offhand way. A whole variety of cultures disdain romantic love, seeking other, less intensely emotional bases for courtship and marriage and confining romantic ideals to literature (Briggs, 1970; Harré, 1986b; Goode, 1975).

Anthropologists are not alone in finding empirical bases for the emphasis on culture over biology in emotions research. The third facet of constructionism, in addition to theory and cross-cultural comparison, involves growing emphasis on change. Sociologists and historians have demonstrated that, even in American culture or in that of Western Europe, emotions change substantially over time. They have pointed to the eighteenth century, to the mid nineteenth century and to the mid twentieth century as points of particularly significant change, though other instances, from earlier periods and other cultures, are open to inquiry as well in a field that is still building.

One sociologist has described how the demands of service jobs, like bill collecting or flight attendance, have led to strict emotional requirements that alter experience not only at work but in personal life as well. Airline stewardesses are sedulously trained to control their anger, even in the face of infuriating passengers, with the result that they not only mask their unpleasant emotions in flight but have difficulty sorting out their emotional responses elsewhere. Their emotional experience and their repertoire of possible judgements expressed through emotional display change, in other words, because of job conditioning, and both also differ from the emotional experiences and judgements most common in American society before the twentieth-century rise of service-sector jobs (Hochschild, 1983). Jealousy changes. In Western society before the nineteenth century, jealousy was often approved, because it provided the emotional stimulus for defence of honour. The Old Testament's God, in this sense, was quite properly a jealous God, and the etymological relationship between jealousy and zeal showed through in cultural values. During the nineteenth century, however, an increasingly commercial, middle-class society began to look down on an honour-based culture, arguing that its products, in such behaviours as duelling, brought unwanted violence and disruption. In this atmosphere jealousy was redefined to apply almost exclusively to love; it was now attributed more commonly to women than to men (since women were assumed to be more conscious of affairs of the heart); and it began to be disapproved, as petty and possessive. The early twentieth century saw a heightened concern about jealousy, evident in new anxieties about sibling rivalry (a new concept) and resulting from less structured contacts between men and women and a growing approval of sexuality. By the 1970s, most middle-class Americans had learned the most recent cultural version of jealousy, arguing that the emotion was immature and had no place in an adult relationship (Stearns, 1989; Pines and Aronson,

1983). Definitions of love change. Nineteenth-century Americans were urged to view love as a transcendent, spiritual experience, and there is evidence that many of them felt this emotion in courtship, marriage, and friendship. By the twentieth century, with different standards, transcendence declined and love became more commonly associated with sexuality (Seidman, 1991). Disgust changes. A persuasive French study shows how bodily smells that once passed unnoticed became positively repellent by the early nineteenth century, leading to the rise of perfumes, supportive new hygiene, and changes in a host of relationships between emotion and the senses (Corbin, 1986).

The key points are clear, as evidence increases particularly in the area of emotional change. Cultures vary markedly in the emotions they define and the expressions they promote. Cultures also change owing to new religious beliefs, new economic forms or other shifts such as alterations in death rates or (crucial for the shift in the love–sexuality equation) available birth control devices. Constructionists, who admittedly like to spend a certain amount of time venturing abstract statements and tweaking the noses of the naturalists through provocative questions, have an arsenal of concrete illustrations on their side. By processes that require further study, but that certainly embrace the socialization of children, different cultures generate distinct emotional rules. These rules then shape individual reactions to emotional stimulus and both individual and social reactions to the emotions of others; they become embedded in the emotional process from the first cognitive phase onward. Whether members of a culture cry or not in response to anger, whether they emphasize shame over guilt – a host of basic emotional reactions flow from the distinctive standards of a particular time and place. Individual emotional personalities then oscillate around the common norms within the culture, with deviance labels applied to those who drift too far from the centre.

One of the basic indications of emotion's dependence on cultural context involves language. Emotional displays are themselves symbolic, conveying judgements sometimes without words. But cultures also develop words for emotion, which provide further evidence for interpretation through discursive psychology. Untranslatable terms like *fago* are dramatic instances of distinctive emotional symbols. But so are neologisms within a single culture. The introduction of the word 'tantrum' into English in the eighteenth century, for example, signalled a new need to be precise about types of anger and to be able to designate certain kinds of displays as reprehensibly childish. The evolution of the term 'lover' towards increasingly sexual connotations in the later nineteenth century, or the emotional warning signs conveyed by American adaptation of the word 'sissy' in the same period, are two other instances of language–emotion connections that require analysis through cultural context. The same holds, to take a still more recent instance, for the curious American fascination with the word 'cool', to designate among other things an approved emotional style, as this emerged over the past half-century.

The question of focus

A recent study of jealousy, in a fairly standard psychology mode, using questionnaire results, notes in passing that expressions of this emotion vary with national culture. Frenchmen when jealous most typically get angry; Dutchmen get sad; and Americans typically check with others to find out if their jealousy has been inappropriate or annoying. Another study finds that American men and women express jealousy differently, with women more likely to break a relationship when it has caused jealousy, but jealous men more likely to use their emotion to try to reinforce loyalties within the relationship (Salovey, 1991). These findings, particularly concerning national differences, are remarked without significant comment. They illustrate the theoretical proposition that jealousy is a blended emotion that can therefore take angry or sad paths, and they lead to further definitional discussions of the emotion's function.

For a constructionist, in contrast, the indications of cultural variation are absolutely crucial, an obvious focal point for further research. Why do experiences of jealousy vary between France, say, and the Netherlands, or between American men and women, and when and in response to what factors did the difference begin to emerge? What kinds of judgements, of oneself and others, do different ways of displaying jealousy suggest? What results do culturally distinctive expressions of jealousy have, in terms of individual coping, responses to the emotion in others, and public mechanisms such as the law?

Of course constructionists and universalists dealing with emotion share certain concerns. Very general working definitions of an emotion enter into cultural research, simply to organize the presentation at least provisionally. Questionnaire results about how emotions are perceived and what coping mechanisms they lead to help organize cultural inquiry.

But the insistence that essential features of emotion are shaped by culture leads to a distinctive kind of research agenda. First, it requires any definitions to be tentative as well as general. No constructionist would be happy with a definition of jealousy that focuses (as is the case in recent psychological studies) on the romantic relationship alone, for there are many instances in other cultures (and possibly even our own, despite the vogue of the romantic focus) where jealousy has other objects. A much looser definition of jealousy as a response to real or perceived threat to a valued object or relationships may work, but the romantic framework is too confining.

Second, the initial basic step in investigating an emotion involves exploring the culture, not venturing general hypotheses about characteristics and functions. Exploring the culture, in turn, means gaining a comparative sense – how the emotion in question is different from one case to the next – even if the end result is primarily to understand one particular cultural expression, such as the contemporary British middle class. Exploring the culture also means locating the emotion historically.

Are its current manifestations changing significantly? If the emotion has been fairly consistent over recent time, when and in what circumstances did its formulation emerge? For these comparative and historical reference points are vital to any effort to determine how an emotion is regarded and experienced, and what functions it serves, in any particular case. Context is crucial.

Through a grasp of context, emotions' role in individual lives, relationships and the larger society can be probed. Here, the student of emotional culture will share interests with other kinds of emotions researchers. But the different starting point not only shapes far more careful definitions. It also determines different kinds of research designs and questions and, as we will see, a broader approach to why and how emotions function.

A case study: grief

One of the best ways to cut through the general points about basic emotion and cultural construction involves examining a particular emotion. Among the several well-studied possibilities, grief offers particularly interesting opportunities for assessment, easily illustrating the advantages of the constructionist approach while also intruding the persistent problem of a natural or 'universal' emotional substratum.

Grief reactions vary, not only from one culture to the next, but also over time. Some cultures downplay grief, or quickly turn what we might think of as an occasion for grief into a display of anger. Some take pride in empathy with others' grief, while others divert or disdain. Within Western history, grief has undergone several reformulations in the past 200 years, in response to economic demands, religious expectation and demography.

Before the nineteenth century, West Europeans and Americans seem to have minimized grief through relatively low-key family relationships plus death practices that allowed adjustments in advance of outright demise. A fairly long dying period, typically from respiratory disease, allowed family members to gather around and reduce grief-enhancing guilt that appropriate measures had not been taken. Grief began to intensify by the later eighteenth century, and became one of the most characteristic emotions of Victorian culture through the subsequent century (Ariès, 1981; Lofland, 1985).

Heightened grief related to the acknowledgement of more fervent love. Victorian convention held even the temporary absence of a loved one to be a real sorrow, as Nathaniel Hawthorne put it in a letter to Sarah Peabody in 1840: 'Where thou art not, there it is a sort of death.' Children, themselves the focus of greater or at least more open affection, were schooled to expect grief. In the 1870s, indeed, American toy manufacturers sold coffins for dolls, so that girls could gain the appropriate emotional experience. A Protestant minister captured the bittersweet depth of

Victorian grief in a family advice manual of 1882: 'It may truly be said that no home ever reaches its highest blessedness and sweetness of love and its richest fullness of joy till sorrow enters its life some way.' Poems in children's readers conveyed the Victorian conviction that death led to a reunion of loved ones in heaven (a very novel perversion of Christian belief): 'Oh, we pray to meet our darling / For a long, long, sweet embrace. / Where the little feet are waiting / – And we meet her face to face.' Outpourings of grief ran through popular songs and private letters and diaries. And it translated into unusually elaborate mourning rituals, including black-draped house façades as well as sombre clothing and funeral rituals. Victorian death practices certainly reflected middle-class wealth and status concerns, but they also mirrored an unusually open embrace of grief (Stearns, 1994).

This tone began to change around 1900, in Western Europe and perhaps particularly in the United States. The features of grief that had seemed most attractive to Victorians, the capacity to take a person out of normal reality in reaction to death or loss, now became menacing. Dread of death and excessive response to death of another began, in popular portrayals, to seem unmodern. A flurry of magazine articles after 1900 argued that death was really rather pleasant, not worth any particular fuss. More generally, outlets such as the *Fortnightly Review* contended that, thanks to medical advance and a more healthy attitude, 'death is disappearing from our thoughts.' Lavish funerals were attacked as wasteful, and the traditional grief concepts that gave rise to them were blasted as 'vulgar and morbid'. 'Probably nothing is sadder in life than the thought of all the hours that are spent in grieving over what is past and irretrievable.' During World War I, popularizations argued that grief was an affront to soldiers' bravery and the war effort, a theme that emerged again in World War II. And even aside from war, modernity and grief continued to battle: 'Modern knowledge offers to the intelligent person today a conception of living which is a positive answer to the old death fears.'

Growing hostility to grief showed clearly in a movement away from elaborate funeral markers and particularly from protracted or showy mourning. By the 1920s, many mourning conventions were declining rapidly, and etiquette handbooks welcomed the resultant simplicity and emotional control. Therapists picked up the new message as well, and viewed most 'grief work' with their patients in terms of recovering from grief as rapidly as possible, and minimal public display (Stroebe et al., 1992). Parents were advised to keep signs of grief from children. *Parents' Magazine* cautioned against 'conjuring up a heaven of angels and harp playing', for 'inevitably the small girl or boy will discover that mother and father are not certain about the after life. Such a discovery augments the fear of death.' 'Let us give the facts to the child' (when evasion was impossible) 'with as little emotion as possible.' Grief had become not only an unpleasant but virtually a dangerous emotion. Emily Post and Amy Vanderbilt added the stamp of modern etiquette: grief was rude, an intrusion on other people. 'We are developing a more positive social attitude toward others,' wrote Vanderbilt in her 1952 best-seller, 'who might find it difficult to function well in the constant company of an outwardly mourning person' (Stearns, 1994).

The transformation of American grief culture had several sources, thus picking up the multiple causation common in cases of significant shifts in standards. Dramatic changes in the actual incidence of death, and particularly the rapid decline of the infant death rate between 1880 and 1920, helps explain both the timing and the direction of the new standards. People grew more emotionally attuned to death fighting (and possibly, deep inside, more truly frightened of death and so more reluctant to open up through grief) than to emotional acquiescence, and they could realistically assume that death at an inappropriate age was becoming rare. The increasing rigidity of work rhythms, as industrialization steadily advanced, discouraged the disruption of mourning periods; in an advanced industrial society, grief proved impractical. A decline of religious certainty, though not uniform in the United States, also weakened the particular grief culture that had surfaced with Victorianism. Finally, the more general movement away from the embrace of emotional intensity, part of the larger redefinition of emotional culture during the second quarter of the twentieth century, solidified the specific rethinking applied to grief.

The substantial change in the modern history of grief, combined with well-established anthropological evidence about the wide variety in grief reactions – and even the virtual absence of overt grief in some cultures – makes it obvious that grief must be understood in specific contexts. What kind of grief is manifested, what kind of grief is accepted, and to some extent what kind of grief is actually experienced varies greatly depending on the cultural cues that guide the cognitive part of emotional response. A constructionist approach is unavoidable if grief is to be understood.

Yet the possibility of some innate grief response cannot entirely be discounted. Historians who have worked on the pre-1700 period, when signs of grief were by Victorian standards modest, have noted a clear emotional record of such events as children's deaths, and a category also in doctors' records for patients whose grief seemed excessive. Neither of these points contradicts the finding of a culture rather neglectful of grief – indeed, they may confirm it – but they also suggest limits to the impact of this culture on actual emotional experience. The same point crops up in dealing with the results of the cooling of grief in twentieth-century culture. New standards had effects not only in institutional expressions of emotion but in personal perception and reaction to others. Grief did decline. But important cases of intense grief persisted. By the 1950s, many grief-stricken individuals formed support groups with other, emotionally comparable individuals. By the 1970s some therapists were questioning the tendency to treat grief as an illness to be cured. At least in Western culture, possibly in the human species, the construction of grief may interact with a substratum of natural emotion. Construction shapes this substratum and its social manifestations, but it may be constrained in the process. Emotion, again, consists of deep-seated responses as well as profound cultural guidance mechanisms. Both must be attended to in any full assessment.

This means that contemporary studies of grief, whether actively interested in history and anthropological comparison or not, must include attention to the directions of current culture. Assumptions about innate grief and its functions may help guide such studies, but examination of tensions created by relatively recent cultural changes is far more significant in understanding what grief is all about and what issues it creates. The sensitive observer must also be aware of subcultures of grief and their own trajectories, in relation to mainstream trends. Various ethnic communities in the United States, for example, have particular traditions of grief that interact with the directions of the larger culture. Effusive grief among southern African Americans contrasts with the typically much more restrained reactions of Americans of German origin; each subculture must deal with its relationship to the guidelines of the larger society, including changes, needs and influences, and with its ability to handle whatever 'natural' grief exists. Only by manipulating these various strands can a major emotion be understood. As therapists reopen debates over what to 'do' about grief in modern society, the appeal for a synthetic approach is not merely an academic exercise (Stroebe et al., 1992).

Causes and results

Approaching emotion as an expression of culture, variable in place and time, not only alters the essential starting points of emotions research towards comparison and historical perspective. It also addresses issues normally omitted from or at least downplayed in more conventional analysis, which in turn heighten the understanding of emotion itself.

Whether the focus rests on a particular emotion like grief, or a larger emotional style linking a number of emotions according to a valuation of intensity or a division between pleasant and unpleasant emotional experiences, grasping emotion as a facet of culture inevitably forces a consideration of causation. Emotion is no longer a natural experience that requires no particular explanation. While it may have some roots in a natural impulse, its real expression is shaped by a specific context. It responds to some functional needs of a given society and culture, though functionalism must not be too narrowly constructed. In the case of grief, we saw that major changes resulted from alterations in the actual experience of death and from wider shifts in the definition of society's needs relating to support for medical advances that sought to prevent traditional death rates and to the decline of religion.

Anthropological inquiries into emotionally distinctive cultures have not been rich in causation analysis, because the cultures are assumed to go back in time and are taken as given rather than explained. Several well-established historical cases, though all derived from Western European and United States society, more clearly set some guidelines on what kind of causes to look for in dealing with why a particular emotional context exists. Multiple factors usually combine to set a particular configuration. Changes in economic structure often loom large. In the early twentieth century, the rise of corporate organization and consumerism prompted a reconsideration of previous emotional standards, towards new emphasis on regulating emotional intensity in the interest of smoother group cohesion. Changes in family and demography also enter in, as with the decline of the child death rate and its impact on love and grief around 1900. Shifts in the nature and hold of religion but also other cultural changes, including previous shifts in emotional standards themselves, expand any narrowly functionalist inquiry. Changes in beliefs about disease may also enter in. Growing concern about high blood pressure and other sources of organic deterioration, and particularly heart ailments, taking hold by the 1920s fed new concerns about emotional intensity and specific attacks on anger or the use of fear in children's discipline. By the 1970s health warnings were extended into personnel training for flight attendants and other service personnel (Stern 1985; Stearns, 1994; Hochschild, 1983).

Causation analysis is not easy and, applied to any particular cultural formulation, it lacks scientific precision. It cannot be tested in conventional scientific fashion precisely because no context can be replicated entirely; it is *sui generis*. Exploring what shapes the context for emotion nevertheless amplifies our understanding of what a particular set of emotional standards itself involves.

At the same time, the constructionist approach invites new inquiry into the results of a particular emotional configuration. Exploring functions through cultural specificity inevitably leads to a reassessment of emotions' impact. Naturalists have long invoked functionalist analysis, trying to figure out, often through speculation rather than evidence, what role a particular emotion might serve in maintaining or advancing the species.

Their approach has typically been more philosophical than empirical, however, because of their insistence on generalized functions regardless of context – the definitional impulse – plus the fact that the results of emotions require social observation in some form. Laboratory settings at best suggest what people may do with an emotion. Constructionists working through field observation, or the sociology of family or workplace, or (despite some limitations of data) with historical materials, assemble considerable information on what emotions yield. A new spirit in psychology, based on recognition of cultural specificity but also the need for a new appreciation of observational techniques, can only enhance this fledgling approach. Promising efforts in the vein including linkages between questionnaire data on individual proclivity to an emotion like grief or jealousy, and stability of family relationships where different emotional styles yield decidedly different results (Salovey, 1991).

An understanding of emotion as the outgrowth of culture changes the assessment of emotions' results in another respect as well. Naturalists tend to look primarily at the impact of emotions on individuals: how they cope, how they express. The individual result is undeniably significant, and constructionists offer insights in this area. But emotions have a wider dimension as well, precisely because they are evaluated and promoted according to wider cultural standards.

The most obvious contribution of the new approach to emotion to the analysis of results focuses on specificity. It is fruitless to push generalized definitions of the functions of an emotion too far. Sadness may prompt self-isolation in American society, but in other societies it enforces group mechanisms or may heighten individual prestige as a badge of pious humility. The impact of an emotion depends on the standards involved.

Young American women in the late nineteenth century could openly proclaim their jealousy, with some assurance that this might motivate others to modify the behaviour that provoked this emotion. By the late twentieth century, an experience of jealousy most commonly made a middle-class American feel embarrassed and eager to conceal or to flee the jealousy-producing relationship, while tending to elicit from others, not a modification of behaviour, but accusations of immaturity and possessiveness. Emotion display had results in both instances, but these had become much more complex by the later period. At the same time, different societies and different periods have different goals, and emotional standards shift in keeping with these differences. Grief, in the Victorian decades when both intense love and death were common, served to bring emotional support to a stricken individual and often helped bond a family in the face of crisis. Families had loosened by the mid twentieth century, and individual satisfactions held a higher place. Grief in this situation often disrupted fragile family ties: few marriages could survive the emotional impact of the death of a child, for example, in the United States; grief avoidance was more clearly in keeping with the new set of priorities (Stearns, 1994).

While constructionism complicates assessment of emotions' functions, because of the need for context specificity, it also highlights the impact emotions have. Emotions effectively mediate between basic forces in a society and desired relationships among people. For example, as the American economy focused on corporate management and the service sector, beginning in the 1920s, it sought smoother, less contentious relationships at work. A key mechanism towards these goals involved new job training and new childhood socialization in the reduction of anger. As the new anger standards in turn were internalized, the emotional tone of many jobs did change, and the emotional basis for work-related protest was reduced. This was no overnight process, for a full generation was required before clear results could be measured (Moore, 1978; Stearns and Stearns, 1986). And of course other factors entered into phenomena such as the downturn in strike rates that began in the late 1950s. Nevertheless, emotional redefinition, once time had elapsed for its internalization, played a significant mediating role between initial cause and resulting new behaviour.

Overall, constructionists who start with emotional cultures look for three kinds of results or functions. The first involves individuals themselves. What happens to individuals in a grief-expressive culture compared with those living under standards that discourage grief? Here is where evidence of basic emotions, not fully amenable to cultural change, has to be handled. Yet standards affect individual expression and self-assessment, which feeds the emotional experience in turn. At the same time, cultural change often helps explain emotional problem areas for some individuals. Anxiety about jealousy ran high between the 1920s and the 1970s in the United States, and was likely to trigger appeals to therapists or child-rearing experts; this was when middle-class norms were changing in the United States (Clanton, 1989). Anxiety has lessened in the past two decades, as what had been new norms were internalized and adjusted to varied personal styles.

But individual emotional expression is not the only result of emotional culture, and the constructionist approach invites new attention to the wider range. The second impact area involves reactions of others. While some emotions may trigger uniform reactions – if we see fear in another, we may ourselves become afraid, in a process of emotional contagion (Hatfield et al., 1992) – many reactions depend on cultural values. One culture's normal, accepted emotional pattern might induce shock or disdain in another. Societies enforcing new standards, like those that attacked open grief, try to persuade many people not to respond to outdated emotional signals. The general point here is that emotions communicate, and express judgement. The constructionist addendum is that communication is culturally specific, and we need to pay more attention to responses of other people.

Emotions and emotional standards, finally, affect public institutions. Laws change in the light of emotional values. Mental cruelty divorce criteria, instituted in the United States in the late nineteenth century, answered to Victorian beliefs in the importance of active, anger-free love; no-fault divorce laws, spreading from the late 1960s, explicitly answered to a new emotional culture that sought to avoid emotional intensity. The public impact of emotional standards feeds emotional experience itself. New work expectations – like the current fashion for 'Quality management' programmes in the United States, whose training manuals explicitly urge against 'becoming emotional' – affect emotions on and off the job. Public impact, however, has a potential complexity of its own. While some laws and programmes work to fulfil the dominant emotional culture, others may move in opposite directions, to serve as release. A twentieth-century emotional culture in the United States that increasingly urged parents to help their children avoid fear-producing situations, also saw a growing array of books and films designed to attract a youthful audience by artificial evocations of fear. Much leisure culture in the twentieth century, in fact, including spectator sports, worked against routine emotional rules, providing symbolic outlets. Here too, emotional norms have impact within a specific cultural context (Griswold, 1986; Stearns and Haggerty, 1991; Jacob, 1988).

Emotions form a vital part of personal experience and of the inter-actions among individuals. They also work into larger social and ritual frameworks, contributing to patterns in religion, leisure, even political life. 'Basic' functions, like the role of anger in preparing for combat, do not necessarily disappear, but the canvas fills out as constructionists explore the larger social framework.

Serious work on emotions and their role in personal and social life must contend with a variety of emotional expressions within a complex culture. There is also the issue of individual variance. Everybody knows, and personality psychologists in recent research confirm, that some people are more jealous, more aggressive, more empathic or more melancholy than others. The universalist approach to emotion long tended to ignore these varieties, but recent research emphasizes distinct styles – differences in 'reactivity' – that are often genetic at base. Cultural constructionists, bent on defining norms within a particular society or subgroup, have also downplayed personality variants. Empiricists who produce questionnaire findings on the varied jealousy or grief proclivities of different individuals clearly point to a vital subtopic (Salovey, 1991). Because they tend to ignore the particular standards of a culture, however, they may downplay the stresses that encourage some styles over others. Even more clearly, they have difficulty explaining where the styles come from beyond genetics – that is, how cultural norms and innate proclivities interact. A modified constructionist approach, which takes the findings on varied personality types but reads them into the promptings of the wider emotional culture to see how they are encouraged or how they require concealment or adjustment, will enhance this facet of emotions research as well.

The marriage between a new psychology and cultural analysis remains the most promising hope for future results in understanding emotion and its personal and social impact. A synthesis with some of the naturalists' findings may emerge, but it is the exploration of the interaction between culture and individual that demands primary attention. This exploration will derive from a new sensitivity to context and to social causation. It will look at the results of emotion not simply through individual expressions but as a connection between individual behaviours and the larger society, with emotions channelling social signals and affecting social behaviours in turn. It may even identify emotional problems not simply as personal vagaries but as products of tensions stemming from cultural change. The attempt to cram emotions research into the most obvious scientific categories of universality and laboratory replicability has narrowed the field and distorted our understanding. The alternative is available, and though it comes initially from outside psychology's domain a culturally sophisticated psychology will extend its findings and improve its capacity to explore emotion as a vital link between self and others.

Paths to explore

The great strides in emotions research in recent years – sometimes supplementing, sometimes replacing older beliefs on the subject – leave a host of topics open to further inquiry. Every discipline involved in emotions study can generate a substantial list of emotions, expressions or functions that have scarcely been treated at all. The most obvious challenge lies, however, in blending disciplinary approaches and moving beyond the increasingly sterile either/or debates between constructionists and naturalists. The process of transmitting culture-specific emotional rules to children lies at the heart of the mixing of innate and learned characteristics in emotion. It invites comparative study that however is also open to evidence of common emotional patterns. Interdisciplinary interest in the functions of emotions must transcend the common impression that emotions need only concern students of personality, though it can build in personality psychology as well. Naturalists, until recently the dominant figures in emotions research, issued powerful but oddly simplistic verdicts about emotions' functions which did not encourage application to political life or work behaviour or even, until recently, family relationships or friendships. Constructionists, with their interest in emotion as intermediary between wider social forces and personal styles and results, invite more extensive claims, as they show how emotional norms relate individuals to institutions, albeit in culturally specific contexts.

3 Constructing Divinity

Nancy C. Much and
Manamohan Mahapatra

Kalasis: conduits to divinity

In *Rethinking Psychology* Much (in press) outlines a prospectus for a (trans)cultural psychology. Its agenda was based upon the investigation of (1) indigenous theories and (2) the interconnectedness of three co-creative semiotic systems: persons, social structures and cultural symbol systems. In this chapter that theme is developed with a case study: the interplay of meanings in the constitution of the life form of a woman of Orissa, a *Kalasi* or possession oracle. According to the envisioned scheme, it is possible to consider her role as possession oracle from the point of view of personal meanings and values, of social statuses or positions, and of local cultural symbolic contexts. The focus of the analysis is upon the cultural discourse that accommodates the role and status of possession oracle, and upon the semiotic skills of the oracle herself as she transforms herself from her ordinary persona to a 'moving divinity' (*Thakura chalanti*).

Orissa, a state on the eastern coast of India, just south of West Bengal and Bihar, remains in many ways an 'enchanted' world, where a remarkable feature of the ordinary life is the extent to which all aspects of daily environments, domestic, occupational and commercial, are saturated with symbols of the sacred world, reminding participants, at every encounter, of the here and now presence of a sacred order permeating, even as it transcends, the objects and events of the material and social world. Here also various arts of ritual are outstanding in countless cultural performances designed to draw onlookers into the realm of discourse with the gods. Not only uneducated farmers and labourers, not only traditionally trained priests and temple servants, but college graduates, office workers, business people, bankers and technicians, as well as professors, doctors, engineers and statesmen, are eager to participate in these discourses.

Among the most popular of ritual arts in Orissa are the many possible performances involving a *darshan*, a vision or viewing of persons or objects who are in one way or another special conduits of divinity. Objects, animate and inanimate, may be conduits of divinity, that is, 'containers' into which the God can be invoked and persuaded to dwell, or in which the deity chooses to dwell, and which for that time possess the living power of the God or Goddess. Such are the icons worshipped as the God in the temple, or the *salagram*, a natural stone, found in the river Ganduki in Nepal, said to be a form (*rupa*) of *Vishnu*. But personal conduits are of a special type. The difference between performances involving ritual discourse with object conduits and those involving discourse with personal conduits of divinity is the apparently intense satisfaction of not only viewing the divinity and having oneself heard by the divinity, but having the divinity respond immediately and directly to oneself, in words and gestures that can be apprehended as human discourse. *Darshan* may also mean an inner vision or a vision in a dream. The *darshan* that is a vision or dream may also speak to the beholder, but relatively few are privileged to have a private *darshan* of this type. In Orissa, several varieties of personal conduit exist, each with its own specific style of discourse. We discuss one particular variety, the *Kalasi*, and one exemplar (an excellent one, we thought) of the *Kalasi* tradition.

Kalasis are possession oracles. They draw their generic name from the Goddess Kali, the Great Mother, who, in one or another (or several) of her forms (*rupas*), possesses a chosen few of her human devotees. Men and women both may become *Kalasis*. However, women predominate and certain forms of the Goddess, e.g. *Santoshi Ma*, are said to possess only women. At some point in their lives, *Kalasis* are chosen by the Goddess as vehicles for her possession. Generally it is said that the person's devotion to the Goddess draws her to that person specifically. *Kalasis* do not generally do preparatory *sadhana* or yogic practices to invite or invoke the first occurrences of trance states. From the experiential point of view of the *Kalasi*, it is the Goddess who initiates the possession relationship. The Oriya (i.e. Orissan) *Kalasi* whose performance we recount told how the presence of the Goddess had been with her from childhood, until finally she had by circumstance been introduced to the *puja* or worship for *Santoshi Ma* in Bengal, and after that the Mother had begun to speak to devotees through her. We have given this *Kalasi* the pseudonym Basanti Devi, where *Devi*, following local custom, designates her as a married woman. Though *Devi* is also a term for the Goddess, in this context it has nothing to do with marking her as a *Kalasi*; it is only the common social index of her status as a married woman.

Basanti Devi's earliest inclinations, as she recalls them, were consistent with the demands of divine possession. Her first experience of divine possession goes back to her childhood. There were various experiences of possession and of the felt presence of the Goddess, as well as other signs that the girl was favoured by the Goddess. The Goddess had even advised Basanti Devi about marriage and she had followed the command of the Goddess in choosing the time for her marriage. The Goddess had always been present to warn her of dangers. A cobra, the mascot of the God Siva and his consort, stayed near her in childhood (a possibility in Orissa, where village houses are open on many sides and snakes not infrequently enter). In childhood she developed devout habits and a concern with purity well beyond the standard for ordinary persons.

MM: When did this Goddess appear here?

Ma: From 1978 the Mother came here. I was a child. When I was six or seven years old. At that time *Kanaka Durga* and *Mangala* appeared in [*lagaiba*] me. Then the Mother appeared. In accordance with the words of the Mother, when I was 13 years old and 14 came, I got married. My marriage was held at the time given by the Mother. The Mother would always come – when there would be some difficulties the Mother would come. If there was to be any loss [*kshyati*], she would come and tell that.

MM: The Mother told this in dreams?

Ma: No. The Mother would possess [*lagaiba*] me and say. She would possess me [*myself*] and speak.

MM: When you were six, seven years old, *Kanaka Durga* and *Mangala* appeared in you, then from when did *Santoshi Ma* come?

Ma: I went to Calcutta, *Babu* and all the children went. He learned driving there. He stayed there for 3 or 4 months. At that time the children were telling me about *Santoshi Ma*. The children in Bengal. [*Children means devotees here.*] Seeing from them, I told my children, this is the *brata* [*a vow to practise a set of rituals and restrictions for a deity*] of the Mother, do it. From there, I started the *brata*. I had started the *brata* for three or four times. [*It is done weekly.*] *Santoshi Ma* appeared [*i.e. possessed Basanti Devi*]. When *Santoshi Ma* appeared, the Mother [*i.e. in possession of Basanti Devi*] talked with them [*the devotees*] in Bengali . . . First when I was small, when I was born, that cobra [*naga sapa*] always would come and always stay near me. And then when I became six to seven years, when I was small, there is a God in our village. When I was small from those days I would go to the God's temple always. Again, from my childhood, I do not eat *ainsa* [*flesh foods, abhorred by Santoshi Ma*] or eat in anybody's house [*for reasons of maintaining purity*]. Everything of mine was separate. [*Separate cooking was done for her, her food was separate from the rest of the family.*] Then till today I have not taken *ainsa* or *usuna* [*parboiled rice, more susceptible to pollution than sun-dried arua rice*]. No onion or garlic, nor [*do I*] eat in anybody's house. It was going on like that.

The public possession trance of a *Kalasi* generally occurs in the following way. At specific times and places, and after ritual preparations, the Goddess enters and merges with [*lagaiba*] the *Kalasi*. At this time the ordinary person in the body disappears into the background and the Goddess acts and speaks through the *Kalasi*'s body. *Kalasis* generally describe themselves as not retaining their own 'sense' [*hosa rahuni*] at the time of possession and deny having any memory of what they said or did while possessed. Under possession the *Kalasi* is the Mother. In Orissa it is only the Goddess, in her various forms, who takes possession of human bodies. The Gods are more aloof and do not enter human bodies for the purpose of *darshan* of their devotees. In Orissa both males and females may be possessed by the Goddess. At the time of possession the *Kalasi*, male or female, is addressed as *Ma*, 'Mother'. Female *Kalasis* are usually addressed as 'Mother' at other times as well, a recognition of their special association with the Goddess and mark of their special prestige and respect in the community. Other senior women are also called 'Mother' (*Ma*) by persons junior in age or rank. But *Kalasis* are also called 'Mother' even by persons who would normally be their social superiors, in a society in which relative hierarchy is conversationally marked in practically every extended encounter.

During the times of transformation and possession, and those times only, *Kalasis* are expected to speak and behave in ways quite different from what is normally acceptable social behaviour. These ways of behaving are, however, patterned and meaningful symbolic deviations from the norm and not random disinhibition. The changes in appearance, demeanour, speech and behaviour that a *Kalasi* undergoes during possession mark her/his transition from an ordinary community member to a 'moving God' (*Thakura chalanti*).

Like other possession oracles, the Oriya *Kalasis* are held to have special powers when possessed by the Goddess. Their actions and speech are understood as the actions and speech of the Goddess and their special powers under possession are understood as attributes of the Goddess and not of the person in her ordinary state. During the time of possession, devotees gather around the Mother hoping for advice and cures for their psychological and physical problems, court cases, school problems, family problems and illnesses.

Becoming the mother

We describe here a series of ritual discursive actions through which Basanti Devi, beginning as a devout housewife and village woman, transforms into the living Goddess. Basanti Devi most graciously permitted Nancy Much to view her *puja* and transformation from a privileged position inside the *Thakura ghara* (God's house or room) and allowed us to record and photograph her in her trance state. We are most thankful to Basanti Devi and most appreciative of her superb skills as a *Kalasi*. We agreed that among *Kalasis* she is a splendid example of devotion to her sacred art. The following is Nancy Much's account of watching Basanti Devi become the Mother.

> It is Friday, the day on which the possession of *Santoshi Ma* ordinarily occurs. Basanti Devi is a short, plump and attractive woman, with a warm friendly countenance and pleasing manner, not without a sense of humour. When asked what kinds of people visited the Goddess, she told us three kinds came: some were true devotees, some came just out of curiosity and, since the possession of *Santoshi Ma* attracts many ladies (and she herself has four pretty daughters), some boys come, mainly for the purpose of watching the girls. Sometimes, she said, the Mother would beat them with canes (*beta*, light bamboo canes, which are carried by *Kalasis* when they become the Goddess) and verbally abuse them; once she asked a boy to squat and rise 108 times, holding on to his earlobes, a symbolic punishment which shames. Before possession Basanti Devi performs *puja*. She is assisted by three daughters. The *puja* for the possession of *Santoshi Ma* begins sometime after 11.00 a.m.
>
> The *Thakura ghara* is a small rectangular cement building without windows; about one-third of it is filled with the elaborate *gadi* or shrine, the ritual seat of 108 *rupas* of the Gods and Goddesses. At the centre of the *gadi* is a larger than

life *rupa* of *Santoshi Ma*. Basanti Devi told us that because 108 Gods and Goddesses were worshipped there, other *Kalasis* could also visit her shrine, perform their *puja* and attain possession.

The place of her *puja* is at a small fire pit in front of the *gadi*. Around this pit are placed a number of *puja* objects, a brass pot of water covered with bel leaves, a *dipa* or ghee lamp to the right of Basanti Devi, a *dipa* in front of the pit, four bananas, white tagara flowers, a jar of *ghee* (clarified butter) for *ahuti* (oblations to the fire), some coconut fibre (for the burning of resin of the sal tree) and an earthen chalice (for burning the resin). There are also some wooden sticks for creating the fire. To the front right of the pit close to the *gadi* are plates of *bhoga*, or food offerings, balls of a coarse gram mixed with raw sugar or *guda*, and one plate of broken coconut, which our driver has brought as his offering.

Basanti Devi, whom we spoke with earlier, has now bathed and changed into a new red sari; the purchase tag is still visible on the sari's edge. Her hair is neatly bound. There is an ordinary wife's vermilion (*sindur*) mark on her forehead. Basanti Devi has the bearing and demeanour of an ordinary respectable Hindu village wife. She wears a sari with which she covers herself well. Her voice is soft. Her smile is soft. She does not laugh aloud. She stands and walks with shoulders slightly curved forward, head slightly downward and glance tending more to turn downward than upward or outward. (These details are mentioned because they will be invoked later as part of the 'discourse' of the transformation.)

The *puja* begins. Basanti Devi seats herself behind the fire pit. She sprinkles the area with water to purify it. She builds a four-sided structure from the sticks in the fire pit; it looks like a matchstick house. The structure is made to allow air to flow to the fire. A wick is put in the middle. One daughter lights incense sticks and puts them on the *gadi*. A tall *dipa* on the *gadi* is also lit. On the *gadi* are canes (*beta*), peacock feathers, two *malas* (garlands of 108 beads for doing *japa*) of *rudrakshya* beads (sacred to Siva) and two bells (*ghanti*). Another daughter prepares some resin powder which is kept on a scrap of newspaper and puts the fragrant resin in the earthen chalice.

Basanti Devi performs the main acts of the *puja*, builds the small wooden structure, then sets it aflame, lighting cloth wicks from the *dipa* in front of the fire pit.

A daughter lights the coconut fibres lying in the earthen vessel on top of the resin incense, creating profuse fragrant smoke. Soon the air becomes thick with incense smoke. While this is going on, one of the daughters begins reading a book of verses in praise of *Santoshi Ma*. One of the daughters rings a bell. At some point a gong begins to be beaten continuously.

Basanti Devi gives the area around the pit another sprinkling with water. She peels the four bananas that have been placed one on each of the four sides of the pit. *Ghee* in a small glass jar is liquefied by holding it over the *dipa*. When it is fed to the fire, the fire rises high. This is an oblation (*ahuti*) to satisfy the fire. Basanti Devi puts the bananas into the fire. As the fire dies down, a *bel* leaf is lit and held in Basanti Devi's hand before her face. She holds it to her forehead and mouth and finally throws it into the fire with both hands. This is *pushpanjali* (petals and leaves), the concluding offering to the Goddess. The leaf rubbed against Basanti Devi's face has made her vermilion 'spot' into a long streak down the centre of her forehead.

As the fire dies down, Basanti Devi, who is now in the climactic transformation (and is henceforth referred to as the Mother), moves off to the left side of the pit and kneels down before the *gadi*.

Her daughter continues to recite the verses. *Hulahuli*, a long, shrill vibrato cry, is made by various devotees outside the door. While kneeling before the *gadi* the

Santoshi Ma begins to tremble violently. The trembling is not spastic but rhythmic, her entire body shaking as one unit. While the Mother is trembling, her very long black hair falls out of its knot and hangs loose down her back. She arises. Her countenance has changed dramatically. When we spoke to her earlier, she had a round-faced, pleasant countenance with poised expression. Her face now has taken on an angry appearance with the lower eyelids raised at the inner corner and darkened. The forehead is not creased but is sternly set and stony, giving a different set to the eyes. The mouth also is sternly set, giving her a fierce look.

The supplicants outside are making loud *hulahuli*. A number stand outside in postures of worship.

The Mother howls (not a *hulahuli*, but a long howl). She rises. Her daughters put garlands of flowers around her neck. Not only her face, but her posture and manner of movement have changed dramatically. During the initial part of the possession the walk is somewhat heavy footed and stiff. She walks to the outside, backing out of the door of the *Thakura ghara*. There at some point she stands still for a moment, her face set. Then again she approaches the *gadi*. Many times she walks out and back to the inside of the temple again. Her demeanour continues to change. She no longer has the held-in, rounded posture with down-curving shoulders typical of traditional village women. The 'veil' of her sari is now off her head and her walk has become upright and strong-shouldered, a confident, arrogant, even swaggering posture.

On one trip back to the *gadi*, she takes a plate of the *bhoga* and offers it around to her visitors. People take fragments of the sweet parched pulse balls. On another trip, she enters the temple and gestures to her daughter for her *rudrakshya mala*.

At this time the Goddess begins taking flaming wicks from the *dipa* and putting them into her mouth to extinguish them, tossing her head and laughing. Each time she does this she laughs wildly. Gradually her laughter becomes more and more predominant and the stern set of her face less. But her smile now is very different from the one she had as an ordinary woman. Her smile is very bold, confident, sometimes mocking, sometimes playful, even seductive. I happen to think she looks quite beautiful this way, and makes a wonderful representation of the Goddess. I smile in aesthetic appreciation. It gives one enjoyment to see her. Most of the onlookers, however, wear serious, even fearful expressions and many remain in postures of worship. I look at her daughters to make sure my smile will not be misunderstood. But they too are smiling to see the Mother. The Mother herself is often half laughing or teasing as she talks.

The Mother takes from the *gadi* a handful of canes (*beta*) and peacock feathers. Again, holding her *beta*, she makes repeated walks to the outside and back into the *Thakura ghara*. On the first walk outside the *Thakura ghara*, her feet are washed (water is poured over her feet). Her devotees bow their heads to the ground at the edges of her *paduka* or 'foot-bathing water'. As she walks to the outside, she sometimes whacks a male supplicant with the *beta*. This is not in anger but is taken as a blessing. The man, smiling, bows his head and shoulders and cowers a bit.

Finally she walks to the end of the veranda where the *singhasana* or lion seat is. She assumes her seat there when she is ready to call her devotees before her. Worshippers, supplicants and inquirers stand around thickly on the veranda or just outside it. As she assumes the lion seat, a woman in a rose-coloured sari comes before her and lovingly sings *bhajans*, songs of praise of the Goddess. The Mother embraces the woman, who weeps, then stays to sit near her. People do not approach her but rather she calls them to her. Next she calls a man. She not infrequently slaps men on the shoulders or side of the head with the canes. But I did not see her do this with women. Women dominate this place in numbers and men are visibly more fearful and shy of approaching the Mother than women are. A male devotee sings *bhajan* in her praise from the background. The Mother begins her *hukum* or commands.

As the reader will readily see, a lot of social-symbolic communication has already gone on during the *puja* and transformation, even though as yet nothing at all has been mentioned of the Mother's speech. Much (1995) argued that discourse analysis should routinely include context analysis, the idea that much important symbolic communication occurs in the environmental and action contexts surrounding speech. The *Kalasi*'s *puja* is an excellent example of how important that context can be. Without the *puja* and other signs of transformation performed by Basanti Devi prior to the public speaking which follows, the conditions for speaking in the voice of the Goddess would not have been properly and effectively set. During the *puja* and transformation she does not say anything, except to utter *mantra* too softly to be heard. Yet she has communicated an extraordinary amount and has done the foundation work for establishing her transformation to a Goddess moving in the world. People have seen an elegant ritual performed with concentration, and then, before their eyes, the transformation of her identity from that of a housewife to the wild, unpredictable and dangerous, though compassionate, Mother. This drama is enacted in an environment saturated with sacred symbols, symbols of the divine realm and the person's relationship to it. It is constituted by a series of actions each of which represents a form of communication with the divine realm, and ultimately stages of merging with it. The symbolic objects worn and carried by the *Kalasi* are all iconographic 'attributes' of the Goddess, standing for the attributes of her personality and her specific relationships to other deities (especially Siva) and to the world of humanity. Every symbolic object and action (of which there are perhaps hundreds altogether in the *puja* and transformation) functions to focus the attention or consciousness of Basanti Devi, as well as onlookers, upon the ambience of divinity and the impeding merging of the ordinary world with the divine.

After the transformation, the Mother will give *hukum*, or the commands of the Goddess. We discuss this discourse later. Let us first consider the cultural symbolic, social and personal meaning contexts in which performances of this kind occur.

Ecstatic states and cultural discourse in Orissa

Along with other cultural scholars (see particularly Kakar, 1982; 1992; also Obeyesekere, 1981) we are dissatisfied with a simple comparison of mystical, visionary and ecstatic experiences with what in the modern West are known as the various manifestations of neurotic or psychotic states. Anthropologists and cultural psychologists have given a variety of psychological interpretations to the trance and mystical states experienced and enacted by South Asian devotees. We do not know of any one work which has yet made an attempt at a comprehensive taxonomic ethnography of these manifestations of consciousness and behaviour, even for a particular area. We can only say at this point that, even within the small circumference where we worked in Orissa, 'mystical', 'ecstatic' and 'trance' states appear to be of a number of distinct types, involving apparently different manifestations of consciousness (as described by those who experience them) and certainly different manifestations of behaviour, including both speech and other symbolic behaviour.

Obeyesekere's (1981) analysis of personal meaning for the Sri Lankan female ascetic ecstatics that he calls 'Medusas' focuses on the forging of personal identities and adaptive solutions to life's existential problems, from combinations of the symbolic needs of the personal unconscious and the symbolic materials and social discourses available within a culture. In Obeyesekere's analysis, the process of becoming and behaving as an ecstatic is a psychodynamic one, a choice of the unconscious, which generates certain identifications and states of consciousness. As Obeyesekere also shows, the psychological and social discourse of South Asia both singles out and encourages ecstatic and mystical states of mind. Since these states are not considered to be aberrant, they are not aberrant. Yet Obeyesekere's analysis of the causality involved in the ecstatic states themselves remains generally within a standard psychoanalytic framework, in which ecstatic states are the psyche's attempts to compensate for disappointing realities. The difference is that, in the Sri Lankan cultural context, these states, if properly conducted, are not aberrant, and so may in fact function as culturally adaptive mechanisms instead of 'symptoms'.

With respect to the understanding of ecstatic states, we find Kakar's (1992) interpretations illuminating. Kakar interprets Indian mysticism and visionary experiences as the cultivation of a particular style of consciousness closely related to creative imagination and artistic response. This interpretation articulates perfectly with the general aesthetic context of the ritual arts of India. The association of the aesthetic with divinity in South Asia is explicit in the theory and production of classical dance, music and drama (Singer, 1972), where each artistic act itself is an act of worship and an offering to the God, performed *primarily* for this purpose, and secondarily for the purpose of bringing those who hear and view into contact with a realm of sacred meanings. Indeed in traditional temples, performances of music and dance were conducted with no one but the deity as a necessary audience. An elaborately developed theory of aesthetics and emotion forms a basic cultural symbolic underpinning for these performances (Neuman, 1990; Rawson, 1978; Singer 1972). *Pujas* in all their variety are also artistic productions. Persons are trained in the ritual art forms. All of *puja* or ritual that we have seen in Orissa is notable for its aesthetic qualities and the artistic arrangements of sight, sound, smell, texture and movement, and sometimes gustatory sensation. These combinations can readily move onlookers to a feeling of communication with a 'sacred order', a magical meaning-saturated realm of order, beauty and awe. Many means are used for this evocation, even in ordinary *puja* practices, e.g. combinations of music, incense, the carefully choreographed presentation of foods and flowers, the use of rich cloth and other valuables, melodious utterances of *mantra*, accompanied by graceful bodily postures and the hand gestures, known as *mudra*.

The purpose of ritual arts seems to be to produce in the *practitioner*, as well as those privileged to share the performance, an intense imaginative experience of communicating with (e.g. speaking with, seeing, feeling, identifying with, *merging* with) divinity, and the presence here and now of a sacred world, awesome, fearsome and beautiful.

Forms of creative imagination, particularly visionary imagination such as eidetic imagery, that is imagery that has the quality of a real object of perception, along with forms for its public expression are intensively cultivated. The products of this imagination are not necessarily original or idiosyncratic productions. Specific sacred images exist as standard forms to be achieved as eidetic images during the practice of *sadhana*. The ritual arts often explicitly include instructions for concentrated private discursive acts on the part of the practitioner, using Harré's (1984) distinction between private and public discourse, in preference to the more usual but less precise distinction between 'internal' and 'external' events. Harré's distinction recognizes that private events, e.g. thoughts and feelings, may have their origins in social discourse. Many ritual practices involve the private rhythmic repetitions of Sanskrit syllable strings called *mantra*. The evocative power of *mantra* is a subject too complex to address in this chapter. They ultimately enable the performer to identify with the 'power' encoded in the syllables. Some ritual practices also involve concentrated efforts of visualization. Once evoked as private eidetic imagery, a ritual image, becoming the object of absorption, is intended to create certain states of consciousness or feeling states in the person. These states (somewhat like attitudes, but not quite reducible to that) are supposed to enable that person to activate natural (e.g. bodily) and social (e.g. emotional, public-discursive) processes. Basanti Devi, the *Kalasi* whose performance we described, 'sees' a visual image of the Goddess just before she is possessed.[1] Original visionary combinations occur in mysticism, but the cultural environment is virtually saturated with iconographic elements of the sacred world. Personal visions, including 'divine' dreams, are constructed of these culturally shared iconographic elements, and so are part of the discourse of the cultural construction of a special order of reality.

Under this interpretation, it is possible to focus upon the idea of creative imagination and the culturally constructed possibility of cultivating it as a skill, founded upon the existence of a highly organized cultural discourse and system of socially transmitted practices, that recognizes visionary experience as a culturally shared and legitimated social reality, and affords opportunities for the cultivation of these skills as something akin to art forms.

The ecstatic behaviour of *Kalasis* is one genre among the ritual arts. The *Kalasi*'s trances are controlled (including well-choreographed 'wildness'), well organized and purposeful, and share with other Indian visionary or mystical skills the fact of being elaborately cultivated by special culturally agreed methods (e.g. the *sadhana, bratas* and *pujas*).[2] There are norms for behaviour while under possession. Ordinary people readily make judgements distinguishing genuine *Kalasis* from people who suffer hysteria or 'spirit possession' (manifested by pathological dissociative acting-out conditions), and who are irrational or are 'mad' or 'mentally ill' (*pagala, unmada, manas roga*). The persons locally recognized as truly adept in ecstatic states of consciousness generally lead disciplined and well-organized lives, and their trance behaviours, though these deviate from 'normal' acceptable discourse and action, also follow well-recognized *cultural norms* for appropriate conduct within the genre.

There are at least two important conditions of Indian culture which afford the possibility of private visionary states becoming socially verifiable events.

One condition involves the different epistemic value placed upon artistic productions and acts of creative imagination in Indian culture. Indian culture places a much greater epistemic value on certain classes of 'subjective' events (including dreams, visions and inferences resembling 'delusions of reference') than is common in Western culture (Kakar, 1981; 1982). These are understood not as mere expressive reflections of someone's subjectivity, or even of group subjectivity, but rather as reflections of an order of reality existing parallel to but also in interaction with the material world and the social structure of domestic and community life. The epistemic value of these forms is related to the more general Indian hypothesis that rational discursive cognition is not the highest form of intelligence or the best mirror of reality. Direct intuitive insight, free from 'logical' thought, is felt to be superior in capacity to apprehend the really real (Kakar, 1981).

Some, though not all, subjective or visionary events are considered to be sources of knowledge about reality. Informants can make explicit distinctions and discriminations about those imaginative events in any recognized category, as to whether they are or are not valid knowledge: e.g. which dreams, which visions, which trances etc. are 'real' and which are delusory. There is not an indiscriminate acceptance of acts of imagination as 'real' but rather a well-developed social discourse which affords the reality of some acts of imagination in so far as they meet certain criteria, which usually include (1) some consistency with shared iconographic knowledge and (2) aspects of the life context and practices of the person and the degree to which epistemically valid acts of imagination are cultivated according to the rules of specified practices. One practitioner of *sadhana* and yoga explained to us the difference between the times when a person will get 'real' dreams and the times when dreams will be mere dreams and nothing more:

Pandit: We see dreams [*swapna*] always, so that is not a big thing. But one thing is that we are household persons [*ghruhi loka*]. We are amidst many kinds of rubbish [*abarjana*], so how shall we get the right thing? So whatever we do and see, that is a [*plain*] dream. That is not a 'good' [*su: enjoyable, auspicious, true*] dream. Because the 'good' [*su*] dream is completely true. But that which is merely a dream, is not true.

Neighbour: *Agyan* [*Sir*], our dreams are of three kinds, [*ordinary*] dream, *susakti* [*good power*], and *Saurya* [*those of Surya, the Sun God, indicating enlightenment*]. These are the three stages [*or conditions*] of dreams.

Pandit: The dream which we see at the time of doing *sadhana* will be neither this side nor that side [*i.e. they will be 'straight', true, accurate, not distorted*]. It is always true. Because then there is concentration [*ekagrata*], there is sincerity [*nistha*], and fear [*bhaya*], and devotion [*bhakti*] – four things are mixed together.

In North American culture, private experiences are epistemically disvalued unless they are expressed in the approved art forms of the culture, say poetry, literature or the visual arts, or unless they occur in the context of the discourse genre known as psychotherapy, whose purpose is to explore subjectivity and bring it into a more adaptive relationship with the culturally constructed model of 'objective' reality. In the case of art, private productions may be cultivated as a form of creativity, subject however to cultural principles of control and organization. If the products of subjectivity meet these criteria, they may enter the public discourse and be shared in this way. The situation for imaginative events in India is not *entirely* different, in so far as ritual and mystic forms also have criteria for genuineness and quality. However the difference does extend to fundamental epistemic issues concerned with the nature of reality and kinds of mental events that best reflect it.

Indian culture is explicit, too, in its recognition of imagination and the imaginative interpretation of perceptions as potent psychobiological resources. The power of psychological states or states of consciousness to effect physical and social changes is also explicit in Indian discourse. According to Oriya belief, fear (*bhaya*) can make people physically ill and frustration can make them behave as if they were 'mad' or 'possessed by a spirit': the 'disease' will disappear when the frustration is resolved. Village shamans and their clients may be surprisingly sophisticated in their recognition and deliberate use of what we call the 'placebo effect'. They possess and appreciate the idea that powerful suggestion, especially accompanied by certain dramatic evocations and other material symbolic means (e.g. talismans), can make a person's symptoms disappear when they are psychologically caused, or can give the person the needed confidence to succeed in some social challenge. Even the sceptics admit that shamans often do work cures but they say that it is 'only psychological' – as if effecting a psychological cure for psychogenic or psychosomatic symptoms were an insignificant thing! What they mean turns out to be one of two things: either that the cure is 'merely' psychological and not genuinely magical (!) or genuinely sacred; or that it is 'merely' psychological and not genuinely medical. The so-called 'placebo effect' – the power of suggestion, and the power of belief – is explicitly recognized and cultivated in Indian folk medicine. The clients of *Kalasis*, and often *Kalasis* and other folk healers themselves, explicitly state that if the client does not have the faith, the cure will not be effective. Kakar, himself a Western trained psychoanalyst, has reported sending a client to a shaman when the man could not benefit from psychotherapy because he did not understand, and so did not have faith in, psychodynamic discourse. Psychotherapy was *less* real to this client (as it is to many Indians) than spirit possession and exorcism. The shaman, Kakar (1982) reports, at least alleviated the man's debilitating symptoms. Kakar discusses, in this work, the varieties of recognizable psychotherapeutic interventions used by Indian traditional healers. These often include interventions in family relationships and the reintegration of the patient with social support systems, as well as the giving of empathic support, the provision of protective parent figures or, more generally, self-objects and symbolic adjustments of identity through the (often ritual) restoration of the positioning of the self in the social structure (e.g. by symbolic transformations of guilt, shame, blame and so on and 'giving permission to' the patient's needs.) Among healing effects, the 'placebo effect', or the therapeutic evocation of faith and confidence, seems to merit more investigation in its own right as a potential therapeutic resource. We wonder why such effects are scientifically discussed in the Western literature primarily as 'noise' in studies trying to ascertain the physiological actions of pharmacological agents.

The second condition is the existence in Indian culture of 'art forms' unrecognized as such in the West. These are the ritual arts and they are developed to an exquisite degree in India. Many experiences described, for example, by ecstatics or yogins suggest an imaginative capacity so cultivated and focused in aesthetically stimulating ritual practices that it attains great intensity and becomes a potent personal creative resource and cultural resource for the construction of shared psychological and social realities, in a society where there exists a discursive agreement that 'knowledge' lies in educated (cultivated, purified, instructed) subjectivity. Specific and rigorous practices are learned and employed for the cultivation of these abilities.

To us the most outstanding feature of the entire 'magical' universe of traditional Hindu culture is its skilled use of ritual with imagination, drama, humour and beauty to evoke or bring to the forefront a 'magical' (that is a meaning-saturated, value-laden, surprising and sometimes awesome) world of order, from just behind the mundane, chaotic, sometimes harsh, images presented by the material 'reality' of the ordinary social world. This 'magical' world is understood as an order of reality in its own right, correlated with, though not identical to, the 'ordinary' world. We agree with Kakar (1992) that mysticism (and 'magic') is closely related to creativity, imaginative and aesthetic skills. These skills act as a creative power applied to the art of discursively constructing meaning in personal life.

The social identity of *Kalasis* in Orissa: prestige, centrality and autonomy

One aspect of the ecstatic's psychological and social development is the changes in social position, including such factors as prestige, autonomy and control, initiated by becoming a possession oracle. Readers familiar with Obeyesekere's (1981) account of Sri Lankan women who are ascetic ecstatics (Obeyesekere calls them, metaphorically, 'Medusas' because of their snake-like matted hair) will recognize certain similarities between these women and the Oriya *Kalasis*. Differences will be equally evident. The cultivation of ecstatic states in South Asia, as Obeyesekere shows, *may* initiate a person into a life style which offers an alternative to the demands of the ordinary domestic and community life. His analysis emphasizes in particular how women, otherwise destined to remain under the control of husbands or other male or elder female relatives, or to be exploited by powerful outsiders, find exceptional freedom as well as prestige (if ambivalent prestige in this case, for they also become outcastes of 'normal' or 'polite' society) by adopting the life of wandering ascetics. Most of the women in Obeyesekere's set of case studies had experienced painful losses and disappointments in domestic life prior to becoming ecstatics.

Oriya *Kalasis* display a different pattern of development in their social relationships. Most significantly, they remain within family life and the life of the village community. While Obeyesekere's ecstatics belong to a kind of local counter-culture, the Oriya *Kalasi* women do not. Except when under possession, their dress, demeanour and conduct are just what would be expected of an ordinary decent person of their gender and caste (*jati*). Moreover, they take on the additional discipline of ritual responsibilities and maintenance of personal purity, including dietary restrictions. The ritual obligations of *Kalasis* are more rigorous than those of ordinary *jati* members. The caste status of Oriya *Kalasis* is within the middle range (high middle to low middle). They are not Brahmans, since most Brahmans would consider the specific kind of trance behaviour required of *Kalasis* too undignified to be consistent with the social prestige they hold by birth and maintain by their own set of ritual practices. Some Oriya Brahmans do become visionaries and practise *other* kinds of ecstatic or mystic states, sometimes in relatively public circumstances.

The *Kalasi* whose *puja* we described is a *Teli* or oil seller by caste. She is married and has several teenaged daughters and a son. She lives in a house in a village on the outskirts of an urban centre in eastern Orissa. Her husband runs a roadside restaurant along the road adjacent to their property. Her small shrine house or *Thakura ghara* is also there in the same compound. We asked Basanti Devi about her daily activities. In the interview transcripts, as before, Basanti Devi's voice is indicated by the speaker designated *Ma*. In the following passage, Basanti Devi tells how she coordinates her daily household and ritual obligations:

Ma: The other women, after getting up in the morning, they may salute at the feet of their husband or not. When we [*we is the polite way of referring to oneself*] will get up in the morning we will salute at the feet of the husband. Then we will get up, then do the daily works, then the clean-up work [*i.e. sweeping the house etc.*]; we will do all these things. Then we will go to take a bath. After taking a bath we will have *darshan* with the God [*go to the Thakura ghara to see the God; no puja is done at this time*]. Then after having the audience of *Surya* [*Sun God*], offering water, after *darshan* of *Thakura*, we shall return. Then the Mother's *puja* starts after we come. After this I wash the feet of my *Babu* [*her husband*] and will drink that water. Then we [*i.e. herself*] will eat something. Not all the women are doing these things . . . It was in the past. Now nobody is doing this. When all our daily work was over or when in the morning the food offering [*bhoga*] is over, *Babu* eats and then we have nothing to eat with my family . . . There is the 'hotel' [*roadside restaurant*] for the children. It is in front of my house . . . *Babu* gives the breakfast and rice; they eat those. We do not cook separately for the children at home; the *Babu* does the cooking for the hotel and sends food for the children . . . My cooking is done here [*in the Thakura ghara*]. After the *Babu* eats. I do not take onion, garlic, fish or meat etc. At night when the *Babu* returns home, finishing his work, or has gone to someplace, after returning from there, after *Babu* eats, then I eat . . . When we go to sleep at night, we meditate on the God [*dhyana karibi*] and sleep. We do *japa* [*repetition of a mantra or the name of a deity*]. We have that, either of the Mother or of the Father [*Goddess or God*], we will do *japa* for 108 times . . . Still then after I eat, then I do the *japa*, touch my head on the feet of the *Babu*, then I sleep. I sleep for 10 to 20 minutes. I cannot sleep more. When I cannot sleep, I do my work [*meaning her meditation*]. Only I do the *japa*, nothing else . . . All the *pujas* in the yearly cycle will be observed here. As there is *puja* throughout the year in *Sri Kshetra* [*Puri, site of the Jagannath temple*] all those will go on here like that.

In Orissa, persons who are recognized as truly adept in visionary and ecstatic states, whatever their *jati*, typically enjoy more social prestige than they would otherwise have. They also acquire a kind of social importance or centrality that they would not otherwise enjoy. These special talents are alternatives to wealth, political power, *jati* and family position for achieving prestige and enhanced position in society. Prestige is earned by their special powers and by the obvious favour or blessing of the divinity which they enjoy. It is reinforced and amplified by otherwise living a life *visibly more devout* – more disciplined, austere and devoted to worship – than others. The *Kalasi* earns her reputation in part by displaying these expected qualities, which are indices to her often discerning public that she is a genuine *Kalasi*.

Once a woman is recognized as a genuine *Kalasi* by her family and community, her position in the family and community changes. If a woman is successful in establishing her reputation as a genuine Mother, she receives a considerable supply of that commodity so valued by Indian society, and often little available to its women – prestige. Her recognition confers an increase of power and prestige which may reach a degree that is not normally possible for a woman and is possible for few village men. While maintaining the norms of respect towards her husband and in-laws, socially she may tacitly count for more than they. The *Kalasi* becomes more central within her own household. Her work is now the work of the Goddess, and husbands, in-laws and children, once convinced, respect it. Of course, relatives and others may be sceptical at first and *Kalasis* may have to demonstrate to others' satisfaction that they are possessed by a real deity (*prakruta thakura*) and not by a *preta* or spirit. The devotional goals of a devoted *Kalasi* are demanding and become a centre of household activity. Others within the family may relieve her of some of her usual chores. Basanti Devi's husband, who cooks at the restaurant, relieves her of cooking for the family.

The respected *Kalasi* not only enjoys an elevated position in the community, but becomes a special nucleus of community activity and discourse. Once or twice each week, the *Kalasi* is surrounded by a greater or smaller crowd of people. People approach her regularly for advice in all kinds of matters, including resolving their family problems and curing their illnesses. Some villagers may be ambivalent or indifferent to a *Kalasi* in their own village, even a reputed one. They may themselves prefer to visit a *Kalasi* outside their own village (perhaps for reasons of privacy). But she will also draw many outsiders from neighbouring localities into her circle of activity. Reputed *Kalasis*, such as Basanti Devi and another village woman we interviewed, attract many visitors from outside their village, from urban centres, and sometimes even from distant places. On certain ritual occasions, particularly the *jamu jatra* or fire-walking festival, the *Kalasi* presides as a centre of public attention and leader of devotees in group performances.

Considerable community activity may develop around a *Kalasi*. Grateful recipients of oracular cures and remedies contribute money to the ends of the Goddess and arrange rituals for the expression of their gratitude. When her reputation spreads, outsiders, many of higher status, come to her for advice and also contribute funds and other resources to projects the *Kalasi* undertakes in the name of the Goddess. Devotees support the *Kalasi*'s work by contributing money for the expansion of the local Goddess worship, e.g. the purchase of land, the building of small temples and *dharmasalas* (places for travellers to spend the night), the construction of *rupas* or sculpted images, or the construction platforms for the fire sacrifice (*yagna mandap*). The *Kalasi* herself is the nucleus of this activity, since she is constantly consulted in all relevant matters. It would be bad form for the *Kalasi* to use contributions for her personal financial gain, but her 'ownership' or custodianship of these various projects is implicit.

In certain limited but psychologically significant respects, Oriya *Kalasis* also have substantially increased autonomy in comparison with other village women. Most Oriya village wives are not free to mingle with mixed company or make themselves the centre of attention to crowds of outsiders (or even converse with them) on a regular basis (or at all). The *Kalasi* has the opportunity to socialize and mingle with other people of mixed types, to share discourse with them, to relate to them, and to hear their personal narratives and stories. In this way she receives far more social stimulation and a much more broader view of at least the local world than most village wives. Most wives are also not empowered to initiate entrepreneurial projects (e.g. temple building, road building or establishing local ritual practices) as the *Kalasi* does. She undertakes these things by the instruction of the Goddess (while in possession) and not on her own initiative. Nevertheless the *Kalasi* is the personal centre and manager of these projects.

Again, there is the psychological satisfaction, perhaps not trivial, that a person may derive from engaging in the kind of emotional and social expression permitted the *Kalasi* under possession but not permitted to ordinary respectable women in normal social discourse, and in many respects not within the family (or especially not there). In possession, the *Kalasi* acquires a different kind of feminine personality than most women are allowed to have − socially ascendant, perhaps flirtatious and seductive, laughing aloud, or angry and threatening, profound and prophetic, by turn. The intense emotional and social engagement signified by this behaviour belongs to the freedom of the Goddess, who is a Mother to everyone. It is not otherwise appropriate for respectable wives, who must downplay emotionality, particularly anger, sexuality and self-assertion, within the family and community (with the exception perhaps of anger, which can be expressed towards outsiders) and for whom such public behaviour would tarnish prestige.

The Oriya *Kalasi* enjoys a psychological, particularly emotional, freedom within the boundaries of her trance states that is not generally available to Indian women. Enhanced freedom and latitude of emotional experience may in fact be among the general attractions of the experience of at least certain trance and mystical states which may allow persons to exercise their capacities for feeling and knowing in ways not permitted to them in mundane life. This is consistent with the idea that these states are related to creative experience and to other art forms. This may be part of what accounts for the apparently intense satisfactions of visionary states that motivate the mystically inclined. If we adhere to the interpretative context we have set up in the preceding section, we would conjecture that these are akin to the intense aesthetic satisfactions of a skilled artist (musician, dancer etc.) completely absorbed in and merged with a performance.

We conjecture that these satisfactions are a powerful motivating factor in their own right, and in many persons. Participation in the identity of the chosen deity may be sufficient, even without other social advantages, to motivate cultivation of these states. We suppose this to be the case because in Indian society, and perhaps in the West as well, many people have been known to *give up* social advantage and prestige for the pleasures of a contemplative or aesthetic life. We suggest that this is a particular mode of psychological satisfaction and integration especially focal to certain persons but, as the ritual arts of Indian culture would suggest, capable of making a contribution, through communication, to the personal integration of a more widely distributed population, which would account for the popularity and prestige of these persons and their performances.

Speaking as the Mother: *hukum*

During her possession itself the *Kalasi* is in a rare position of practically absolute social ascendancy over the audience of supplicants. She may command, criticize, scold, demand self-punishments and even whack them lightly with thin canes, as well as predict, advise, comfort, praise, bless, reassure and bestow her loving ministrations on their illnesses and personal problems. Few persons in India or North America enjoy, even temporarily, such supreme discursive ascendance as a well-respected *Kalasi* in divine possession. The style of interaction is described in more detail below.

The Mother, assuming her position on the *singhasan*, calls devotees before her and gives *hukum* or directives, predominantly advice on how to remedy personal problems and illnesses. Occasionally she also makes unsolicited predictions about various events of local importance. She calls the men to her, addressing each as 'boy' (*balaka*), and she calls the women, addressing each as 'girl' (*balika*). Her interactions with each supplicant are typically brief. Most seem to be persons who have come to this *Kalasi* before and her discourse refers to things already known between them. *Kalasis* may use various means for curing supplicants of physical, social and mental problems. These include driving out the problem by using *beta* to lightly beat the body, cleansing by sweeping the body with the *beta*, giving talismans, giving of *paduka* (the ritual bathing water poured over the Goddess – either the sculptured image or the feet of the *Kalasi* – mixed with flowers, sacred leaves or other ritual offerings), commanding food prohibitions, giving home remedies, prescribing devotional practices, giving practical and moral instruction, and giving items and substances imbued with sacred protective power through prior ritual, especially the incantation of *mantra*. *Kalasis* vary in their emphasis on these remedial methods. This *Kalasi*, to judge from our observations, has a preference for the giving of sacred items, prohibition of *ainsa* and *khata* (flesh and sour foods), the prescription of devotional practices and the use of moral instruction and scolding. The following is a small sample of the Mother's *hukum* following the *puja* described. Although we are limited by considerations of space to presenting only a very small sample of the *hukum* discourse, we have tried to select cases that typify the characteristics of most of the *hukum* we recorded with this *Kalasi*. Phrases indexing the divinity of the speaker, when adopting the Mother's voice, are marked in the text in bold.

Case 1

> *Ma*: Get up, *balika*. Whatever I shall tell you, will you follow it [*manibhuta*]? For 32 days you will have to stop **khata** and **ainsa**. Well done. Do you understand? Where is the bottle? Bring it. [*The Mother will give her a type of 'holy water'.*] The water of the **five-face pot** [*pancha mukhi khumba: a jug with five holes around its circumference, used in some puja to the Goddess*], you give, washing the **sword, trident and snake** [*ritual items, emblems of the deities in the Thakura ghara*]. You have not given the **water of the snake washing** [*sapa dhua: i.e. have not bathed the snake, telling me a lie*]. Go. Look, *balika*, every day after **taking bath**, do the *darshan* of **Baba** [*Father, i.e. Siva*]. Tell me who is *Baba*?
> *Man*: Siva.
> *Ma*: Siva. Come back after the *darshan* **in the temple**. After taking a little **bel leaf** then come and take the *paduka*. But for 32 days stop **khata** and **ainsa**. Don't eat that. If you eat it, **you will be put to great difficulty**. I told in advance, when you come in the next *pali* [*turn*], come bringing a torn cloth [*to bathe in it and then throw it away*]. And you will take a **bath**. Understand? [*The supplicant will wear the torn cloth and take a purificatory bath, then she will throw the cloth away.*] *Balaka*, did you remember?
> *Man*: Yes.

The case involves a man and a woman. They have asked the Mother to accomplish something for them but we do not know what. The Mother and the supplicants share that knowledge between them. The Mother, however, is telling the supplicants that they have not fulfilled her ritual instructions correctly and completely. They have lied to her, saying that they have done what they have in fact not. They have forgotten what she has told them to bring. They must complete the ritual instructions and then return.

Case 2

> *Ma*: Oh *balaka*, did you inform me anything? After that, you remember. The house in which you have fallen into trouble **you have put Me** there with your three children [*laughing*]. But everything depends upon you. You are the main one. Everything will be all right if you arrange everything. You are the person who has given the birth. I come afterwards. You are first. First you will **bless** them and then we will see.
> *Woman*: You do the work. You are the person who will save.
> *Ma*: I will only save but you have given them birth. But *balika*, you remember, **I shall keep everybody in peace by engaging them in work**. Whatever you have thought, to stay together [*this concerned perhaps a joint family who were going to separate because of quarrel*], **the thing which has broken, can that be put together**, my *balaka*?
> *Woman*: No.
> *Ma*: **But you all will stay peacefully. I will give peace.** And the *balaka* for whom you are so sorry.
> *Woman*: Yes, yes.
> *Ma*: Whose *balaka* is he? One will suffer disease [*roga heba*], if another will take the medicine, will he be cured? But you bring him. Bring him, **I shall cure him**. Understand? Then take. Why I say, do you know? The **things which he accepts** [*perhaps he eats khata and ainsa*], those are **my enemy** [*satru*]. For that, I say no. Tell him **after taking bath**, he will eat this. Take.

The supplicants, apparently husband and wife, have presented two problems. One has to do with disruption in the joint family; perhaps the joint family is about to separate because of a quarrel. The Mother promises to give peace to everyone involved, engaging each in their own work, but she says that the family cannot be brought together again. A second problem concerns a boy who is sick. The Mother complains that the supplicants have put too much of the burden on the Mother's shoulders; that the supplicants themselves, as the parents, must take responsibility – at least to bring the patient to the *Kalasi* in person. She cannot completely cure the patient by only giving something to the parents. Besides, the patient has been eating *ainsa* and *khata*, which work against the powers of the Mother. Yet the Mother does not refuse to give some interim treatment. She gives some *paduka*, with simple ritual instructions, and asks the supplicants to bring the patient in person the next time.

Case 3

> *Ma*: Hey, *balika*, tell me, for how many **palis** I told you to come? How many **palis** I told you to come? Have you come? I told you **khata** and **ainsa** are prohibited. Out of greediness [*lobha*], you ate. The *balaka* says that my *balika* was not cured. How will she be cured? You sit down and get up for **108** times, holding the ears. Get up, get up. Don't you know that **khata and ainsa are My great enemies [*parama satru*]**? Stand up. Will you do this wrong action [*bhul kama*] again? If you wanted to eat [that], why did you take **My thing**? Take. [*She **gives the woman paduka**.]* If you make the mistake again, **I will not leave you [*alone*]**.
>
> *Male bystander*: Whatever the Mother says, you do that.
>
> *Ma*: Okay, *balika*, give her **a flower and a little vermilion from My head**. Every morning **after taking a bath, eat three three-stemmed bel leaves**. Why don't you take? [*She gives paduka*.] Take. If you make a mistake again, **I will not leave you**.

The husband or male relative (*balaka*) of the female supplicant (*balika*) has complained to the Mother that the woman was not cured by Mother's instructions. The Mother scolds them for not following her directions and then saying that she has not effected a cure. They were told to come to her for a certain number of times, on successive Fridays. They did not. And though they accepted materials for her ritual cure, the woman failed to abstain from meats and sour foods during the period of the cure, which polluted her so that the cure could not be effective. The Mother asks the supplicant to enact ritual self-punishment but then tells him to arise. The Mother gives further instruction and *paduka* for the supplicant's cure but threatens that if the supplicant makes this mistake again the Mother will not leave her in peace.

Case 4

> *Ma*: Come *balika*, where is that child? Didn't I tell you not to take My child to the hospital [*daktara khana*]? Heh? What was the necessity? Now what

happened? Quiet! Why did you not bring him immediately [*to the Mother*]? I told you not to take him. If you go there again, don't come to me. I told you, no, My child will not go to the hospital for the medicine card [*prescription, dispensary card*]. Take [*this*]. **Twenty-one bel leaves** and *misri* [*rock sugar*]; crushing it, feed it to that child for 21 days. Do you understand?

Woman: Yes.

Ma: Yes. Don't give any other medicine. Where is the bottle? Have you come for a walk [*i.e. are you just here for a stroll*]? Shall I tell you always? Heh? **In a flower, give him a little**. Next time [*pali*] when you come, bring the *balaka* and come with a container. Go.

Ma: Hey *balika*, tell the other *balika* to come here. After **getting hukum** from Me, who told you to go to the hospital? I told you not to. Sit down and get up, holding the ear. If my *balaka* would have come, **I would have beaten him**. He did not come. Stand up. It is the mistake of the *balaka*.

A woman had brought a sick child to the Mother and the Mother had ordered a ritual cure along with a home remedy. But the parents had then taken the boy to the public hospital clinic for treatment. He has not got better and the mother of the boy has returned to the *Kalasi*. The Mother scolds the woman for taking the child to the medical centre instead of staying consistently with the cure given by the Mother. The Mother finally blames the woman's husband (*balaka*) for the error; it must have been he who insisted that the child be taken to the hospital. The Mother, ever forgiving, refusing no one, gives further materials for a combination of home remedy and ritual cure.

Case 5

Ma: I have also **told you what will happen**. Oh, my *balika*, **I explained this to you in a dream**. On that day of **My birth festival**, you went to sleep crying. You said, 'If I do not get the **darshan of my Mother** on my birthday, I shall say that my Mother is not there.' Did you get **My darshan**? You go. Go, **don't touch anybody**. [*Mother gave her paduka*.]

A woman supplicant has come to see the Mother. The Mother tells her that she has already come to her in a dream and told her what was to happen. She refers to the day when the devotee was weeping in despair of her desire for a *darshan*, in this case a vision of the Mother. The Mother now asks her, did I not then appear to you in a dream? There is no denial. She gives the supplicant some *paduka* and tells her to go, protecting herself from the (potentially polluting) touch of others.

Case 6

Ma: Come *balaka*, come. As I did not call you, you went back?

Man: Mother, it is your kindness.

Ma: No, don't leave your own place.

Ma: Hey *balaka*, from the beginning, you were **worshipping Me in the form of Adyasakti Mangala**. Today you have come to Me but *Mangala* is very much pleased [*santusta*] with you. **Nothing untoward will happen whether you were**

successful in all your works or not. Why did you make a mistake in the middle of it? Will you eat? Eat.

Man: In the middle? I don't remember.

Ma: Shall I tell? Shall I insult My son among so many people?

Man: I don't remember. I beg apology to the Mother.

Ma: See, *balaka*, in this **Kali yuga [dark age]**, all that you have accepted – is that true? Don't accept those things again. Are you telling the truth? Did you fear?

Man: Yes.

Ma: **If you accept those, I shall be very much dissatisfied** [*asantusta*].

Man: No, I do not accept.

Ma: Did you not eat?

Man: I was eating. Sometimes in the middle [*of fulfilling my vow*]. I left that [*gave it up*].

Ma: What did you do recently, 15 days back? What did you do? Where had you been 15 days back? What did you do there?

Man: I don't remember, Mother.

Ma: What more shall I tell you, *balaka*? But I said, look *balaka*, **if you can say no to these things and if you do all those things the way you were doing before, you will be in that type of position where you were before [*i.e. a better position*].**

Man: Now the man has fallen into trouble [*referring to himself*].

Ma: Why did I say? Don't you understand?

Man: –

Ma: One day, it was *sankranti*. What did you do? Think awhile. I am telling you for the last three years. **From there your downfall came.**

Man: The pain and mental suffering are bad.

Ma: **All those things have come from that,** *balaka*. Do you know why I am telling you this? Because **you will not be respected very much. I will not leave you on the wrong path. I am telling you this on oath.** You accepted both of the things on the **day of *sankranti*.** So your *Babu* [*probably employer*] was dissatisfied and punished you so much. I am telling you today, take shelter near the **Baba [*Siva*].** Sit down and get up **108** times. **Take shelter. Henceforward, all peace will come.** Whatever I will say, will you do that?

Man: My work, can you not do it? My work, whatever sorrow is there in my mind? [*Can you not remedy my situation?*]

Ma: Why am I telling you this, my *balaka*? **Why did I make such a great oath [*if I could not do it*]?**

Man: You will drive away this sorrow? You can take away the sorrow that is in me?

Ma: Remember, **if you give up these things, I shall fulfil your desire.**

Man: For me, Mother, ten families are crying.

Ma: You see, *balaka* –

Man: It is all right, if you can do everything.

Ma: All right. But remember, **I shall fulfil your work.** But whatever I have stopped [*made you stop*], you will not touch it even for a day.

Man: No. Not at all. My life breath will go for Mother.

Ma: Give an **areca nut** from the **gadi** [*a symbol that a person has taken a vow before the Goddess*].

This middle-aged male supplicant is obsequious with the Mother. The gist of the conversation is that bad conditions have developed in his work and family life, which he begs the Mother to resolve. But, though he has been a devotee and pleased *Mangala*, he has done some serious backsliding in the middle of his efforts, on certain moral promises he has made to the Mother. The error he made involves indulgence in something shameful and the Mother will not insult him by mentioning it in public. A culturally plausible implication is that the man has been getting drunk and/or visiting a brothel. This he also did on a holy day, *sankranti*. Though at first he denies understanding the allegation, he later agrees to it. The Mother asks for ritual punishment. The supplicant begs her to rescue him from the pain he has caused to himself and his family. The Mother agrees. She will give him peace and restore his situation; but only on the condition that he will obey the injunctions of the Mother and give up the ruinous inclinations that are too shameful to mention.

The socially shared illusion

The discourse of the Mother has a special name, *hukum*, commands. During the *hukum*, a socially shared illusion is created wherein participants have the experience of *darshan* and receive personal attention and advice directly from the Goddess. In saying that the *hukum* is a socially shared illusion, we are not particularly distinguishing it from other kinds of socially shared illusions of Indian or Western culture, e.g. psychotherapy or academic symposia, business meetings or artistic performances. It is not the 'supernatural' aspect of the *hukum* which makes it an 'illusion' but rather its socially constituted facticity, without which it would not be experienced as meaningful in the way that it is. In the remainder of this chapter, we focus upon the discursive properties of *hukum* which help to constitute the *darshan*, the presence of the Goddess, as a public social experience rather than a private subjective state of the *Kalasi*.

The *Kalasi* is distinguished from other personal advisers (e.g. magicians or *gunia*) in Oriya culture by being an oracle, a living conduit of divinity, holding divine knowledge and power for the time of possession.[3] The ritual transformation described above establishes her in this identity, which endures within the limits of the trance (usually some four hours for Basanti Devi). This is accomplished through the use of a complex series of symbolic objects and actions which both invoke the trance in Basanti Devi and inform onlookers of the occurrence of the transformation. During the period in which the *Kalasi* is in divine possession, her speech is regarded not as her own, but as the speech of the Mother. Just as the *puja*, followed by visible changes in behaviour, expression and bearing, marks the trans-formation, the speech of the *Kalasi* giving *hukum* continues to distinguish the divine identity of the speaker from that of an ordinary person. It continues to hold the attention of the audience (and perhaps the speaker) upon the apprehension of a divine personality. Having ritually and dramatically created a transformation of consciousness and social presence, becoming the embodiment of the Mother, the *Kalasi* now manifests this identity with her speech. This is the *darshan* of the Goddess.

Recall the ongoing choreography of altered bodily appearance, the specific changes of posture, movement, countenance and demeanour, the style of wearing clothing, hair and the vermilion mark, the various accessory details, the garlands (*rudrakshya malas*), peacock feathers and *beta*, which are all references to the divine identity, and support the discourse of *hukum*. The constitutive features of the *hukum* are discussed in what follows.

Some of the discursive characteristics of *hukum* are obvious. It contains a high proportion of imperatives and implicit imperatives (not marked in the text). But that is *hukum* almost by definition. The possibility of speaking in this way, however, marks the speech as that of someone who is in a very special position of social and moral ascendancy. The Mother, speaking to adult men and women, some of whom are senior to her in age and/or other determinants of status, speaks to everyone as though he or she were a child, calling the men *balaka* 'boy' and the women *balika* 'girl'. Even very elderly persons will be addressed or referred to in this way. This helps to establish and hold in focus an important feature of her relationship with devotees, namely that she is speaking to them *as a mother to her children*. The constitution of this relationship is, we speculate, an important part of what gives her the licence to engage in the emotive and expressive freedom she displays, which is so much in contrast to the normal discursive behaviour of adult women.

This discourse feature also helps to place the Mother in a position of unilateral power. She scolds and criticizes and even extracts symbolic punishments and occasionally whacks men across the shoulder with the light thin canes she holds. Rebukes are generally meekly accepted, at least to the face of the Mother. If a supplicant is known to have complained of ineffectiveness of advice, the Mother scolds the supplicant as any mother would scold an unruly child. The fault is found to be with the supplicant, who has not been faithful in carrying out the directions for treatment; he or she has failed in part of the ritual procedures or has eaten *ainsa* and *khata* during the period of abstention. The supplicant's choice is to recognize her and follow her advice or to look elsewhere for *darshan* and consultation.

The omniscient and omnipotent aspect of the *hukum* experience is a particularly interesting facet of its social construction. How is this impression discursively maintained? One outstanding feature of the discourse that contributes to this impression is the way the Mother does practically all of the talking. Others generally only supplicate or assent. There is a power differential here, but there is still more to this than meets the eye. Goddesses have superhuman knowledge and powers. Often the *Kalasi* would seem to know, without asking, what the problem of the supplicant was. Though she is diagnosing various kinds of distress, she only occasionally asks anyone a question (other than rhetorical ones) about their situations. She generally seems to already know what she needs to know, including where the person had gone wrong or failed in following the instructions of her *hukum*. The only response she seeks is affirmation of her assertions. And this she does frequently. By contrast to actual informational questions, she makes ample use of rhetorical questions and requests for confirmation, which were not generally denied. The Mother might even dispute those who denied what she has said, and tell them they are lying. An impression is thereby created of shared knowledge between the Mother and each of her supplicants respectively.

The unquestioned reception of *hukum* (at least to the face of the Mother) contrasts not only with Basanti Devi's normal speech, but with the discourse of certain other cultural counsellors including magicians or *gunia*, who often seem to be in a more publicly accountable position, allow their rationales to be questioned, and respond to their client's arguments and dialogical expansion of his problems. Perhaps it is not quite accurate to say that the *Kalasi* did not allow her rationales to be questioned and did not encourage a dialogical expansion of the supplicant's problems, for people did not seem to try. It was as if they generally knew that this is not within the norms for *darshan* of the Mother.

Of course, many supplicants are returning to the Mother after several visits or more. And Basanti Devi has undoubtedly obtained information about some of her devotees in casual conversations outside the *hukum* and through the local networks of report. Many if not most people would also be reluctant to contradict a powerful *Kalasi* in possession, face to face, even if they felt her to be mistaken. They will rather return to their homes and conduct their discussions and criticisms there. The audience in this way collaborates with the *Kalasi* in producing a shared illusion on the basis of ambiguity. It is an illusion of shared agreement or mutual knowledge that cannot be easily penetrated by outsiders or casual observers. And outside the bounds of a renowned *Kalasi*'s sanctum, for every narrative account of disappointment, one can collect another enthusiastic narrative account of the *Kalasi*'s brilliant successes in curing illnesses and in remedying other personal and financial problems.

Some further constitutive features of the *Kalasi*'s speech during *hukum* make special contributions to the social experience of the *Kalasi*'s divine identity and remind everyone that she is speaking in the voice of the Goddess. Each of these features functions by indexing the divinity of the speaker or the sacred powers operating in her environment. (Examples of these features are marked in the text with bold font.) A quick glance through the *hukum* cases will confirm the prevalence of these features in the *Kalasi*'s discourse, *in addition to* the other features already mentioned. One thereby gets a sense of the multi-layered constitution of the shared illusion. Besides displaying apparent foreknowledge of the supplicants' situations, desires and downfalls, the *Kalasi* makes predictions about future events, often the outcomes of supplicants' personal situations but occasionally also public and/or mystical events (a notable case of this type was not included in the text because of its length and complexity). She is able to tell people whether their desires will be fulfilled or not. Divine beings have supernormal powers and so they can promise or threaten things that ordinary persons could not possibly deliver. During *hukum*, the Mother made promises and threats of divine or karmic punishments if the supplicants failed to keep their vows to her. Since her promises and threats are of a kind that ordinary persons *could not* keep, they index or presuppose the speaker to be someone of divine identity. The personal predictions and the impersonal prophecies which were present in the *darshan* we observed, though not included in the cases presented above, also distinguish and index the presence of a Goddess speaking through an oracle.

One might think that such prediction and promises would provide an easy way to deconstruct the illusion, but they do not. The Mother predicts and promises many things in the *hukum* and threatens to punish those who give her their promise to take up beneficial disciplines and then fail to keep their promises. But since all of these pertain to some unspecified future period, it is impossible for anyone to assess their accuracy at the actual time the *hukum* is given. Those who are disappointed rarely come back to announce such things publicly before an audience at *darshan*. To do so may be to be publicly shamed, since one's own failings may be exposed in such a conversation and the faithful may be more likely to believe the Mother than the complainant. Therefore those present know not the outcome but only the assertion of potency and intention. Again, the typical cases for local gossip, or the collection of outside accounts of past and present devotees of *Kalasis* (we did not at the time seek out devotees of this *Kalasi* specifically), yield stories of disappointment and stories of satisfaction in approximately equal measure.

Finally, a striking feature of *hukum* is the *Kalasi*'s constant reference to sacred symbols and the symbols of ritual: abstinence from *khata* and *ainsa*, water from the five-faced pot, snake-washing water, *darshan*, the *pali*, and *gadi*, the purifying bath of persons or the ritual bathing of deities, the vermilion from her forehead, *paduka* or remains of her rituals, the ritual number 108, the bel leaf, the repetition of the names of Gods and Goddesses, the ingesting of sacred substances, instructions to perform ritual, the lighting of ghee lamps, the holy festivals, the satisfaction of the Gods, the dark age or *Kali yuga*, the holy day or *sankranti*, the taking of shelter in the God or Goddess, the ritual use of areca nut, and so on. A continual stream of the Mother's discourse focuses the attention of the onlookers and supplicants back to the atmosphere of sacred power symbolically surrounding the encounter. This is, of course, in addition to the multiplex iconography involved in the appearance and accessories of the *Kalasi* herself.

The stream of references to sacred symbols during *hukum* continues to connect the speech with the visual symbols and actions that were part of the transforming *puja* and with the ongoing behavioural iconography: the changed bearing, smile and laughter, hair style, manner of wearing the sari, vermilion mark, wearing of the *mala* and carrying of the canes and peacock feathers, and so on, mark the identity of the Goddess. The discursive behaviours of speech and action during *hukum* are both based upon and continue to index the transformation brought into existence during the *puja*. They continue reaffirming the presence of a divinity – for who else would dare to speak and behave to others in such ways? Yet the fact of speaking or behaving like this, in itself, is not sufficient to establish the presence of a divinity. The features of speech and iconographic symbols of the ritual work interactively as features of the discourse that establish the *darshan* of the Goddess and position the *Kalasi* as a genuine conduit of the Goddess, a 'moving God', a being distinct from her ordinary identity as a devout woman. Taking what we imagine to be the experiential point of view of the *Kalasi* herself, these same ritual and discursive acts first invoke and then mark a transformation in consciousness and experience of identity and enact the *Kalasi's* own experience of the self merged with her vision – a shared cultural vision – of (one variant of) the feminine divine personality. The features of the discourse and the particular behavioural and iconographic attributes associated with the possession state must also function to focus and hold the *Kalasi's* attention upon her personal experience of the divine presence.

Many Oriyas, keenly aware of the 'placebo effect', the idea that it is largely one's faith or belief in something that makes it effective, will tell one outright that everything depends upon one's faith. Some disparage the remedies of *Kalasis* and *gunia* as being merely psychological and only due to the person's belief. Others, including some practitioners of the healing arts, admit that faith and hope are extremely important, even decisive, in effecting remedies, not only because they affect client compliance but because attitudes themselves are potent psychophysical resources. The basic difference between the Oriya culture and Western science in this respect is that many Oriyas regard the 'placebo effect' as a legitimate therapeutic resource, the idea that a 'divine' or a 'magical' (there is this distinction in the local culture) remedy will be effective only if the person for whom it is intended has faith in it. This is not necessarily perceived as a flaw in the remedy; rather it is believed to be in the nature of the healing process. Perhaps part of the measure of brilliance of a *Kalasi* is the extent to which she or he is able to elicit the experience of faith based upon the ability to evoke the reality of a living Goddess and so amplify a supplicant's attitude of protection and the promise of well-being, and the accompanying confidence to pursue with hope a course of self-discipline and remedial action.

Conclusion

In this chapter we have discussed aspects of personal and social psychology that belong traditionally to the psychological conception of 'personality'. Personality theory in its various forms includes concepts such as temperament and disposition, characteristic patterns of feeling, thinking and response and their articulation with the social world, and transient 'states' of consciousness or awareness – broadly speaking, moments of knowing and perceiving. Such moments are 'states' of the organism in the sense that they are set apart as having a distinct bounded focus and duration – but are dynamic rather than static conditions of the organism. For example, feelings and emotions such as anger, attraction and fear can be considered psychic states or states of awareness. They have subjective as well as biological and behavioural components. Robert Levy's essay 'Emotion, knowing and culture' (1984) is especially recommended for a discussion of the relationships between feeling, knowing and awareness in emotions.

It is not within the intended scope of this chapter to review and analyse Western personality concepts and theories. Let it suffice to say that personality constructs at present are controversial in Western academic psychology and clinical and anthropological psychiatry and appear to be undergoing radical reconceptualizations within several distinct traditions, including trait and individual difference theory, theories of emotions, post-Freudian psychodynamic theory, cultural psychology and biological psychiatry (Kakar, 1981; 1990; 1992; Klein, 1981; 1988; Klein and Rabkin, 1981; Kramer, 1993; Lutz, 1988; Lutz and White, 1986; Mischel, 1968; Obeyesekere, 1981; 1991; Roland, 1988; Rosaldo, 1980; 1984; Shweder, 1977; 1979; Shweder and Bourne, 1982; Shweder and Miller, 1985; Wolf, 1988).

We therefore limit ourselves here to using the term 'personality' in the most general and common-sense way: to indicate simply that in our own local culture there is a roughly shared terminology for describing our sense that we ourselves and others have *patterned* ways of knowing, feeling, perceiving and responding, and that these patterns seem to vary across persons, situations and perhaps cultures. From these patterns of communicated subjectivity we also sometimes infer psychic 'structure' and psychic 'organization'. Perhaps, as suggested by the experientialist psychology of Johnson (1987), these are metaphorical constructs derived from our more concrete experiences of the structure and organization of our bodies. We might add here that Indian ethnopsychology also has representations of subjectivity that are continuous with its representations of the organization of the body; these employ central metaphors somewhat different from our own, metaphors focusing upon dynamic *fluidity* (e.g. humours), balance and 'osmotic' transactions between person and environment (see Kakar, 1982; Marriott, 1990).

How much of the conceptual groundwork for our observations of personal patterning and continuity is constructed by the cultural categories of the ethnopsychology with which we grow up is here left as an open question (but see Shweder, 1979; Shweder and Bourne, 1982; Shweder and Miller, 1985).

There is a long-standing academic controversy concerning whether, to what extent and in what ways personality organization is variable across cultures, and to what kinds of socio-cultural contingencies personality development responds. Some classic and still current conceptualizations of these questions can be found in the works of psychological anthropologists such as R. LeVine (LeVine, 1973; 1990; LeVine et al., 1988), R. Levy (Levy, 1973; 1984), Sapir (1986) Spiro (Kilborne and Langess, 1987; Spiro, 1984) and B. Whiting and J.W.M. Whiting (Whiting and Child, 1953; Whiting and Whiting, 1975; Whiting, 1977; Whiting, 1980; Whiting and Edwards, 1988; Whiting, 1990; 1992). These views in general recognize both universality in developmental potential, and developmental responsiveness to culture-specific contingencies.

A recent trend has been increasing interest in more strongly 'culturalist' and 'social-constructionist' positions, focusing upon the description of cultural variation in emotion, interpersonal and intrapersonal dynamics, social skills and values, with an eye towards how socially communicated cultural symbol systems and encoded values create or constrain the cultural possibilities for realizing various potentials: ways of knowing and responding, organization and dynamics of personality components such as emotion, culturally defined modes of pathology, and local languages for describing 'personality' (Lutz, 1988; Lutz and White, 1986; Rosaldo, 1980; 1984). Some theorists have also taken an interest in the question of historical perspectives within changing Western Euro-American culture (e.g. Harré, 1986a; 1986b; Heelas and Lock, 1981; Wolf, 1988), inspired by various observations of historical change, for example that philosophical 'virtues' and 'vices' on the one hand, and the predominance of different clinical syndromes and complaints on the other, seem to be changing across time, along with the culturally most favoured behavioural styles.

Here we focus briefly upon the idea that personality forms or components could be regarded as *skills* for purposes of comparative analysis (including differences across persons and across cultures). This conception emphasizes the idea that features of personality function to articulate the organism with the object environment. The object environment is social — animate and inanimate, but always communicative or symbolic and meaning laden. Different cultures, and various social systems within them, emphasize and privilege rather different personality skills.

Among the striking findings of comparative studies in cultural psychology are observations of patterns of response and behaviour that are considered aberrant or anathema in Western ethnopsychology but seem to be normative, adaptive or especially skilful in other cultures. Varieties of shamanism, mysticism and trance are especially well-known examples (e.g. Kakar, 1982; Mumford, 1989; Obeyesekere, 1981; Tambiah, 1985; and many others have studied these personal skills in cultural context). Other examples include Rosaldo's (1980; 1984) work on the dynamics of envy/rage and cooperation/achievement among the Ilongot, Kakar's (1981) work on the developmental patterning of intimacy, individuation and gender identity in north India, and Herdt's (1982; 1987) work on masculine gender socialization and universal stage-specific mandatory homosexuality among Sambia males.

All of these studies and others point to the fact that certain personality patterns that have by and large been considered aberrant in modern Western psychology are allowed for, expected or especially admired in other local ethnopsychologies, or in other historical periods of Western culture.

These studies in the cultural psychology of personality are analogous in their implications to the earlier work of Cole and his colleagues in culture and cognition. At the time that Cole began his work (the 1960s and early 1970s) the dominant cross-cultural perspective on cognition and cognitive development derived from the universalist viewpoint of Piagetian developmental psychology. This perspective measured and evaluated the cognitive performances of other groups against performance criteria developed for white middle-class Euro-Americans growing up in a particular kind of educational environment. The criterion performances, it turned out, could be shown to be deeply embedded in the demands and practices of that specific cultural environment.

In cross-cultural comparisons, the ethnocentric bias of this work led repeatedly to conclusions that non-Western peoples were inferior in the development of their cognitive processes. At that time a popular sympathetic view was expressed as the 'cultural deprivation' hypothesis. This view was favoured as a non-racist explanation for the poor measured cognitive performances of non-Western peoples and black children from impoverished families in the United States. The position was that the relative paucity of opportunities for intellectual stimulation in the local culture deprived children of opportunities for full intellectual development.

Cole and his colleagues (Cole and Scribner, 1976; Cole, 1975; Cole and Means, 1981) began from such a universalist viewpoint when they were invited by the Liberian government to try to understand the mathematical 'deficiencies' of Liberian Kpelle children when they attended Western-style schools, and to help design interventions that might help these children succeed. These researchers became pioneering investigators of the ethnographic contexts of learning, reasoning and intellectual skill. The Liberian Kpelle with whom Cole worked did indeed perform poorly on most of the laboratory tests Cole designed to measure school-related cognitive abilities.

But Cole was impressed by the fact that the Kpelle, among whom he lived, did not seem in any way to be cognitively defective or incapable when he observed their spontaneous cognitive activities and performances naturally situated in the contexts of their accustomed everyday life tasks. Nor did their life contexts suggest to Cole a general deficiency of opportunities for cognitive stimulation.

Cole began to wonder whether something was wrong with the laboratory tasks and the criteria. In a series of studies, the investigators showed how local contexts of meaningful performance, local values and relevance structures – i.e. local opinions about what was considered worth knowing in which situation and why – had shaped cultural training situations such that people were encouraged to cultivate certain kinds of cognitive performance (e.g. mathematical reasoning, categorization) in relation to the pragmatic contexts of everyday life, while other culturally irrelevant performances were neglected or discouraged. It seemed impossible to segregate abstract 'ability' (an assumption taken for granted by the universalist-developmentalist tradition) from specific performance contexts. Cole and his colleagues demonstrated that the apparently aberrant or immature thought patterns and 'incapacities' of Kpelle – relative to Western designed cognitive tests – were in fact better understood as indicators of differently organized patterns of skill and expertise, learned in conjunction with the relevant performance contexts of a local cultural environment. There was a local universe of relevant skills. The same would, of course, be the case for middle-class Euro-American school culture. There is a local universe of relevant cognitive performances. Others are often not encouraged, or are definitely discouraged, and may be considered aberrant if they appear. Put simply, one learns to do what it is relevant and acceptable to do in one's local culture. Contra Piagetian theory, there seems no particular reason to suppose there are transcendent abstract skills that must transfer to extremely unfamiliar contexts. To manifest that assertion, we suggest that many professors and other professionals of our generation will recall their own initial sense of opacity when first confronted with personal computers. They already knew how to write; they generally knew how to type; most knew elementary logic: but all of that did not make the machine in front of them transparent. Not, at least, until someone taught them how to use it.

Part of the experimental agenda of Cole and his colleagues was to design categorization and arithmetic tasks that Kpelle informants could perform well, while American college graduates teaching in Africa could not. This proved to be eminently achievable. The cognitive skills of Kpelle were not inferior but were shaped by the cultivation of cognitive skills according to local pragmatic contexts of use.

In a similar vein, Kakar (1981; 1985; 1990), Obeyesekere (1981; 1991) and others have criticized Western ethnocentric personality theories for a bias that repeatedly concluded that non-Western peoples are less robust by Western standards of ego development, are poorer at reality testing and are generally closer to the regressive or pathological end of the developmental spectrum. These cultural psychologists and others have also shown that coherent and enriching revisions of the basic theories can result from revising those theories to accommodate the phenomena of other cultures without pathologizing them.

We suggest that from the point of view of a social and cultural psychology, personality patterns – dispositions, patterns of knowing and feeling, awareness and response – are aptly considered skills. A neonate enters the social world with a certain range of potentials, some universal or widely shared, others particular to a subset of individuals. The social cultivation of some of these potentials may be universally mandatory for survival (Geertz, 1973). But many others may be cultivated or not, depending in part upon existing cultural contexts for learning, knowing and performing. In one culture the conceptual and social resources for cultivating certain varieties of human potential (e.g. eidetic imagery, trance states, dreaming) may be scarce. Related skills may not be considered important and the insistence upon personal expression of such skills may be considered aberrant, in part because there are few or no legitimated cultural institutions for cultivating them in well-organized and socially productive forms. Comparative observations of other cultures illustrate that it is a real possibility that certain of our culturally defined aberrations could be talents in disguise, found in forms that are organized, disciplined and controlled, well integrated with social institutions and interpersonal relationships, and articulated with cultural goals.

It is already amply evident that cultures value and train for different personality skills, emotive/expressive and social-relational skills (Heelas and Lock, 1981; Lutz, 1988; Lutz and White, 1986; Roland, 1988; Rosaldo, 1980; 1984; Schwartz et al., 1992; Tambiah, 1985). Seemingly, some kinds of potential abilities and skills are irrelevant to the values of some cultures (e.g. contemporary Western culture), do not articulate well with cultural values and goals, are not encouraged, and so are associated with aberrance and appear primarily in disorganized and poorly inte-grated forms – because they are not generally institutionalized or cultivated as productive, creative behaviours. A salient case of contrast is presented by the various contemplative, mystical and ecstatic skills valued, taught and cultivated in South Asia but ignored and generally pathol-ogized by mainstream contemporary Western society. The pathologized and marginalized potentials of one culture may be recognized talents, and so developed into socially and personally adaptive skills, in cultural contexts where these skills are accepted, where they can be cultivated in well-organized institutional forms, and where they are integrated with local social structures and cultural goals. If our own theoretical psychology is to be a genuine transcultural psychology, it will benefit substantially from the contributions of other indigenous psychologies that offer possibilities for knowing and experiencing that have not yet been accounted for by our mainstream psychology – as yet still an indigenous theory studying itself.

Notes

1 *MM*: 'She asks, two to four Goddesses are appearing in you, *Mangala*, *Durga*, *Barabhuja* etc.; how could you know which Goddess comes to you at what time? How do you know this?' *Ma*: 'She shows her own form [*rupa*]. It is like this.'

2 *Sadhanas* are complex practices for obtaining specific powers; *bratas* are vows to a deity to perform specified rituals and observe certain restrictions, usually food restrictions, for a certain period, usually in order to obtain a particular blessing; *pujas* are all of the ritual practices involving offerings to the deity. *Sadhanas* and *bratas* usually involve *pujas*.

3 It should be mentioned here that other kinds of sacred oracles do exist in Orissan culture, as well as other kinds of sacred healers who are not, however, oracles.

PART II
COGNITION IN PUBLIC:
the Psychology of Decision and Action

4 Attribution

Derek Edwards and Jonathan Potter

Attribution theory is concerned with the ways in which ordinary people, acting as 'intuitive scientists', explain human actions and events to themselves. In the classical version, attributions are a perceptually derived species of social cognition in which people assign causal explanations to events, situations and actions. Despite the fact that the theoretical foundation of classical attribution theory is essentially perceptual and cognitive, research methodology relies on verbal descriptions of events, verbal communication of instructions, and verbal formulations of causal explanations. Experimental subjects are provided with linguistically formulated vignettes which make descriptive statements about the world (e.g. 'John laughed at the comedian') and are asked 'Why?' Language is part of method rather than part of theory, enabling experimenters and subjects to communicate sufficiently so that subjects' causal thinking can be assessed.

Recent developments and alternatives to the classical model have started to place much more emphasis on the central role of language, and it is these studies that we shall focus on. In one approach (e.g. Au, 1986; Brown and Fish, 1983; Garvey and Caramazza, 1974; Semin and Fiedler, 1988), the process of attribution is studied in terms of categories that are built into the linguistic system itself and, particularly, into the semantics and presuppositional structures of the different verb classes that people use to describe and explain people's actions and states. These studies make the important point that language is by no means a transparent or neutral system for conveying information; rather, the words that people use to describe simple, everyday actions and states carry with them powerful implications for the causal explanation of those events. We shall call this approach the *linguistic category model* (after Semin and Fiedler, 1989). In the second approach (e.g. Hilton, 1990; Hilton and Slugoski, 1986; Turnbull and Slugoski, 1988), the emphasis is on the pragmatic and structural features of conversation, which are considered to underlie both the cognitive and linguistic natures of everyday causal attributions. We shall call this second approach the *conversational model* (after Hilton, 1990).

In a recent review of studies in attribution theory, Hewstone noted that 'the attention now being paid to linguistic factors is long overdue' (1989: 93). Our view is that these approaches still do not pay sufficient attention to the nature and dynamics of ordinary discourse. We argue that fuller recognition should be given to the importance of discourse and that doing so leads to a more thorough re-evaluation of attribution theory's perceptual basis than has yet been recognized (cf. Billig, 1985). The approach we recommend here is that causal attributions, both inside and outside the laboratory, can fruitfully be studied as social acts performed in discourse and not merely as cognitions about social acts, which happen to be expressed within conversations. Discursive psychology disputes the 'window on the mind' epistemology of language that is generally implicit in attribution theories and possesses wide-ranging implications for other cognitive studies that are also based on it.

Discursive action model

To deal with attribution theory's particular concern with everyday causal reasoning, we shall begin by outlining an alternative set of principles, which can be termed the *discursive action model* (DAM). DAM is not a model in the cognitive sense of specifying a series of mental processes that possess psychological reality. Rather, it is a set of principles at a meta-level somewhat like Heider's (1958) original formulation of attribution theory, which outlined the kind of theory it is, the kinds of phenomena it encompasses, the set of considerations that any study of attributional reasoning should have to take account of and the kinds of empirical work that would have to be done to substantiate and test it. It also provides a principled basis for a detailed critique of how more traditional attributional studies have dealt (often implicitly) with language and discourse. There are three major principles, each of which has three components. They are summarized as follows:

Action
1   The focus is on action, not cognition.
2   Attributions are discursive actions.
3   Attributions are situated in activity sequences such as those involving invitation refusals, blamings and defences.
Fact and interest
4   There is a dilemma of stake or interest, which is often managed by doing attribution by means of factual reports and descriptions.
5   Reports and descriptions are therefore constructed and displayed as factual items by a variety of discursive devices.

6   Reports and descriptions are rhetorically organized to undermine
     alternatives.
Accountability
7   Reports attend to agency (causality) and accountability in reported
     events.
8   Reports attend to the accountability of the current speaker's action,
     including those done in reporting.
9   The latter two concerns are often related, such that component 7 is
     deployed for component 8, and component 8 is deployed for
     component 7.

We expand on these principles in the following sections.

Action

DAM is a model of action, not of cognition. This is the primary and major
departure from perceptually and cognitively oriented approaches, including
the recent language-based approaches. Attributions are defined both
operationally and theoretically as things people do, not as things people
perceive or think. They are defined as discursive actions, done in and
through language, deploying but not accounted for by language's semantic
structures. In DAM, attributions are studied as discursive actions
performed in everyday life, as a constitutive part of activity sequences that
involve interpersonal or intergroup issues such as blame, responsibility,
reward, compliment, invitation and so on. DAM topicalizes these activities,
rather than attribution *per se*, and analyses attribution as an element in
these activities.

Fact and interest

The performance of attributions as a constitutive part of discursive activity
immediately raises a dilemma of stake or interest: an interested or
motivated account risks being discounted on just that basis (e.g. 'He would
say that, wouldn't he?'). Much of the power and value of the discursive
approach to attribution stems from its concern with how participants
handle or manage interest by performing attributions indirectly or
implicitly. One of the major ways of doing this is by factual reporting.
Attributions can be communicatively accomplished as upshots, or implications, of ostensibly disinterested (or interest-managed) factual reports.
One way of warranting a report as factual is to describe events as ones
that are perceived directly, or by means of graphic description and
sequential narrative that imply or invoke the perceptual clarity of being
there. Other ways of warranting factuality include the provision of
eyewitness reports, corroborative evidence, appeals to common knowledge
or consensual agreement, and so on (cf. Edwards and Potter, 1992; Gilbert
and Mulkay, 1984; Pomerantz, 1984; Potter and Edwards, 1990; Woolgar,
1988). The point here is that in ordinary conversation, factual reports are

designed in such a way as to imply specific attributional explanations of the events described.

Because descriptions and attributions occur as part of interested social actions, DAM is concerned with how factual reportings are rhetorically designed. This means that everyday reports and descriptions are likely to be designed in ways that anticipate their possible refutation or undermining as false, partial or interested and that they are likely to be designed to undermine, in turn, alternative versions. Analysis needs to focus on the rhetorical design of descriptions. A principal discursive location for the production of factual discourse is where there is an issue, conflict or dispute; it arises as a feature of rhetoric. This reverses the conventional attributional model, which starts with factual statements and proceeds inferentially from them.

This emphasis on the action orientation of event descriptions and factual reports is a major feature of the discursive approach. It means that we have to re-examine the practice in traditional studies of presenting people with decontextualized statements from which they are required to draw attributional inferences. Such studies might be seen as offering the virtue of experimental control, that is, of removing the dynamics of event construction while revealing the inferential processes that ensue from them. However, the problem is not with the notion of cognitive inferences but with the cognitivist metatheory to which this is attached. It may be that people do not ordinarily figure out a definitive (for them) causality for events and then put it into words; nor may they ordinarily respond in an automatic, 'calculus' manner (Brown, 1986) to descriptions as given pictures of the world from which explanatory inferences have to be drawn.

Discursive psychology suggests that reports and descriptions are constructed communicatively and that language offers great descriptive flexibility for doing so, precisely for the attributional implications that such reports can carry. Furthermore, because these constructed descriptions and reports are embedded within the performance of situated actions and are interactively responded to by other participants on that basis, this means that attributional inferences are an integral part of communicative actions in which descriptions and versions of events are closely bound up with establishing their possible explanations. In situated talk, we suggest, explanation is not a neutral business of making the best sense of experience, with language serving to inform the investigator of how and what people think. Rather, it is part of a social process of reality construction in which participants have a rhetorical stake or position and orient to what each other says as similarly positioned and possibly contentious.

Accountability

In reporting events, speakers routinely deal with issues of agency and responsibility, in other words, with the kind of issues that concern attribution theory. However, there is another level of accountability that is systematically omitted (or controlled out) from attributional studies: that of the current speaker or writer. At the same time as they are reporting and constructing explanations of events, speakers are accountable for their own actions in speaking, for the veracity of their accounts, and for the interactional consequences of those accounts. This is the notion of accountability which has been explored more by ethnomethodologists than by social psychologists. The notion of 'footing' (Goffman, 1979; Levinson, 1988) is useful here in pointing to the basis on which an account is offered, whether from direct experience and involvement, or as a factual report that is based on the testimony of a reliable witness, as a disinterested passing on of possibly contentious information, or as reported speech, and so on. Footing plays a central part in accountability. The interactional work performed in reporting events, including attributional issues for speaker and audience, may be accomplished indirectly through the way in which reported events and attributional issues in them are handled. Conversely, establishing footing, or one's personal accountability for the veracity of a report, can work towards claiming credit for, or distance from, the reported events.

Even for events in which the reporter had no direct part, actual reports invariably display the speaker's interest, or attempt to display a disinterestedness in described events, and are likely to be dealt with rhetorically, as potentially interested versions, by coparticipants. Within a discursive psychology of attribution, the current speaker's accountability for what is said, in terms of such talk's occurrence within an interaction sequence, comes before issues of accountability in the report itself. The omission of this feature from conventional studies of attributional reasoning is therefore a significant one. As with the constructed nature of factual descriptions, the removal of interest by means of experimental control can only be understood as a removal, with the ensuing results properly interpreted, when we have developed an understanding of how such issues normally operate. We shall argue that the omission of these things is perhaps more like Ebbinghaus's efforts to study memory without meaning; the worry is that the baby may have been thrown out with the bath water.

In summary, DAM enables us to highlight three important limitations in the current linguistically oriented work: (a) a failure to properly theorize the relationship between linguistic and psychological analysis, (b) the use of methodologies that are insensitive to the sequential organization of natural discourse, and (c) a failure to recognize how descriptions and versions of events are constructed by speakers and writers to perform social actions. These limitations are inflected in different ways in the various studies that make up both the linguistic category approach and the conversational approach. Taken together, they have the effect of pushing attribution theory towards an idealized, normative account of causal understanding that does not do justice to the complex social and rhetorical contexts of attributional accounting in natural discourse. We shall begin with a critical examination of the linguistic category studies.

Blaming words can be dangerous: the verb studies

Serious interest in the possibility that attributional phenomena might be reducible to linguistic ones began with a study by Brown and Fish (1983) in which two classes of verbs, which describe either behavioural or mental interactions between persons, were shown in a series of experiments to carry different implications for attributions of causality. When behavioural action verbs, such as *help* or *cheat*, were placed in simple sentences, such as 'Ted ____ Paul', causality was predominantly assigned to the agent, Ted. When the action verb was replaced by a mental (state) verb, such as *like* or *notice*, perceived causality switched to the stimulus argument, Paul. A linguistic pattern was also noted, which was later confirmed empirically by Hoffman and Tchir (1990), for agentive verbs to form agent-attributive adjectives (e.g. obey/obedient and help/helpful), while those adjectives derived from stative verbs typically described patients (e.g. praise/praise-worthy and like/likeable). While Brown and Fish (1983) have proposed that these linguistic structures were derived from cognitive universals, Hoffman and Tchir (1990) have argued for a more Whorfian effect of language upon cognition. In a subsequent study Van Kleeck et al. showed that the causality implicit in verb categories 'significantly moderated . . . but did not overpower' (1988: 89) the influence of basic attributional information about consistency, distinctiveness and consensus (as defined by Kelley, 1967).

Developments of the verb category approach to attribution have included Au's (1986) demonstration that, in addition to the action/state pattern established by Brown and Fish (1983), there is also a subclass of action verbs that carry patient-causal implications. This important study is acknowledged as incorporating and advancing the earlier work and will therefore be a focus for detailed attention. The other major development is the work of Semin and Fiedler (1988; 1989). This work extends the number of attributional verb categories to four and suggests a linguistically based progression from agent to patient causality, as we move from verbs that describe simple actions to straightforward adjectival state descriptions. We shall give detailed attention to this work also.

Our argument is that the powerful statistical significances reported in these studies do indeed point to important insights into the cognitive reality of the semantic analyses on which they are based. However, they also point to a degree of circularity, that is, to the fact that what is being demonstrated is the robustness of semantic analysis rather than discoveries about how people explain events. By presenting people with decon-textualized sentences, devoid of stake and interest, invented by the experimenter and lacking any context of discursive action, people are invited by the experimental methodology to simply confirm intrasentential semantics. As psycholinguistic studies they are interesting, but their relevance to attribution theory is restricted to pointing out that language is a primary medium for expressing causal ideas and that the subjects in these studies are competent speakers of a language that has structures that allow them to do that. The discursive approach suggests that the psychology of attributional explanations will remain invisible, in the absence of an empirical framework in which alternative and variable descriptions are possible and can be responded to interactionally as such.

Causes: agents, stimuli and speakers

If we consider what is meant in these psycholinguistic studies by the cause of an action or experience, there are at least two possible senses: (a) the direct cause of the action or state of affairs labelled by the verb, and (b) the person or thing considered responsible for bringing it about in the world that the action or state labelled by the verb came to happen. It is this second sense, concerning worldly causality, that is essential to the claim that these studies are investigations not merely of linguistic mental structures but of causal attributional ones. However, it is not always clear which kind of causality is being invoked.

Take, for example, one of the most clear-cut cases of semantic causality. The verb *telephone* (as in 'Betty telephoned John') was one that, in Au's (1986) study, achieved a 100 per cent rating as agent/causal. It is clearly something we know or assume about people who make telephone calls, that they do so intentionally. Nonetheless, we can put the verb into a more complex sentence: 'Having gotten a message on her answering machine to call him back urgently, Betty telephoned John.' In this case, we are forced to distinguish between the case agent (Betty) and the situational responsibility that caused Betty to make a phone call. Further reversals of situational responsibility might arise if we are informed that Betty had instructed John to call her urgently if situation X arose. Of course, it might be argued that by constructing these more complex sentences or scenarios, we are going beyond strict psycholinguistic concerns, overriding the verb's natural or implicit causal structure, and invoking extraneous situational considerations. However, situational considerations and responsibility type (b), given in the previous paragraph, are basic to the entire practice of assigning responsibility for scoldings and criticisms to the scolded and criticized, rather than to the scolder or critic. Rather than addressing these crucial attributional issues concerning the relations between descriptions and events, the verb-category theory turns to presuppositional semantics.

Au's definition of causality in 'interpersonal' verbs is taken from Fillmore's (1971) treatment of presupposition in contrasting pairs such as *scold* and *praise*, where *scold* presupposes that the object (person) was responsible for doing something bad, while *praise* presupposes that the person did something good. Here, the cause is again semantic (type (a) given in the first paragraph of this section), rather than to be found in some real or presumed situation of use. Such presuppositions are intrinsic to meaning: that is, they are part of what anybody would have to understand to be counted as a competent user of these verbs.

The claim that attributional causality is part of these verbs' intrinsic presuppositional semantics is basic to Fillmore's analysis, and it is something we do not dispute. If words did not carry meanings of this sort, they would not be available for performing discursive actions, for constructing causal versions of actual events. What is at issue is the psychology of attributional explanations. Au interestingly questioned the psycholinguistic reality of Fillmore's analysis:

> As compelling as this analysis may seem ... it remains an open question whether people are as sensitive to the presuppositions of interpersonal verbs as sophisticated linguists like Charles Fillmore. For example, if John scolded Mary, one may think that it was because John was in a bad mood or was an irritable person, that he scolded everyone in sight, and that she did not deserve to be scolded. But one can also imagine that John scolded Mary because she blundered again or because she had been pestering him all day, that anyone in John's position would have scolded her, and that she deserved to be scolded. (1986: 104–5)

Fillmore's linguistic analysis is taken as an empirically testable one, as if it might be possible to discover that people are unaware of, or even disagree with, his intuitions. However, it is important to note what is being suggested here. Fillmore's analysis is of the presuppositional semantics of these verbs. If empirical testing could in some sense prove him wrong, then it would prove him not to understand these verbs as others do or else as having to revise his analysis. In fact, Au's set of alternative readings for why 'John scolded Mary' have nothing to do with disputing or proving Fillmore's analysis, in that they all assume its correctness. The notion that Mary perhaps 'did not deserve to be scolded', far from disputing the presupposition that *scold* blames Mary, relies directly upon it. What Au was pointing to here is properly a matter of situated discourse, that is, the appropriateness of John's attribution of blame, not Fillmore's analysis of the word's meaning, that it involves such an attribution.

The notion that somebody might scold another person undeservedly draws our attention to how words perform social actions. There are three levels of responsibility at stake in Au's example: what Mary did; what John did in scolding or praising her; and what the current speaker (excluded from all of the experimental studies) is doing by calling John's action a scolding or a praising and what he or she is thereby doing with respect to Mary. In Au's (1986) study, the event is merely given, taken as true, so that the attribution of responsibility is taken to be for the event, not for the sentence. Our argument is that the psychology of language and causal attribution requires a study of the situated deployment of such verbs, in which all three sorts of responsibility are taken into account, and in which they are likely to be psychologically important in reverse order: current talk and speaker first, John second, and Mary third. From the perspective of discursive psychology, what Mary purportedly did is not the *starting point* but rather the *product* of such talk.

In keeping with DAM, then, we should extend our two kinds of responsibility to include a third: (a) the direct cause of the action or state of affairs labelled by the verb, (b) whoever or whatever is held responsible for bringing about the prior conditions for whatever worldly event is labelled by the verb, and (c) the current speaker's role in describing events such that (a) and (b) obtain. The importance of the speaker's responsibility for a particular discursive construction of events is not merely that it adds something that was omitted from the linguistic category studies. Rather, its importance lies in the difficulties it raises with the cognitive metatheory to which these studies are allied, which claims for them a larger explanatory relevance with regard to how people ordinarily understand and explain events in the world. The decontextualized sentences have no speaker, no occasion of utterance, and hence lack the kind of discursive and rhetorical backdrop in terms of which descriptions and explanations are ordinarily produced and understood. The 'event perception' kind of theorizing is sustainable only by virtue of this decontextualization, which systematically obscures the action orientation (Heritage, 1984) of descriptions in talk and text, including how they might be marshalled precisely to invite particular (and possibly contentious) attributional inferences. As a consequence of limiting the emergence of central features of discourse (its action orientation and its constructed nature), these studies risk becoming circular, confirming the verbs' inherent semantics rather than offering anything of wider psychological interest.

What we are dealing with here appears to be an artefact of decontextualization. Because the sentence is presented as speakerless, as merely given, it is also presented as motiveless, as unoccasioned. Subjects are invited by the experimental methodology to treat verbal descriptions as unmotivated, unsituated and true depictions of the world. We suggest that being thus stripped of all but the word's intrinsic semantic and presuppositional content, the experimental subjects confirm mere semantics – that praising somebody consists of saying what a fine person they were for doing something good. We conclude, then, that while these studies are useful in demonstrating the cognitive reality of semantic analyses, they shed little light on how and why people ordinarily offer and respond to verbal explanations of events. In situated talk, praise can be sycophancy and faint praise can be damnation.

Description and reality

The treatment of mental-state verbs as implying causality, in all of these studies, rests upon a theoretical assumption that recasts all meanings in terms of actions. Thus, not only are semantic agents the causes of the

actions labelled by action verbs, but also the stimulus is glossed as a kind
of causal agent for experiential verbs. 'For instance, in *Ted amazes Paul*,
Ted elicits "amazement" and is therefore the Stimulus, whereas Paul
experiences the amazement and is therefore the Experiencer. Ted, rather
than Paul, is generally viewed as the causal agent of this interpersonal
event' (Au, 1986: 105–6).

This action-based approach to the meanings of both action and state
verbs is developed further in the linguistic category model of Semin and
Fiedler. Here, a fourfold distinction is offered: direct action verbs (DAVs),
interpretative action verbs (IAVs), stative verbs (SVs) and adjectives
(ADJs). According to this scheme, each type of description represents
increasing abstractness, as we move from simple, objective descriptions of
actions (DAVs such as *kick*, *kiss*, *telephone* to interpretative action
descriptions (IAVs such as *help*, *hurt*, *challenge*), then to experiential state
descriptions (SVs such as *like*, *hate*, *admire*), and finally to descriptions of
enduring traits (ADJs such as *dishonest*, *extrovert*, *friendly*). The base
definitional terms are the DAVs, which purportedly offer a neutral
description, where 'no interpretation of the action is involved, merely a
description of it' (Semin and Fiedler, 1988: 559). The other three verbal
categories are then founded by degrees of contrast on this basis of
objective description, as involving increasing degrees of interpretation,
though even for IAVs, 'their external reference can easily be established
and the truth value of the statement can be examined' (Semin and Fiedler,
1988: 559).

The status of the division between DAVs and IAVs is of central
importance for Semin and Fiedler's psychology of thought and language,
as well as for the linguistic foundations of the model, and for discourse
analysis. Its importance for the linguistic category model is that it appears
to offer grounds for transcending mere semantic analysis and addressing
the relationship between language and cognition. DAVs are defined as
offering a direct description of reality. Once reality can be objectively
described, a benchmark of comparison is established for looking at how
other, more interpretational, kinds of descriptions are able to serve their
various social-psychological ends. However, not only is there, at the very
least, a question mark over its naïve realism, but also the linguistic basis
for the distinction is not secure. The state and action dichotomy originated
in generative grammar, in explicating a basis for syntax. However, Semin
and Fiedler provided no *syntactic* justification for the distinction; instead
they relied solely on interpretative, semantic considerations, which we shall
argue are dubious in any case.

Take *kick*, for example. The status of this verb as a DAV is assured
semantically by the fact that, as with other DAVs,

> there is at least one physically invariant feature shared by all actions to which
> the term is applied (e.g. *kiss* always involves the mouth, *phone* always involves
> the phone, *kick* always involves the foot, etc.). In contrast, there is no physically
> invariant feature in the case of IAVs, which refer to a multitude of different

actions that may have nothing in common (e.g. there is no single common feature shared by the different instances of *helping, hurting, challenging,* etc.). (Semin and Fiedler, 1988: 559)

However, consider the sentence 'John kicked his opponent' as a description of an event that is claimed to have taken place during a soccer game. Within the laws of the game, their interpretation, their definitions of foul play and of sanctions against misconduct, and a disputation about whether a penalty is to be awarded, this sort of description can be read as accomplishing important interpretational work: blaming and warranting, categorizing actions, attributing intent, and so on. In soccer, the referee's decision may be taken as an operational definition of foul play or of a goal (if the referee judged it so, it was a goal, foul, accident, etc.). Possibly endless or unresolved disputes about how to describe the world are resolved by means of an operational definition, a practical resolution.

In discursive psychology, ethnomethodology, and conversation analysis, this practical action basis of descriptive adequacy emerges as so pervasive a feature of ordinary talk that the choice of what are ostensibly more direct descriptions can serve to accomplish an interpretation as a description. What is to count as mere description, and as the objective reality that descriptions merely refer to, are, in other words, rhetorical accomplishments. Action descriptions can serve rhetorically as externalizing devices (Pomerantz, 1986; Potter and Edwards, 1990; Potter and Wetherell, 1988; Smith, 1990; Wooffitt, 1992; Woolgar, 1988), that is, ways of accomplishing versions, categorizations and explanations such that they appear to be simple, uninterpreted and unmotivated descriptions. The significance of this for attribution theory is that it has failed to address how people themselves construct and deploy descriptions. Rather, in most studies, reality has entered predefined by the analyst in terms of vignettes, such that a whole dimension of psychologically important attributional activity is systematically excluded, with the effect of promoting a severely limited event perception theory of the process.

Semin and Fiedler recognized that there are problems with the notion of description: 'The interpretative versus descriptive contrast alone is insufficient because interpretativeness is a matter of degree rather than an absolute feature. Many DAVs have an interpretative component, although IAVs involve a greater depth of interpretation. However, it is difficult to specify such a criterion explicitly' (1988: 559). The criterion they offered was that of 'invariant features', which we have discussed for the verb *kick*. Nonetheless, this also fails to distinguish between DAVs and IAVs for three reasons:

1   It ignores the essentially classificatory, speaker's action nature of all description. It is precisely the classificatory work of words, as they occur in situated descriptions, to claim such invariances in the world; however, this claim is by no means a guarantee.

2   The linguistic resources for those speakers' actions are given in the
     fact that just about all words have semantic invariances. Otherwise,
     they would be semantically useless, and we would have to classify an
     infinity of different situational uses for each word. Even statives and
     adjectives have invariances, but, of course, those invariances are not
     ones of action. Indeed, it is precisely because *hurting* (classified as
     IAV) has an invariance related to the effect on the patient, that it need
     have no invariance related to the action of the agent.

3   The notion of invariant features also suffers from the weakness that
     the features in question are not those that distinguish each word's
     particular meaning, and which therefore govern its choice. Thus,
     'calling always involves vocal sounds' (Fiedler et al., 1989: 273).
     However, talking, shouting and so on also involve vocal sounds, even
     more so perhaps, because patently 'what do we *call* this' does not
     imply vocal sound, just as other DAVs such as *hold* can refer to
     different kinds of actions (e.g. 'hold this for me', 'hold on, what do you
     mean?', 'I'm putting you on hold'). The point is that this approach
     becomes reliant on the possibility of a simple, direct mapping between
     words and reality of a kind that, as we have noted, has been strongly
     questioned on both conceptual and empirical grounds.

Semin and Fiedler's linguistic category model fails therefore as a set of
linguistically justifiable semantic categories, though at least some of its
distinctions are derived from well-founded linguistic work. However, it
fails also as a psychology of relations between language and non-linguistic
events, and it is in this arena, that of event descriptions and explanations,
that its relevance to the psychology of attributional reasoning is most at
risk.

The arbitrariness of taking actions as the foundation for description and
attribution can be examined by taking, instead, mental states as the
criterion. In fact, mental-state descriptions can be relatively direct, while
actions are more abstract. Consider, for example: 'The beast terrified John.
John fled from the beast.' *Terrified* is much more clear about John's
mental state than *fled*, which may, however, imply something about John's
mental state. Mental-state descriptions are indirect action descriptions no
more than action descriptions are indirect mental-state descriptions. What
we need to do, and as discourse analysts have started to do, is to examine
the nature and deployment of descriptions, as constructed within text and
talk.

In this section, we have argued that the linguistic category model's
typology of verbs rests on two arbitrary foundations. First, the sole
criterion for the classification is that of action. The other categories are
defined as being less descriptive of actions, rather than studied for the
descriptive work that they actually do. The findings of Semin and Fiedler
(1988), that the more abstract statements are more informative about their
sentence subjects than DAVs, is a tautology, whose obviousness is

obscured by the formulation of such sentences as abstract descriptions of actions, rather than direct descriptions of states. Second is the notion of realistic, objective description, which is the basis for the link between language and event explanations, and the criterion against which other sorts of more interpretative or abstract descriptions are defined as such. These problems stem from a failure to recognize the categorical nature of all description and from treating language as a kind of window on mind and world, rather than as a medium of social action.

Causal questions and causal answers

One of the possible artefacts in all of these studies, and one which concerns the researchers themselves, concerns ecological validity: that the findings about subjects' attributional reasoning may be unnatural, unspontaneous and produced by asking them to make causal inferences that they might not otherwise have done or in a form that they might not have freely chosen. Brown and Fish (1983) provided subjects with a booklet listing sets of simple statements such as 'A loves B', and requesting subjects to answer 'Why?' Additional materials included sample responses and included the instruction to focus the explanation on either A or B, but not both. Similarly, Au's methods included a sentence completion task, with items such as 'John thanked Mary because . . .', and the subjects' responses were then examined: 'If a subject responded, "John thanked Mary because he was grateful to her," the completion was counted as attributing the cause to the Agent. If the response was "John thanked Mary because she had done him a favour," the completion was counted as attributing the cause to the Patient' (1986: 109).

Note that the two sample completions offered by Au are not mutually exclusive and could easily be parts of the same subject's extended discourse: 'John thanked Mary because he was grateful to her for doing him a favour.' Indeed, for Mary's favour to be the occasion for John's thanking, presumably some relevant characteristic in John must be assumed: if not gratitude, then at least politeness, or even deviousness (to encourage Mary to repeat her generosity in the future, or whatever). Similarly, we are given as contrasting attributional responses, 'John interrupted Mary because she had been talking for an hour', and 'John interrupted Mary because he had something to say' (Au, 1986: 110). Again, these are not exclusive possibilities and could easily be formulated without contradiction by the same speaker. Au's methodological procedure can fruitfully be examined, using the discursive approach (DAM), as a kind of instructional conversation. It requires subjects to (minimally) write something relevant to adequate reasons for thanking, blaming, criticizing, interrupting and so on. However, if this is what we are interested in, participants' constructions of adequate explanations for conduct, then we might do better to study it more directly, with real talk, as conversation analysts do (Atkinson and Heritage, 1984). Such work is designed precisely to reveal what Au is drawing upon in these subjects: how people display themselves and others, in talk, as accountable for interpersonal actions, in interactions, and in reports of interactions. For example, interruptions have been a prime focus of interest (Levinson, 1983), transcribed for their occurrence as parts of situated talk, such that issues of what counts for participants as an interruption (rather than merely overlapping speech), how it is accomplished and responded to in an accountable manner, that is, as excusable, intentional, rude and so on, are just the kinds of analytical issues that can be illuminated through an examination of the surrounding talk. So the experimental use of decontextualized, simple statements and direct, causal questions may well obscure rather than reveal the nature of spontaneous attributional reasoning.

Dialogue and mind: the conversational model

Although recommendations have been made (e.g. Billig, 1982; 1987; Lalljee, 1981) that attribution theorists might fruitfully take some note of discourse analysis and of speech-act theory, there have as yet been few empirical studies of attribution in ordinary discourse. Those that have appeared do not treat discourse in its relatively raw, transcribed form, where meanings can be examined for their sequential placement and occasioned nature. One approach begins by categorizing talk into classes of utterances, determined by the analysts' interest in, say, how arguments develop in path and branch structures (Antaki and Naji, 1987), how attributional statements serve a variety of personality functions (Harvey and Weary, 1984), or how subjects impose different readings on narrative materials (Howard and Allen, 1989). Another approach (Hilton, 1990; Turnbull and Slugoski, 1988) makes little attempt to study naturally occurring discourse at all but takes certain abstracted features of conversation (such as Grice's maxims in Grice, 1975) as a model for cognitive attribution processes. Through a critique of this work we shall argue for the virtues of studying real discourse.

Conversation and everyday explanation

Although Antaki's work on ordinary explanations shares some of the same concerns as attribution theory, it is directed at a much wider range of phenomena, including lay explanations of all kinds. Its major concern is with their structural organization, with how they occur as 'coherent wholes' (Antaki, 1988: 60) that can be subdivided into component steps, paths and branches. The analytical technique is to obtain transcriptions of lay reasoning, generally involving persons discussing or answering questions about issues that concern them (such as their political allegiances), and then to extract particular sorts of features, such as the occurrence of 'because' statements or the kinds of ideal argumentative structures (data, warrant, claim etc.) proposed by Toulmin. Attributional issues such as self versus other responsibility claims are then amenable for study in terms of how they are invoked in ordinary explanations.

Similarly, Harvey et al. (1988) described a method in which free response, or unstructured, attributions can be extracted from talk and text concerning topics such as close personal relationships or combat stress in Vietnam War veterans. Again, the method involves the extraction and coding, using predefined categories, of types of causal attributional statements. Real text and talk are studied not in their own terms, as discourse, but rather as an ecologically naturalistic source of data, which can be selectively searched for spontaneous attributional expressions. Cody and McLaughlin (1988) analysed precoded observational data, such as survey data or field notes taken in traffic courts, such that the study of natural discourse is bypassed altogether.

By focusing on naturally occurring data, however, these studies have produced interesting and challenging findings. Harvey et al (1988), for example, showed that meaningful distinctions can be drawn not merely between the dispositional versus situational explanations of classical attribution theory but, more precisely, between locus (internal–external) and responsibility (situational–dispositional) as well as several other bipolar attributional dimensions (valence, globality and stability). Antaki and Naji discovered that 'other people's single actions – attribution theory's paradigm case for explanation – were not frequently brought up for explanation' (1987: 119). The largest category of 'because' explanations (34 per cent) were for 'general states of affairs', followed by explanations of events in which the speaker was involved (29 per cent), while events 'involving other people' accounted for only 18 per cent of all instances. This suggests that the classical experimental studies of attribution may represent only a narrow focus of explanatory concern when compared with ordinary talk (see also Abraham, 1988). Antaki (1985) articulated several more of the critical themes that we develop here and themes that are features of DAM: that ordinary explanations occur not as discrete attributions but as parts of larger social actions and arguments, the importance of the speaker's involvement in the events accounted for, and the importance of the definition of events to be explained. In conventional studies, 'subjects . . . are denied the common conversational practice of choosing their own description of an event or disputing a given description' (Antaki, 1985: 214).

Freedom to describe events, rather than merely to explain them, is a particularly important feature of DAM. When examined in context for the interactional work that they do, what appear to be simple descriptions of actions, events, states of affairs and so on will be revealed as accomplishing important attributional work, much as we suggested earlier in the verb studies section with regard to *kick*. Consider the following examples, taken from a conversation-analytic study of courtroom dialogue by Drew (1990; as discussed in Wooffitt, 1990: 14). The council (*C*) for the defence is cross-examining the prosecution's main witness (*W*), the victim of an alleged rape.

1 *C*: [*referring to a club where the defendant and the victim met*] it's where girls and fellas meet isn't it?
   W: People go there.
2 *C*: And during the evening, didn't Mr O [*the defendant*] come over to sit with you?
   W: Sat at our table.

Wooffitt pointed out how counsel and witness produce different and competing, but not contradictory, versions of the two incidents, each of which is 'designed to make available certain inferences to the overhearing jury' (1990: 13). The counsel's choice of the description 'where girls and fellas meet' conveys an impression of the kinds of intentions and expectations that club patrons might have of each other, which are clearly of implied relevance to the alleged offence, whereas 'people go there' neutralizes those implications, just as 'sat at our table' depersonalizes and defamiliarizes the relationship implied in 'came over to sit with you'. The use of the categories *girls* and *fellas* is not merely descriptive but provides a gender relevance for actions, that attendance at the club is something people do *as* girls and fellas (cf. Sacks, 1992). Much of DAM can be seen at work here in the construction of factual descriptions that deal with attributional issues indirectly within a rhetorically organized interaction sequence. In conventional attribution studies, all of that interesting descriptive work is masked by research design, through the provision of disembedded sentences and vignettes, which the disinterested subject is required to treat as mere truth.

A study of motive seeking in conversation by Burleson (1986) did offer an attributional analysis that is based on sequences of activities in a relatively complete transcript. However, there are major questions about the study, and these provide a useful demonstration of important features of DAM. First, the single transcript used (two teaching assistants discussing a failing student) seems to have been selected precisely because it contains reasoning similar to that predicted by Kelley and other attribution workers. Examining the conversation of two aspiring scientists is arguably a soft test of the man-the-scientist model of attribution. Second, there is very little warrant for the interpretations of action made; it tries to fit transcript to existing attribution theory rather than allow any questioning of that theory to emerge. Third, and most important, the interpretations offered embody the traditional attribution emphasis on explanation (of the girl's failure) without questioning what other discursive actions might be performed. It is at least plausible to suggest that the time spent by the two teaching assistants on the girl's failure is a product of a concern with their own accountability: was she poorly taught (by them) or is she being unfairly treated (by them)? A number of features of the transcript that support this reinterpretation were explored further in Edwards and Potter (1992), along with a critical discussion of

Brown's (1986) application of attribution theory to other real-world textual materials.

Conversation and cognition

We turn now to some recent work that defines a conversational model of causal attributional reasoning while retaining an experimental methodology, rather than opting for systematic analysis of real conversations. It is claimed that, 'In locating causal explanation in everyday conversation and interpersonal relationships, the conversational perspective moves the study of causal explanation to the heart of social life' (Hilton, 1990: 77).

However, despite Hilton's argument and its general closeness to DAM, it is notable that the study of everyday conversation plays no part in his method. Rather, and in the manner of Fiedler et al. (1989), the study of conversation is represented instead by a citation of Grice (1975), whose maxims are taken as rules that describe and govern ordinary talk. In a similar vein, Turnbull and Slugoski suggested that 'Grice's (1975) model of conversation is essentially one of a contract between cooperating equals who set out to transmit information in the most clear and efficient manner possible' (1988: 85).

We suggest that there is a major difficulty with this use of Grice for a specification of the nature of conversation. Given that no evidence is offered by Grice, Hilton or Turnbull and Slugoski about the empirical correctness of the model, there is a very real danger of it providing the foundation for an idealization of natural conversation. That is, while it might provide an exemplary model for those wishing to design expert system interfaces or hoping to provide stipulative heuristics for causal reasoning, it would have the effect of prejudging the nature of natural causal reasoning.

It is also what might be termed a *consensus model of interaction*, as the basic cooperative principle states: 'Make your conversational contribution such as is required, at the stage at which it occurs, by the *accepted purpose* [italics added] or direction of the talk exchange in which you are engaged' (Grice, 1975: 45). Again, this presupposition of shared goals makes it suitable for some areas of psychological research, but it is far from clear that the social psychology of conversations, or of ordinary causal explanations, is one of them. One of the points we have been concerned about making is that an analysis of discourse will consider attribution processes in situations of conflict, rhetoric, power and manipulation, that is, situations where people may be struggling for control of definitions and have competing aims. These are, as many researchers have pointed out, precisely the situations in which blame and accountability are at stake and attributional talk will be prevalent.

The conversational model rests on the assumption that ordinary explanations, or attributional inferences, are either overt or covert answers to questions and solutions to puzzles. From the perspective of DAM, this assumption is both idealized and impoverished in that it rests upon the same cognitive metatheory of language, thought and reality as the classical and verb category approaches to causal attribution. In this case, it is a restricted and idealized notion of the conversational contexts that occasion causal explanations, which is sustained by ignoring the nature of ordinary discourse, and focuses instead on the business of rule-governed problem solving. A whole range of rhetorical and pragmatic elements of talk are then swamped by informative cooperativeness, by a cognitive question-answering device that operates like an idealized expert system according to considerations of mutual knowledge. What is not fully recognized is the conversational work done by explanations – these are taken to be merely informative answers to questions – or the subtle, yet pervasive relations between description and inference. The question answerer is, as in the other approaches, unmotivated, disinterested and objective, and is seeking merely to be cooperatively informative. It is a model not of ordinary conversational attributions but of the activities of people, precisely like the experimental subjects in classical McArthur-style studies (McArthur, 1972), whose attributional answers are provided as part of their experimental cooperativeness.

Part of the model's idealization of conversation is its failure to attend to two important features of lay talk stressed by DAM: on the one hand, the constructive work of descriptive discourse, and on the other hand, speakers' interestedness displayed through their descriptions and explanations. The effect of these absences can be seen in two experiments (Slugoski, 1983; Slugoski et al. 1985) that Turnbull and Slugoski offered to test the hypothesis that 'whether a personal or situational factor is identified as causally relevant should depend on the answerer's beliefs about the knowledge being presupposed by the inquirer' (1988: 73). For example,

> Slugoski (1983) had subjects read a detailed case history of a youth who has committed a crime. The case history included personality information about the youth, and situational information about the circumstances in which the crime occurred. Subjects were then led to believe that they would be conversing with a partner who (a) knew nothing at all about the case, (b) knew only about the youth, or (c) knew only about the situational background. Subjects then provided explanations for the crime in response to a 'why' question from their partner. These explanations were scored by raters, blind to the experimental hypothesis, to determine the number of propositions containing personal and situational information . . . subjects who believed their partner to have knowledge about the person conveyed relatively more situational information than did subjects in the no information or situational information conditions. (1988: 73)

As we have noted already with other studies, this sort of experiment gives the speaker no reason for speaking, no stake, no interest. That does not mean it lacks psychological value because it reinforces our understanding of how speakers generally adjust the content of their talk according to considerations of what the hearer already knows. However, DAM requires us again to treat the whole experiment, including its procedural materials and requirements, as a discursive event. With no other reason for speaking and cued by the informational structure of the experiment (they are told $X + Y$; their partner knows only X and asks about $X + Y$), speakers transmit Y. Why else were they told all that information? It is possible that the involvement here of causal explanation is almost irrelevant, that what we have is a demonstration of subjects' sensitivity to a 'given' and 'new' information structure (Haviland and Clark, 1974) and the operation of procedural demand characteristics.

From the perspective of DAM, therefore, there are three major problems with the conversational model of attribution. They take the form of a related set of omissions, each of which has consequences for the adequacy of the model:

1   the lack of attention to the nature of actual conversation
2   the lack of recognition of the constructive work of discourse, in producing descriptions of the world which are constitutive of an understood reality, rather than reflections of reality as given
3   The lack of concern with the interestedness of speakers and actors as displayed in their descriptions and explanations.

One of the omissions highlighted particularly with points (2) and (3) is a consideration of rhetoric.

Rhetoric and truth

Some approaches to causal attribution have attempted to take account either of rhetoric (e.g. Tetlock, 1985) or of reality construction (Howard and Allen, 1989). However, neither of these studies makes proper allowance for three fundamental features emphasized by DAM, that is, for how, in ordinary talk and text, constructions of reality are accomplished by interested parties. For example, Tetlock (1985) showed how, under controlled experimental conditions, the introduction of a requirement to justify an attributional statement can override the fundamental attributional error, whereby observers tend to overestimate personality or dispositional causes of behaviour while underestimating situational constraints:

> Subjects were exposed to an essay that supported or opposed affirmative action. They were informed that the essay writer had freely chosen or had been assigned the position that he took. Finally, subjects either did not expect to justify their impressions of the essay writer or expected to justify their impressions either before or after exposure to the stimulus information . . . Subjects were, however, significantly more sensitive to situational determinants of the essay writer's behavior when they felt accountable for their impressions prior to viewing the stimulus information. The results suggest that accountability eliminated the overattribution effect by affecting how subjects initially encoded and analyzed stimulus information. (Tetlock, 1985: 47)

This passage shows the continuing influence of the pervasive, post-Heider treatment of attributions as kinds of perceptions. The study is couched in perceptual concepts; the essays are stimulus information, which subjects view and to which they are exposed. Also, the study is designed to show how the effects of accountability are at the input, perceptual phase and are not matters of subsequent verbal accounting 'affecting how subjects encoded and processed incoming information, not by merely affecting the types of judgements subjects were willing to express' (Tetlock, 1985: 233).

On the face of it, this study seemed to incorporate the issue of speakers' interestedness in producing descriptions that DAM emphasizes and also seemed to show, contrary to what would be predicted by DAM, that the accountability effect works only when events are first perceived, not when they are later recounted and explained. However, it is not clear that the subjects in this study had the kind of stake in what was going on which would make accountability a salient consideration. The essays to which subjects were required to respond were ones in whose creation they had no part. The idea of accountability here is that of reasoned justification of an argument, exactly like one presents in writing or evaluating an essay. Tetlock's subjects were disinterested observers (students receiving money and course credits for participation), mere readers of the essays they were given. We suggest that it was this disinterestedness, this separation of the attributional judgement from any responsibility for the actions in question (the essay itself and the writing of it), that led to his major finding that accountability is only effective at the perceptual encoding of events and not at their telling.

Howard and Allen (1989) were critical of conventional attribution studies for ignoring the insights of reader response theories, which derive from contemporary developments in literary criticism, and share some assumptions with ethnomethodology (see also Potter et al., 1984). According to Howard and Allen, these theories

> argue against the traditional notion that texts have a single meaning, for which authority lies with the author. Reader response theories suggest instead that many possible meanings of texts are constructed through interaction between textual characteristics and characteristics of readers themselves. This view of reading poses serious challenges for attributional research, much of which relies on presentation of verbal stimuli typically assumed to constitute identical stimuli for all subjects. (1989: 280)

In place of the brief attributional vignettes of the traditional studies, subjects were presented with a published short story; they provided a running commentary on this while reading it and later responded to a set of structured interview questions. The running commentary is taken to provide spontaneous attributional thinking (Howard and Allen, 1989: 284), analysed by means of a coding and frequency analysis of individual responses.

The study produced some results that support DAM. Variability was identified within as well as across individual readers' explanations of events in the story. It is a notable feature of discursive psychology that the kinds of variability in versions of events that complicate or embarrass cognitive notions of mental representation, or which have to be discounted as error or unreliability, are important indicators of the action orientation of talk (Edwards and Potter, 1992; Potter and Wetherell, 1987). Different descriptions, even incompatible ones, will be produced by the same people in different discursive and rhetorical contexts.

Another interesting finding was that attributions for one character in a story were shown to interact with those for another. This can be taken as an instance of the wider principle, also proposed by DAM, for how ostensibly mere descriptions carry indirect attributional implications: 'For example, the more common readers think it is for a woman to knit alone at night (as the mother does), the more they view the daughter as insecure and as unemotional or cold . . . when the mother is viewed as normal, the daughter is viewed negatively' (Howard and Allen, 1989; 292). Of course, DAM also emphasizes that descriptions are likely to be constructed precisely for such attributional effects. For interested parties, a description of a spouse or working partner is available for its implications concerning the speaker. It is therefore available for its possible discounting as interested, and also for how its factuality is warranted. Unfortunately, Howard and Allen's methods do not permit such construction and interest features of the attributional process to emerge. Useful though their results are, there remain some disadvantages with the methods used, even ignoring the artificiality of the running commentary method.

One of these drawbacks concerns how the data were analysed as isolated, coded and counted attributions, listed as simple statements or even as individual words and phrases ('unemotional, cold'; 'a dreamer'; 'an escape from her life': Howard and Allen, 1989: 286). Once context is removed in this way, a study of the situated and occasioned nature of such formulations becomes impossible. Furthermore, the emphasis on readers' constructions of meaning is made at the expense of a speaker or writer's construction perspective; each statement or characterization is taken as a discrete perceptual judgement, an individually variable reader's response.

Disinterestedness is also a limiting factor, where a rather academic story-criticizing framework is reminiscent of Tetlock's (1985) essay-evaluating method. The participants in Howard and Allen's study, like those in Tetlock's, produced their accounts for the experimenter as part of the study's methodology, while the events at issue (the essay or story) were provided for the participants for that purpose and were events in which, and for which, they had no accountable concern or interest. Being neither authors of nor participants in the stories, these subjects were again essentially third parties, vicarious witnesses, with no stake in talking about those things apart from what was involved in being cooperative experimental subjects.

Moreover, we suggest that these restrictions may account for the experiment's most interesting finding, that 'readers form attributions spontaneously, but these appear to be limited primarily to trait attributions . . . spontaneous causal attributions are almost totally absent'

(Howard and Allen, 1989: 294). However, there are at least three reasons for doubting the importance of the low frequency of spontaneous causal attributions. First, there is the point we have just made concerning the academic nature of the exercise and the subjects' consequent lack of any participatory rhetorical stake in the events at issue. Second, the over-whelming preponderance of trait attributions could also be based even more directly on academic factors, in this case, on the participants' use of a conventional, schooled mode of responding to written stories, novels and so on in terms of their characterization – the classic notion of the novel, or *Bildungsroman*, as events stemming from and constructive of character. This would stand in contrast with social science's concern (and that of attribution theory's intuitive scientist) with direct causal explanation. Third, the dichotomy itself between trait and causal attributions ignores the causal attributional work that may be discursively accomplished by means of trait descriptions. Indeed, that is the proper role of charac-terization in one sort of traditional literary criticism, to explain what happens causally in terms of character. Howard and Allen are unable to study this in their data because of their method of isolating, coding and counting each attributional formulation. Their data tables lose the contextual information necessary for examining how trait descriptions might contextually accomplish causal explanations.

Analytic support for the discursive action model

Direct analytic support for DAM currently consists largely of qualitative studies of talk and text. This in turn raises important methodological concerns, especially for psychologists accustomed to the rigours of experi-mental control and statistical analysis. It is an important part of our critique of earlier studies that it is precisely the pursuit of such controls and rigours that has restricted understanding of the subtlety of the relationship between language and attributional explanation. Such studies have failed to encompass stake and accountability and the important role of description in handling the dilemma of interest. It is not that experi-mental methods are intrinsically unable to address these concerns, but rather that they have actually failed to do so.

DAM is formulated not only on the basis of a critique of these studies but also, and primarily, on the basis of scrutiny of stretches of ordinary talk. Researchers into the sequential organization of ordinary talk, and the social actions performed in it, have begun to collect, transcribe and analyse data that for psychologists constitute a kind of natural history of the kinds of phenomena we are interested in, such as everyday explanations, and relationships between language, thought and reality. Although conversational researchers may not see their work in this light, as psychological natural history, it nevertheless highlights those features of everyday talk and thought that we have identified as being important but so far are missing from (or are distorted in) experimental studies. These features include the importance of speakers' concerns with accountability, the interaction-oriented nature of attributional explanation, the use of descriptions to do indirect attribution, and the detailed coherence of indirect attributions when examined in situations of conflict and rhetoric. Although we are not yet in a position to deliver firm empirical regularities, or statistical frequencies, we see this work as both empirically and conceptually prior to that task, as identifying an apparently robust and well-ordered set of issues and phenomena that arise in ordinary attributional discourse.

There are three major strands of support for DAM. First, it is at least consistent with findings in the very large literature on attribution, where evidence for the mechanisms of attributional reasoning is neutral with regard to cognitive or discursive metatheory. Robust findings, for example the ways in which a causal calculus of attributional reasoning can be specified in terms of event variables such as the consistency of situational versus actor variance, can be incorporated into DAM but with a different psychological status. Cognitive theories offer them as features of worldly events that are computed by rational perceivers in the pursuit of definitive explanations. The discursive approach relocates them as conventional rationalizations, as the kinds of considerations that speakers will attend to, and be held accountable to interactionally, in the construction of versions of the world that persuasively carry attributional implications. As for hearers, the idea that particular linguistic formulations of events trigger automatic inferential mechanisms has an important psycholinguistic status as a model of how words are comprehended, but again this needs to be set within a more flexible, constructive and action-oriented discursive psychology of situated descriptions. Indeed, DAM provides a basis for examining attributional experiments themselves as discursive events, rather than simply having to accommodate their findings.

Second, the detailed critique of current research on language and attribution, offered above, points towards the need for something like DAM. The major findings of the linguistic category and conversational models of attributional reasoning are all compatible with DAM, and they are useful in indicating some of the cognitive processes that may be involved in discursive action. The semantic analyses, to the extent that they are well founded, explicate some of the essential tools that language provides for the work done by situated discourse: in particular, for the accomplishment of attributions as discursive actions done by means of descriptions.

The third and most direct source of support for DAM derives from a broad base of research on discourse and interaction, including discourse-analytic and conversation-analytic work. Although only a small number of studies have been carried out using the model specifically on issues of causal attribution, it is possible to point to a much wider range of studies that exemplify and substantiate many of the features of the proposed model. These include a broad range of empirical work in discourse analysis, as well as some findings of conversation analysis (e.g. Atkinson and Heritage, 1984; Button and Lee, 1987), where substantial progress in detailing systematic regularities in natural conversation have been acknowledged by linguists and cognitive scientists (e.g. Clark, 1985; Levinson, 1983; 1988; Luff et al., 1990). Although these studies typically do not directly address the social psychology of attribution and were not designed to do so, DAM can nevertheless be used to highlight what they reveal about the discursive basis of recognizably attributional processes (see also Heritage, 1984). The remainder of this chapter sketches out the nature of this empirical support, which, as we have noted, takes the form of intensive, largely qualitative analyses of spoken and written discourse obtained from everyday contexts.

Although we introduced DAM as a listed set of principles, we are not suggesting that these are empirically discrete. They are facets of a complex whole. For this reason, empirical work cannot be broken down neatly into studies concerned with each principle, although emphasis varies. Moreover, because much of this work is likely to be unfamiliar to a psychological audience, we have avoided merely summarizing findings but have tried also to give an indication of the styles of analyses and kinds of evidence on which these findings are based. For simplicity we will concentrate on three groups of studies: two groups that focus on kinds of activity sequences, involving blame and requests or invitations, and a third group that is concerned with the management of factuality.

Blame negotiation

Blame, denial, excuse and mitigation are the nexus of discursive activities that correspond most closely to the concerns of traditional attributional research. Take, for example, the talk of a defendant under police interrogation or courtroom examination; in the light of DAM we can expect such talk to be organized to attend to attributional issues. We have already cited a brief example of such work, from Drew's (1990) study of cross-examination in a rape trial, where descriptions of places, actions and persons are shown to carry contrasting and highly relevant implications for the distribution of responsibility between interactants. Watson (1983) also showed how, in a murder investigation, the description of victim and motive in terms of group membership categories (white men, black sisters etc.) performs what DAM would define as indirect attributional work. Without straying from truth or accuracy, descriptive categories are deployed that establish the act as representing a group interest and therefore promote the actor as less personally culpable for it than would be the case with a merely self-motivated act of murder.

Indeed, this is recognizable as a more general feature of sympathetic or insiders' accounts of acts of social violence or terrorism, and it serves in such cases to externalize agency beyond the individual actor, to group and circumstance and to situational necessity. More subtly still, Wowk (1984) examined how a murderer's description of his victim's behaviour and speech before the attack implies relevant category membership (that of a prostitute who approached and abused him) and so provides mitigation for the murder by implying provocation, involvement and lack of innocence on her part. It spreads accountability, again by dissolving agency into the social interaction between murderer and victim.

The use of descriptive categories for implying attributional responsibility for actions is also a feature of news reports, as Jayyusi's (1984) analysis suggested with regard to accounts of the actions of Christians and Moslems in Beirut. The deployment of those social categories implies their relevance to the actions concerned, that the people concerned acted *as* Christians and Muslims (cf. *girls* and *fellas* in Wooffitt, 1990). Understandings of motive and cause are thus accomplished by description, such that other equally accurate descriptions would carry different attributional (causal and intentional) implications. It is also important to note that in certain sequences (apologies etc.) self-blame will be the normatively expected option (Pomerantz, 1978). Again, such discursive phenomena cannot be accounted for by a theory that allows for verbal attributions as either straightforward descriptions or errors; they require the kind of discursively embedded model represented by DAM.

A further indirect (descriptive) device for attributing blame is to draw on role and trait talk, where role acting or acting in line with a particular personality type is discursively deployed as a form of attributional accounting. In an analysis of accounts of violent political protest, Wetherell and Potter (1989) found that excuses and mitigations of police violence were constructed by using personality and role talk, such as

I think the police acted very well. They're only human. If they lashed out and cracked a skull occasionally, it was, hah, only a very human action I'm sure.

In a way they didn't have much choice . . . they've got to do their job . . . a lot of people tend to forget that.

In the first example, police action is constructed as natural, only human, and therefore excusable, what anybody might have done in the circumstances. In the second, it is role behaviour that removes responsibility: they acted not as universal individuals, but as policemen, legitimately and under orders (cf. Smith, 1990). So the deployment of group membership categories, whether universalizing ('only human') or specific role descriptions ('doing their job'), appears again as an important but indirect way of performing attributions. They are kinds of consensus accounts that externalize the explanation of actions; ways of saying that anybody or everybody in those circumstances, in that role, did or would have acted that way. The point to note is that these accounts *construct* consensus and do so precisely for such implicational upshots. Consensus is not merely a visible feature of the world, to be picked up perceptually and subjected to a cognitive calculus or perceptual analysis of variance; the events concerned were controversial and subject to a variety of contrasting descriptions. Nor were such descriptions forced upon people by the nature of language. What we have is a situated deployment of discursive resources, of role and trait categories, for the attributional work of explaining behaviour designed for the current interactional business of (in the above cases) excusing it.

The rhetorical deniability of such descriptions is another feature of DAM that has not come to the fore in traditional research on attribution. It is not just that descriptions and their attributional implications will be actually denied or countered in conversations. Participants will in any case orient their accounts, explicitly and implicitly, argumentatively to what others may think (cf. Billig, 1987). We can see this rhetorical organization surfacing quite explicitly in the above example, in the phrase 'a lot of people tend to forget that'. In a recent study that focuses on attributional discourse about political events, Edwards and Potter (1992) analysed how participants (Mrs Thatcher and her Chancellor, Nigel Lawson) used role and trait categories to assign blame and responsibility for the Chancellor's controversial resignation. 'Advisers are there to advise. Ministers are there to decide' (Edwards and Potter, 1992: 133) declared Mrs Thatcher, for example, rebutting the accusation that she had undermined her Chancellor's position by using an independent economic adviser.

Organization of requests and invitations

The indirect performance of social actions is a general feature of conversational interaction (Levinson, 1983; Schegloff, 1988), and one of its main devices, emphasized in DAM, is the strategic production of factual reports or descriptions. That is, producing a report or description will perform an action in such a way that the speaker can, for example, accountably deny that this was their intent. The importance of this for attributional issues can be seen not only in studies involving clear cases of blame and accusation but in ordinary conversational exchanges such as making and declining requests and invitations.

Requests and invitations can be made indirectly, by means of reportings of need, desire and circumstance, or by 'fishing' (Pomerantz, 1980), so that 'face threatening actions' such as requesting and being rejected, or rejecting itself, are avoided (Davidson, 1984; Drew, 1984; Heritage, 1984). This also serves to avoid the attributional implications of rejection; personal wishes may be replaced by situational constraints: *not wanting* is replaced by *can't*, and situational descriptions are formulated for how they imply constraint. The factual reports that are used in invitation sequences and in the account component of dispreferred actions such as rejections and refusals (Atkinson and Heritage, 1984) are prime conversational examples of factual descriptions pressed into the service of discursive attributional work. Again, these kinds of studies demonstrate the importance of locating everyday attributional reasoning within discursive practices, rather than within a cognitive metatheory of persons simply making best sense of objectively available events.

We shall take one example in some detail to illustrate the subtlety of this process. Drew (1984) discussed a sequence from a telephone conversation in which, having been invited on a shopping trip by *N*, *E* launches into a lengthy description of the enduring effects of a recent operation on an infected toenail. Note in this short extract how much attributional business is accomplished by *E*'s factual report and how those attributional implications are visible in their receipt by *N*. This shows how the examination of implication and uptake in discourse is capable of revealing the kinds of attributional reasoning that would otherwise have to be theorized as covert mental calculations.

```
 1  E:  So everybody's been nice in the apartment just like
 2      with my le:g ihh ⌈hh heh heh huh?
 3  N:                  ⌊Yee:::a:::uh::,
 4  N:  Well you- people should be nice to you Emma,
 5      you're a, thoroughly nice person to be nice to.
 6  E:  Oh::: well it was-
 7  E:  They all come up and see how ⌈I am and I have=
 8  N:                               ⌊Well su:re.
 9  E:  to have my foot up on the pillow for two days,
10      you know ⌈and- ·hhhmhhh
11  N:          ⌊Yah?
12  E:  But honey it's gonna be alright I'm sure,
13  N:  Oh I'm sure it's gonna be alri:ght,
14  E:  Yeuh,
15  N:  Oh:: do:ggone. I ⌈thought maybe we could
16  E:                  ⌊I'd like to get      some
17      little slippers but uh,
```

(Drew, 1984: 138, 150. Line numbers are ours: transcription conventions are standard in conversation analysis. Cf. Button and Lee, 1987.)

The report of the infected toenail, both in its conversational placing and in its content (lines 7 and 9), provides for situation-oriented attributional inferences. It is not that *E* does not want to go shopping (as lines 16 and 17 then explicate) but that she cannot. *N* takes up these inferences quite clearly (line 15), making the relationship between factual description and inferential attribution a joint conversational accomplishment. Note also the detailed attributional work earlier in the sequence, where *E* formulates consensus information (lines 1 and 7) and *N* draws appropriate attributional inferences (lines 4 and 5). In many ways, this is like an experimenter–subject dialogue in an attribution experiment. However, *E* does not simply report some disinterested facts about the world and *N* simply draw some cognitive inferences; if so, that would ignore the details of the interaction, its precise content and sequential organization, and the interactional work being done thereby. Note that *N*'s inferences include a moral, norm-referenced imperative ('people *should* be nice to you Emma', line 4); reportings and their implications occur here not as cognitively disembedded ways of making sense of the world, but rather as parts of social interactions. In DAM, fact and inference are studied as conversationally embedded actions, where facts are constructed precisely for their attributional implications, in this case within an invitation–rejection activity sequence.

It takes a study of many such sequences to establish the robustness of these conversational phenomena and their variations, and we can refer to only a few instances here. Pomerantz (1984), for example, provided an analysis of how a refusal to comply with an invitation to take up a home nursing job is accomplished indirectly by means of a factual discussion of how the patient got to need such medical help. The negotiation hinges on details of what happened when some previous medical treatment went wrong and, specifically, on issues of responsibility and blame: 'In reporting just the facts, speakers rely on the recipients' seeing the import of the facts for the issues at hand' (Pomerantz, 1984: 158). These sorts of naturalistic data, examined in detail, exemplify the importance of an accountability component of DAM, where attributional issues of agency and blame for reported events, conducted through ostensibly mere factual description, are a medium for attributional issues in the current conversational interaction. By constructing the patient's condition as in fact resulting from a controversial error and as being possibly difficult and long term, the invitee manages indirectly to externalize the grounds for her rejection of the invitation; it resides not in her own capricious will but in the circumstances of the case.

Management of factuality

One of the central points of DAM is that if attribution is going to be performed through reports and descriptions, then speakers will need to attend to the issue of factual objectivity. That is, they will need to handle the dilemma of stake or interest to show that their report is justified by the facts, or warrantable, rather than merely prejudiced, biased or self-serving confabulation. Thus, an important analytic focus of DAM, and one of the features that distinguishes it from traditional attribution research, is its analytical focus on the discursive devices used to establish objectivity and factuality.

One major group of devices for managing interest is to externalize the account, to place it 'in the world', so to speak (cf. Smith's 1990 case study of the discursive construction of somebody as mentally ill). Studies of the discourse of science have revealed how such devices operate to characterize phenomena as objectively 'out there', to be discovered rather than being products of method, instrumentation or theory (Latour, 1987; Woolgar, 1980; 1988). A prime concern of externalization generally, in ordinary talk as much as in science, is to present accounts as disinterested or unmotivated. Conversely, interest is usable for undermining factual accounts, and again studies have shown how it is deployed for this effect in scientific discourse (Gilbert and Mulkay, 1984; Yearley, 1986), in legal discourse (Atkinson and Drew, 1979; Pollner, 1987), in ordinary talk (Yearley, 1987), and in a study of consensus-based attributions in political discourse (Potter and Edwards, 1990). In the last study, for example, a disputed version of a political event, despite representing a journalistic consensus across 10 different newspapers, is attributed to the journalists' lack of 'a good enough story and so they produced that'. Here, a role account is used to undermine consensus: the journalists' job, to produce good stories, provides an interest basis for discounting their objectivity.

Another device for externalizing accounts, and thereby bolstering their attributional implications, is to produce detailed narratives and perceptually graphic descriptions. The use of narratives provides for a kind of sequential reliving of events, displayed thereby as coherent and believable (Gergen, 1988; Jackson, 1988). Narratives require for their coherence the kinds of causal and motivational connections between persons and events that are the concern of attribution theory. Furthermore, they entail the sort of detailed descriptions that create an impression of direct perceptual clarity, of 'being there'. Thus, John Dean's testimony at the Watergate hearings contained just the sorts of detail and narrative continuity, concerning Oval Office conversations, that rendered it convincing, despite later evidence from transcripts that major elements of that detail were erroneous (Neisser, 1981). A further examination of Dean's testimony (Edwards and Potter, 1992; Chapter 1 in this volume) showed how its graphic reconstruction of fact was carefully oriented to the major attributional issues at stake, that is, to the responsibility for the Watergate break-in and cover-up (the original events) and, simultaneously, Dean's own delicate position as an interested reporter of those events. Similar features are evident in Bogen and Lynch's (1989) study of Oliver North's testimony in the Irangate hearings. These qualitative studies of testimony exemplify much of the scope of DAM, including how factual reports are constructed and marshalled for their attributional implications; how interest is managed and fact externalized; and how accountabilities for current talk and for original events are mutually implicative, all within an overall rhetorical organization of fact, inference and denial.

Concerning the rhetorical basis of factual descriptions and their attributional inferences, Pomerantz (1984) has noted that factual accounts in ordinary conversation tend to be produced in situations where accountability is in question. It is when there is an implicit or explicit challenge that people offer the source or basis of their knowledge. Our own studies of British political discourse concur with Pomerantz's observations concerning the rhetorical context in which detailed factual accounts are produced. The production of detailed narratives in our data followed objections to earlier, less detailed accounts and involved the kinds of graphic description that create an impression of perceptual reexperience:

Mr Lawson sat in an armchair in one corner, next to a window looking out over the garden of No. 11 Downing Street. The Press Secretary, Mr John Gieve, hovered by the door. The rest of us, notebooks on our laps, perched on chairs and sofas in a circle around the Chancellor. It was 10.15 on the morning of Friday, 4 November. (*The Observer*, 13 November 1989, as cited in Edwards and Potter, 1992: 122)

You know the way there are two chairs at the side of the President's desk . . . on the left-hand chair Mr. Haldeman was sitting. (John Dean, cited in Neisser, 1981: 11)

It is within the context of these detailed narratives and graphic descriptions that the crucial, contentious events that carry the burden of attributional implication are placed. Again, it is not that hearers of such narratives are forced to accept them or their implications. Indeed, the production of detailed descriptions opens up additional possibilities for rebuttal, for counter-narratives, and it raises the danger of the entire account and its carefully orchestrated attributional upshots being sabotaged by refutation.

So we also find the opposite kind of device: the use of systematic vagueness (Potter and Edwards, 1990). For example, it has been noted how idiomatic expressions (such as 'caught between a rock and a hard place') operate in inauspicious rhetorical environments, where an account is in difficulty, to complete or round off a description in such a way as to render it difficult to undermine (Drew and Holt, 1988). The very vagueness of application of idioms and other generalized formulations is thus rhetorically useful in providing a barrier to easy undermining, while at the same time using expressions that, of their very nature, are designed as distillations of a common wisdom. So not only is direct refutation difficult, but the would-be refuter is positioned against an implicit cultural consensus. Again, analysis of discourse shows how consensus, one of the major event variables in the cognitive calculus of attributional reasoning, has the status not simply of an abstracted perceptual generalization across objective events but of a discursively constructed and deniable feature of the world and one that is constructed precisely for the business of generating attributional implications.

Similar sorts of attributional issues are displayed in reports of unusual or supernatural phenomena (Wooffitt, 1992), where the use of graphic description, reported speech, and narrative connections bolsters the externality of reported events while paying attention to their prima facie irrationality. Wooffitt picks out the systematic use of an 'At first I thought (mundane X), but then I realized (extraordinary Y)' device, whereby reporters handle the delicate task of deflecting attributional inferences about their own possibly deviant perceptions and cognitions and promote the externality of the reported phenomena. In attributional terms, the reporter's task is to place the version of events as situationally driven, as perceptually vivid, and implicitly consensual (what any normal person would have seen) rather than accountable in terms of characteristics of the perceiver. This brings us to another interesting contrast between perceptual and discursive approaches to attribution. In DAM, the perceptual basis of attribution is itself a discursively constructible (and rhetorically underminable) warrant for how attributional implications are descriptively generated in talk, rather than the psychologist's true story of how attributional implications are actually arrived at.

Finally, a number of studies have concentrated more explicitly on consensus as a phenomenon of discourse. The construction and use of a consensus basis for attributions involve a variety of well-established discursive devices. These include several that Pomerantz discussed in conversation-analytic work, such as the procedure of undermining a version or account by placing it against an alternative one that is already consensually accepted (Pomerantz, 1989) and the deployment of extreme case formulations (Pomerantz, 1986) such as 'everybody does/thinks/knows X.' By constructing certain actions as universal or normative, their attributional explanation shifts from the personal to the situational, from agent to circumstance. Again, examples such as 'any Chancellor of the Exchequer would have been in exactly the same position' combine role discourse and extreme case formulations to construct, in the context of competing versions, an account of action that removes it from the realm of personal caprice.

Consensus formulations are also available for undermining and are designed with regard to that possibility. Potter and Edwards (1990) showed how consensus claims are both made and deployed for rhetorical effect in establishing the facts of disputed events (a controversial political statement made in private to a group of journalists), and, by means of those factual descriptions, in attributing responsibility. We also examined how that same consensus was rhetorically undermined as collusion, how the dispute about consensus and collusion was pursued by means of the production of an independent witness, and how that independence was in turn open to undermining. Here, fact and inference had to be constructed discursively against alternative constructions within a rhetorical process of sense making. This illustrates the importance of DAM's rhetorical principle and suggests the perhaps counter-intuitive view, also embodied in DAM, that facts are the outcome, not the prior condition, of attributional discourse.

Conclusion: discourse and cognition

DAM is offered as a discursive metatheory, contrasted with perceptually based cognitive alternatives. This brings it into conflict with specific cognitive models of causal attribution and with the kinds of empirical methods that cognitive studies have generally used. However, this does not mean a denial of the reality of cognitive processes, or of the validity of those methods. Rather, it calls for a relocation of attributional findings within a wider, discursive model.

We have argued that when people produce and respond to versions and explanations in talk, it is insufficient to take those versions either as neutral descriptions of the world, or as realizations of underlying cognitive representations. DAM theorizes talk as an arena of social action, with constructive and pragmatic relationships to world and thought. The critique that we have offered of both traditional and more recent treatments of causal reasoning is primarily addressed to this issue of how everyday versions of events and their explanations should be treated as situated discursive phenomena.

Cognitive processes (as distinct from cognitive metatheory) can play an important part in such discursive practices in two kinds of ways. First, as we have noted, the established attributional event variables (consensus, distinctiveness, and consistency) can be relocated as rhetorical criteria, as the kinds of considerations that event descriptions attend to when implying attributional causation. Rather than having these variables operate as perceptual abstractions across sets of real and objectively relevant events, event descriptions can be examined for how events are constructed as similar, distinctive and so on by means of the selection of particular events as relevant instances, by their linguistic categorization, and in terms of their rhetorical organization with regard to possible counter-descriptions. We have outlined some empirical work on how the attributional criterion of consensus is discursively constructed, undermined and deployed within sequences of social action.

Similarly, semantic analyses of word meanings are useful explorations of the linguistic resources that speakers and hearers deploy. Participants have to understand the semantics of the words they use to both produce and comprehend attributional implications. Again, however, we have argued that the psychology of attributional reasoning has to place such semantic structures within a larger discursive metatheory in which such resources are put to active and flexible use, rather than being the automatic causes or consequences of event perception. As far as actual, everyday causal attribution is concerned, we have to look to indexicality of meaning and situated deployment, the construction and rhetoric of factual descriptions, and the basis on which certain descriptive terms rather than others are selected.

The second role for cognitive processes in DAM would be in an explication of whatever underlying competences make DAM psychologically possible. We have not attempted such an enterprise here, to formulate DAM as a model of competence, but it would at least be feasible to do so. The point we would make is that this would have to be quite unlike traditional or recent versions of attribution theory. Rather than beginning from a cognitivist metatheory in which attributional reasoning is seen as a matter of figuring out the best sense of perceived events or of how best to inform another person of what she needs to know, it would have to try to provide a cognitive theory of social action, to explicate what makes situated conversation possible, including the rhetorically organized flexibilities of description in which participants engage. That would require, rather than be preferable to, much empirical and theoretical analysis of what goes on in ordinary discourse.

Note

This chapter was originally published as 'Language and Causation: a Discursive Action Model of Description and Attribution', *Psychological Review* (1993) 100 (1): 23–41. © 1993 The American Psychological Association. Adapted with permission.

5 Agentive Discourse

Rom Harré

Mental mechanisms or discourse grammars?

In this chapter I will be outlining an approach to the problem of sketching a psychology of human agency. The discussion will be built around the question of whether we should develop such a psychology by framing it within the theory of mental mechanisms and the metaphysics of causality (that is within cognitive science of the old style) or by trying to develop it within the framework of narratology and the metaphysics of discursive acts (new-style cognitive psychology). It should further be noted that what I am trying to sketch is not a psychology of choosing, but one of executing a choice once made. The problem is not that of rationality but of the will, its strength and weakness. In the course of the analysis the will melts away as a theoretical entity invoked to explain the facts of the executive act, to be replaced by the procedures with which we take and repudiate responsibility for our actions. We shall be abandoning the search for diaphanous mechanisms in favour of the grammatical analysis of certain classes of speech acts as they are employed in specific situations and the teasing out of the conventions of certain kinds of self-referring narratives.

Within our common-sense way of thinking about our world an agent is a being capable of bringing something about. In using our descriptive and explanatory categories to give accounts of what happens in the world of things and people we make use of a distinction between basic, independent, original and true agents and derivative, dependent or vicarious agents. According to our everyday scheme the latter derive their powers to bring things about from the former.

In the mechanistic picture of the universe, sketched for example by Descartes, the motion displayed by a particular body at some definite moment is the result of the impetus to which it has been subjected by the impact of some other body, already in motion. No material thing is ever a source of its own motion. Since, according to Descartes, all activity, be it of inorganic or organic bodies, is the result of motion, the activity to be discerned in the world at this moment is the result of the redistribution of prior motion, back to an original input of motion to the whole material universe by the Creator, who alone is a true and independent source of motion. According to the 'mechanistic' point of view, material agency is an illusion.

In sharp contrast to this is the dynamicist view of the post-mechanistic physics of the field theorists, according to whom there are original sources of activity in the physical world, sources which can, without themselves moving, bring other bodies into motion. A unit electric charge might be such a genuine or originating source of motion. The space around a charge is structured as a field: that is, at each point in the space there is a field energy, specified in terms of the dispositions to induce motion in a test body. In physics the ascribed dispositions must specify the subsequent motion in both magnitude and direction. The contrasting mechanistic and dynamicist schemata for constructing explanations in physics can be represented diagrammatically as follows.

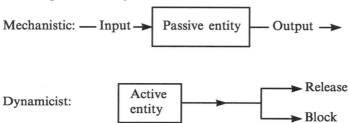

The principle of the conservation of energy requires that the active entities of a physical system should have obtained their energy from somewhere. They do not spontaneously possess energy. A watch spring must be wound up, a capacitor must be charged and so on. However the ontology of the physical sciences is organized hierarchically. Complex entities like watch springs and capacitors are structured aggregates of more basic constituents, themselves active entities. The hierarchy of constituents terminates in primary agents such as electrons, which are nothing but permanent and original charges owing their powers to no prior process of charging. If electrons are not basic but quarks are, then they would possess the basic powers, and so serve as the basic particulars.

What are the basic particulars of the human sciences, the uncharged charges, the primal source of activity? According to the discursive point of view they are persons, the unanalysable source of all discursive phenomena. How is this primal agency manifested? Again according to the discursive point of view it must be manifested in competence in a wide variety of discursive practices. According to this way of thinking, in the sphere of human action, 'agency' and 'skill' are bound up with one another. The analysis of human powers requires a richer conceptual toolkit than does the analysis of the powers of inanimate beings. With these observations as a general guide we can begin the investigation of human agency.

The Cartesian agent and its Kantian successor

A human body, composed of elementary material particles, cannot, on the notion of agency upon which classical mechanics is based, be the source of its own motion. It could not therefore choose between equally possible and equally attractive courses of action. Unless a tiny preponderating force existed it would be forever stuck in the situation of Balaam's ass, starving between equally attractive bales of hay. Nor could it exert itself by an act of willing. How could a purely material being have executive powers? A material body would lack certain of the basic, defining characteristics of a person. It follows that persons cannot be material bodies. To remedy the defect, philosophers added the Cartesian soul. If the (mechanical) physiology of the body cannot account for what seem to be the plain facts of human agency, perhaps they can be accounted for by the hypothesis of the existence of a non-physical component of a person, their mind or soul, which possesses native powers of free choice and 'conation'.

Kant understood very well that this move did not provide an answer to the question 'What is the source of human activity?' If the mind is conceived as a system of basic entities (simple ideas) and forces it is just as much a machine, though of a very different kind, as is the body. In so far as we are aware of our thoughts and feelings they seem like an inner version of the outer world of atoms in motion according to Newtonian laws. The Kantian solution was to put the source of human activity outside the realm of experience. When a person executes an action they are not aware of how they do this, only that they do it. There must, therefore, be in each person a noumenal self, a source of agentive power in both the choosing and the willing sense, that is not available to us by inspection. We know that we are noumenal selves, since we can act as original agents, but we can have no experience of the noumenal self in or as itself.

With some recent exceptions, psychologists have ignored one half of the problem of human agency. There has been much research into how decisions are made, and subtle mathematical models of decision-making processes have been offered in which the psychology of choice has been treated as a branch of the logic of decision-making. We shall open up the question of the nature of the executive aspect of human agency and its psychology by distancing ourselves absolutely from the Cartesian/Kantian idea of an independently active human mind to which such capacities/powers as the will are to be assigned. We shall turn instead to a study of the discursive practices in which our agentive powers are manifested or, to put it more candidly, in which we present ourselves as agents. Concepts such as 'agency' occur in our languages as polarized pairs, teamed with an indispensable 'opposite'. We can only grasp the meaning of what it is to be agentive by contrast with what that excludes, that is what it is to be passive. So in studying the ways in which we present ourselves as agents by discursively embedding our actions in the agentic framework, we must not fail to attend to the ways we have of presenting ourselves as patients, and to life projects and situations that call for one or the other strategy. It would have been misleading to write 'adopt this or that strategy' in making this point. This would have wrongly suggested a machiavellian knowingness in our discursive practices. We usually smoothly modulate from one discursive mode to another. Only when confronted by police, spouses, psychiatrists or jurors do we reflect upon our modes of presentation – and sometimes not even then.

Agency as a discursive presentation

For our purposes the two most important ways of presenting ourselves as agents and our actions in an agentic framework are:

1 for the taking and assigning, accepting and repudiating of responsibility for actions
2 for the demonstration that what happened was an action satisfying some appropriate rule, convention or norm, or was not an action but the effect of some causal process.

Being competent in these two practices is what it takes to display oneself as an agent. From the discursive point of view, being an agent and displaying oneself as an agent are *one and the same*.

For the most part and typically these practices are skilled productions of certain patterns of utterances or written statements, making claims and declarations, with characteristic grammatical forms. For instance in many cultures the main discursive practice for accomplishing (1) above consists in making certain kinds of statements in the first person singular, or some construction that has a similar force. The practices through which (2) is typically accomplished have been analysed with great care by J.L. Austin (1970), and developed and refined in the researches of others (for instance Backmann, 1977). Austin distinguished between the making of excuses, that is, what we say when we are ready to admit the moral quality of what we did but wish to avoid being ascribed responsibility for what happened, and the giving of justifications, in which we admit responsibility but what we say is aimed at changing the imputed moral quality of what we did. Research into agency will involve detailed studies of these discursive practices, their forms and content, and the narrative contexts in which they play an indispensable part.

From the discursive point of view the management of first-person talk and the making of excuses, the giving of justification and the like, are skilled performances, not things that just happen or that are automatically brought forth on the occasion of some stimulation. The possession of these skills has a profound effect on the forms of human association.

For example, it is their possession that makes persons into beings 'fit for the rule of law'. The rule of law is nothing but the rule of discourse, of edicts, declarations, orders and written instruments, rather than the rule of persons. When what is required is fixed by the utterances of a particular person, whim and arbitrary irrationality may be dominant. The rule of discourse may be no more than the rule of custom and tribal practice, when that practice is expressed discursively. But once the source of obligation shifts from persons to propositions, to the rule of discourse, questions of mutual consistency, of logical ordering, of argumentative justification and so on naturally arise. When that happens the rule of custom has become the rule of law. Discursive presentations of agency and passivity then become central discursive strategies in fateful encounters, in the dramas of the law courts, the boxes of the confessional and the couches of psychiatry. An important corpus of material already exists in studies of the discourses of these events.

The agent as the person responsible

Do I have to do a little piece of research into the operation of mental mechanisms to discover if I am the person responsible for some action? Is the claim that I am responsible a matter of empirical fact about which I could be wrong? Indeed no. Taking responsibility for an action is something I do, not something I know or discover about myself, or that someone else might discover about me. We could make sense of the remark 'Despite what you think, you are responsible for that action' if it were supposed to be the announcement of a discovery in cognitive psychology, say about the meshing of certain mental cogs and the tension of certain mental springs. It makes sense right enough, but as a reminder of the fact that responsibility is not only taken but assigned. In some cases it accrues to someone by virtue of their position in some social network of role positions. A parent can, in some circumstances, be held responsible for the actions of a child, an employer for those of an employee, and so on. I would like to distinguish at this point between the psychology of agency as a phenomenon of certain individual discursive practices, and the sociology of agency as a phenomenon of certain collective social practices. The distinction is not absolute and there are important cases where the psychology and sociology of agency may run parallel or together. Such cases can be found in the practices of formal and informal courts of law. For the purposes of this chapter I will draw the boundary of the cognitive psychology of agency so as to exclude the discourses of the law. For an interesting introduction to the problems of a discursive psychology of agency in legal contexts, see Robinson (1994).

In various places (Muhlhäusler and Harré, 1991) I have argued that one of the main ways in which we take and assign responsibility is by the use of pronouns and other personal inflexions of verbs, particularly in the first and second person. The taking and assigning of responsibility is achieved by exploiting the indexical properties of these pronouns. A brief summary of the indexical theory of pronoun use is all that we need at this point.

The basic analytical level is set by the choice of speech act as the functional unit of discourse analysis. A speech act is what is accomplished by an utterance as it is taken up by those who hear it and understand it as intended to have a certain social force. Austin's term for the social force or executive force of an utterance as speech act was 'illocutionary force'. For instance a statement may look like a tentative description, say 'I think that

that shadow looks rather yellow', and yet function in the context of an art lesson as a reprimand. In speech-act analysis the structure of a complex, many-person discourse is revealed by taking the units of analysis as the speech acts accomplished by the utterances of the conversants, rather than say their descriptive content. An utterance becomes functionally a speech act only in so far as it is taken up as such by the others involved in an exchange. A speaker may intend an utterance to have a certain illocutionary force, and produce a speech action that would, if so taken, accomplish that speech act. However it must be completed as such by the others if it is to play its role in the unfolding of an episode in which, for instance, the psychological phenomenon of agency can be displayed when someone portrays themselves as striving! Analysis of features of speech acts, such as the role of pronouns, is relative to the illocutionary force of utterances in context and to the joint 'creation' of that force by those taking part.

In speech-act analysis it is clear that it would be quite incorrect to take first- and second-person pronouns to be functioning as noun substitutes. They are not 'pro-nouns' but indexicals. The term 'indexical' has been used in several ways in the literature. For us the important aspect of indexicality is not the fact that knowledge of the occasion of utterance is necessary for the mythical hearer to complete the sense (that is to disambiguate the reference) of an indexical expression. In the context of speech-act analysis the indexicality of pronouns is best looked on as locative. The pronoun indexes the empirical content and illocutionary force of speech acts with the locations of speakers and sometimes also of addressees in four possible manifolds, that is with the speakers' spatial, temporal, moral and social positions. The way that latitude and longitude are used to index the names of cities, lakes and so on with their positions on the abstract geographical grid is not a bad analogy for the function of pronouns as indexicals.

The grammar of the first person

A very simple example can show that first-person use, analysed within the context of speech-act theory, cannot be anaphoric, that is cannot be explained as a substitute for the uses of proper names. The illocutionary force of 'Jonathan and Luke will take care of the lunch' commits the speaker to nothing. However, 'We will take care of the lunch' is usually taken as a commitment to do whatever has been specified. To make that commitment is also to present oneself and one's friend as agentive with respect to the course of action in question. This distinction in illocutionary force relative to speaker holds even if either Jonathan or Luke uttered the first remark, even though it is hard to see what the point of it would be.

If the role of pronouns is taken to be locative, in the manner suggested, we can show that on any one occasion of use a first-person pronoun has more than one indexical function. It serves to index the content and force of an utterance with the location of the speaker and sometimes of a counter-speaker in several manifolds. To demarcate the range of possible indexings for which first-person pronouns can be used we shall work with the hypothesis that our usage of first- and second-person indexical devices (pronouns and other equivalent devices) is dominated by four manifolds:

1   A spatial manifold, consisting of a discrete set of spatial locations carved out of the continuous manifold of physical space by the spatially located bodies of the relevant speaker/speaker individuals or groups.
2   A temporal manifold, consisting of a discrete set of temporal moments carved out of the continuous manifold of physical time by the actual moments of utterance of those speech actions from which speech acts will be created by speaker/speaker uptake.
3   A moral manifold representing the array of person types in the local moral order, location in which is defined by the speaker's moral standing (reliable, dishonest, careless etc) *vis-à-vis* that of the counter-speaker and others in the relevant community. The manifold of 'moral locations' consists of the shifting and multiple patterns of positions that conversants occupy relative to one another.
4   A social manifold, location in which defines the speaker's social position *vis-à-vis* others in the relevant discursive community.

I shall develop these concepts somewhat in illustrating the thesis of the discursive construction of agency. We could call the above four manifolds the basis for a 'completely enriched language'. In such a language the empirical content and illocutionary force of all first- and second-person utterances would be fully indexed with the speaker's locations in all four manifolds by the use of the appropriate pronoun or functionally equivalent inflexion.

The English 'I' indexes the speech acts it is used to introduce with location of speaker in only two of the four possible manifolds, the spatial and the moral. Locations of the speaker in the temporal and the social manifolds of human life are indicated in other ways. Taking responsibility as a speaker is a highly complex matter since it involves not only one's location in a moral manifold, but also one's temporal and spatial location. One must be in the right place at the right time to perform an action, before one's claim to responsibility for the act can be taken seriously. By the same token the best possible alibi is a proof that one was somewhere else when the crime was committed. One must have the right social location as well, being a person of the appropriate status to take responsibility for the kind of action whose performance is the occasion for a display of agentiveness. In an organization the person whose hand performed the deed may not be the one who is taken to be agentive in the last resort. The ordering of persons in ranks of responsibility and hence of agentiveness is a matter of discourse, of how roles in the company are *defined*. It is not a matter for which empirical research into questions of fact need be undertaken. Of course we may need to know the conventions that are operative in a certain organization as to how responsibility is to be distributed. This may need investigation. But we shall not be uncovering the workings of some hidden mechanism.

In the previous two sections I sketched ways in which certain agent-relevant acts are performed discursively. The next step will be to try to show that when acting agentively one is not the site of the working of some diaphanous mental mechanism, but rather one is embedding an interpretation of what one has done, is doing or is about to do in a narrative in such a way that one displays oneself as an agent with respect to the action in question. The models for a discursive displaying of oneself and one's actions are, I shall argue, the forms by which physical events are explained in accordance with the dynamicist schema. But the function of the discourses constructed according to that schema are utterly different in the one case and the other. In the human case the schema serves to display oneself as an agent, while in the physical case the schema serves to explain an event as the result of the action of the basic physical agents and their forces and fields. The former use is expressive while the latter is explanatory. It would be a serious mistake to transfer the whole metaphysics embedded in the grammar of dynamic explanations in physics to the use of the dynamicist schema in the discursive presentation of oneself as an agent.

Explanations of action

In the discussion which follows each of the basic schemata from the physical sciences will be tried out as a framework for ways of assigning, taking and repudiating responsibility, achieved in the course of constructing action explanations.

The Humean/Skinnerian picture: the mechanistic schema psychologized

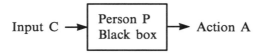

According to this schema an action A is accounted for wholly in terms of some input of stimulus C which is applied to the individual P whose action it is. There are two matters to be accounted for in such a schema. First, the coming into existence of the action must be explained. We could say that the direct causation of the action is the input or stimulus C. This is typical of the classical behaviourist way of explaining actions. However, we may be more interested in accounting for what properties an action A has rather than its merely coming into existence. This we could call the indirect schema for action explanations and it is characteristic of the psychology of B.F. Skinner. Skinner's form of conditioning works on operants, that is behaviours which are spontaneously produced by an organism. The work of the environment, human or otherwise, in selecting from amongst the operants has the effect of determining which kind of behaviour is performed rather than that some behaviour is performed instead of none. In general one uses this schema to construct stories in which one repudiates responsibility. The use of this narrative form displays one as passive and thing-like, not as an initiator. Such a one is displaying himself or herself as 'easily led', 'carried away by . . .', 'dreaming along', 'just doing it out of habit' and so on. It would be very interesting to make a close analysis of the import of these various commonplace uses of the Humean/Skinnerian schema, to look for the similarities and differences between them, and to try to find out with which narrative conventions they are commonly used, and what projects an actor is engaged in when using them.

The agentic schema

In the use of the agentic schema the basic principle is that the individuals using it show themselves as ready or prepared or intending to act, and that they will so act unless they are frustrated or blocked from acting. An action explanation involves two independent clauses, in one of which the tendency or propensity to act is assigned to the person P. The other clause concerns the blockage or release (fulfilment etc.) of the tendency, propensity or intention. A person can be presented as responsible or not responsible for the tendency, impulse or intention to act, and they can be presented as responsible or not responsible for the blockage or release of that tendency, power or intention. This complexity permits the construction of three subschemata of the general agentic form:

1   The person NN is responsible for the tendency or intention to act but is not in command of whether it is released or blocked. For example this subschema could be used to express the situation in which one is actively though impotently struggling with a jammed door.

2   The person NN is not responsible for the tendency or intention to act, but it is they who block or release it. For example one sometimes has a strong tendency to sneeze but one releases it or blocks it oneself. The idea of a self-frustrated intention should have a place at this point. If there were a need to use this story form to account for some happening, this subschema would be the right one to frame it in.

3   The person NN is both responsible for the existence of the tendency or intention and in command of the release, realization, frustration or blockage of the tendency or intention.

Many importantly different narratives share the general agentive form. Obviously 'tendency' stories are very different in many ways from 'intention' stories, though it is easy to think of cases where they would overlap. Philosophers have done a great deal of work on these distinctions, teasing out subtly different structures of accounting for action. The next research stage should involve detailed studies of actual story telling to ascertain the extent to which the various agentive schemata are in daily use, the distribution of such uses numerically, by social category, by occasion, by actor's project and so on.

In setting out both the Humean/Skinnerian schema and the agentic schema I have juxtaposed a diagram with a discursive account of what each can be employed to accomplish when it is taken as a narrative convention. This rhetorical device allows me to put a fundamental question. Are these schemata sketches of mental mechanisms by which action is produced (they could look a bit like vector diagrams)? Or are they pictorially arresting ways of presenting the grammatical rules of two classes of discourses, those which we might employ for repudiating or taking on responsibility and thus displaying our agency or lack of it? According to one point of view in contemporary cognitive psychology, the artificial-intelligence/cognitive-science point of view, the answer to our first question is 'yes'. These are diagrams of mental mechanisms, and cognitive science is in the business of discovering their true nature by a simple use of the hypothetico-deductive method. From the point of view of the protagonist of the other main approach in contemporary cognitive psychology, the discursive point of view, the answer is 'no'. These schemata are simply rhetorically expressive ways for presenting the grammar of self-presenting discourses.

One must ask, how does the person NN show that he or she has a certain tendency to act in some way, or has formed an intention to undertake some course of action? For the most part, in the Judaeo-Christian tradition this is done by displaying that tendency, propensity, intention etc. as a choice among alternatives. It is to the study of the structure of the discursive presentation of an intention (or of a subsequent action) as a 'choice from a set of alternatives' (in the simplest case, all equally possible) that I now turn.

Grammars of agentic displays

First of all one must make it clear to one's audience (and this may sometimes be just oneself) that when one decided what one wanted or came to want, that was one amongst a set of alternative actions which were within one's power. This is the first step in showing that what one did was neither random nor forced upon one. To display one's action as merely random is to embed it in too rich a set of possibilities, and to display it as forced is to embed it in too narrow a set. What is the proper form for doing this, for displaying an action as a matter of choice? We can represent it in a simple formula:

$$[(A1 \text{ or } A2 \text{ or } A3) \text{ and } P] \text{ so } A2$$

This formula can be read in the following way: the first clause sets out a fairly abbreviated set of alternatives amongst which lies that which we actually did, or actually will do. The second clause cites some principle according to which the alternatives are evaluated. The result of the evaluation is our intention to perform the alternative we did or propose to perform. This we shall call the *minimum discursive agentic display*. For example, when tucking into a slice of tin roof fudge pie I may wish to display myself as an agent relative to that pudding and I do so by mentioning an alternative that was on the menu, for example, apple pie à la mode. Then I must cite some principle according to which tin roof fudge pie is to be preferred. I must emphasize that what I am describing here is a discursive practice. It is not to be taken as a sketch of a causal mechanism, the running of which causes me to say to the 'server', 'I'll have the [try some of your] tin roof fudge pie, thanks.'

But the use of this discursive style in presenting what one did as a matter of choice leaves one open to the accusation that one is, as Garfinkel (1967) has called it, a mere 'cultural dope'. One is uncritically employing certain principles in deciding amongst the puddings on offer, without considering the possibility that there may be alternative principles for the making of choices than those currently dominant in the local culture. In order to avoid this accusation one must display the principle that one employed in the first-level 'choice' discourse as itself a matter of choice. The formula for accomplishing this might be something like:

$$[(P1 \text{ or } P2 \text{ or } P3 \text{ or } P4) \text{ and } P] \text{ so } P3$$

In this formula the first clause displays the principle as one amongst other possibilities. The second clause cites some meta-principle according to which, or in the light of which, or relative to which the principle used to make the choice in the first instance is displayed as favourably evaluated. For example the principle I would cite in the first place, when required to demonstrate agency with respect to the ordering and consumption of tin roof fudge pie, might be that I am very fond of chocolate, and so my choosing it rather than anything else on the menu is the act of a rational being. But when I need to display myself as an agent with respect to the choice of chocolate flavoured puddings, I might cite the principle that in the dead hours of the afternoon a chocolate pudding gives one more life than a piece of fruit. And so on. The use of this discursive strategy must *not* be taken to be a way of describing some mental processes that went on when I ordered the pie. Everything cognitive is already out in the open in the discourse.

The 'and so on' which I have just inserted at the termination of my display of agency with respect to tin roof fudge pie points to the way in which such hierarchies of principle citations are presented as indefinitely open. If they are really indefinitely open, how could I ever establish finally that I am some sort of agent? There are two main lines along which this matter might be considered. Wittgenstein's (1953) move is to close the regress of the hierarchy of rules with a basic commitment to one line of action, usually one into which I have been trained. As he says, 'this is what I *do*.' Jean-Paul Sartre (1957) also suggests a means for closing the hierarchy. As he puts it, 'this is what I *am*.' In neither case is there room for any further justificatory move in conversations incorporating this discursive convention.

Alternatively, another way of proceeding to maintain agency, in the light of the openness of the hierarchy of principles that any individual may put to work in agentic discourse, is simply to leave that hierarchy unresolved. This amounts to somehow being seen or taken to be able and willing, if pressed, to produce a yet higher-order principle which could be used to rank the principles on offer as alternatives at the former highest level. The nth-order principle could always be presented as a selection from alternatives according to some $(n+1)$th-order principle. Thus I am capable of presenting myself as an agent, relative to whatever challenge to my hegemony I face. The capacity for cunning development of such hierarchies is what has to be acquired as one of our discursive skills.

Presenting oneself as an agent in the midst of the action is what we have so far examined. It is to the carrying out of that job that the indexicality of 'I' is the appropriate grammatical instrument.

But the presentation of oneself as agent demands a background sketched out in such a way that the speaker is to be seen as able to exercise those powers that agentic talk implicitly claims they have. To complete the task of agentic presentation, the fact that one is free must be discursively established. The older philosophical talk of 'the will' as positive power is at odds with everyday discursive practice in that it is frequently part of a narrative line in which 'freedom' is 'developed' as a positive quality, of the person, the will and so on. Austin (1962), in looking closely at the practices of discursive construction of freedom, pointed out that the citation of freedom, liberty and the like is best understood as a way of ruling out the existence of certain kinds of constraint. To say one is free, perhaps in so many words, is a generic device for ruling out contextually implied specific constraints. 'I'm free tonight' can mean a host of different things, depending on whether it is said in response to an invitation, or during the last hours of serving a prison sentence, or just before a decree absolute. In Austin's vivid but politically incorrect remark, '"free" is a trousers word'; the negative wears the trousers: that is, what is taken to be ruled out determines the sense to be given to the use of the term on some particular occasion. So far we are looking at an observation about usage made in the study, so to speak, by a philosopher of genius. (Interestingly the same point about 'liberty' was made by Thomas Hobbes in the seventeenth century.)

Recent work by Westcott on narratives of freedom, life stories in which a certain range of liberties is displayed (as reported in his book of 1988 and in recent articles), involves the analysis of story lines in which various people display themselves as free agents. The story lines Westcott has collected and analysed are exemplifications of the Austinian principle that claims to freedom are used to rule out the existence of certain specific constraints on action. Westcott (1992) presents the tales of two speakers, who in very different ways and different circumstances present their freedom as the absence of certain social constraints on what they do.

Pathologies of agentive discourse

The grammatical and narratological conventions I have described so far are amongst the devices by means of which people constitute themselves as agents with respect to the conventions of agenthood which their society at some historical moment makes available, for this or that everyday purpose, with these others, on this occasion. The discursive enterprise, as I have argued, is to be seen in the large as concerned with the taking and repudiating of responsibility. The way persons are involved in this depends in large part on whether individuals or groups, such as families or teams, are taken to be the locus of responsibility, and so of agency. The Japanese first-person singular locates the content of the utterance relative to the position of the speaker's body in space, but the moral index is always to some group, family or status collective.

There are two pathologies of agentive discourse, or perhaps one should say pathological forms of agentive discourse, whose usages need examination. One is the discourse of the akratic, the discourse of weakness of will. The other is the discourse of the misplaced 'why' question, the question that presumes that there are causes for actions, and that the task of the person who wishes to understand action is amongst other things to find those causes. To ask an actor for a report on the causes of his or her behaviour seems to be a reasonable procedure. Why, as Crowle reports, is it so hard for actors to find an answer? And yet those same actors can readily produce a narrative of freedom and of an active and undistorted will!

IDKWIDI

In a perceptive analysis of a striking feature of the discourse of the deviant, Crowle (1990) has argued that someone, when challenged to explain what they did, who says 'I don't know why I did it' (IDKWIDI) should be taken seriously. That is, the reply should not be treated as a dishonest evasion of the question. Crowle's argument turns on a demonstration that not only could the person questioned not be able to answer, but the best equipped social psychologists must also fail if the corresponding question 'Why did he/she do it?' is posed to them. The reason is simple enough, but very deep. In order to test hypotheses about contributing factors to the action under scrutiny, the standard methods of investigation require a full permutation of all the factors that might or might not have been relevant. Since the problem is posed to or about just one person, the one under interrogation, this would require that person to have lived just as many alternative lives as there are combinations of presence and absence of variables. Thus the person questioned would have had to have been brought up in a broken home, and also not so brought up, for the differential effect of the presence or absence of this factor to be discovered. Crowle calls this the Ray Charles principle: the singer, when asked about the effects of blindness and poverty on his life, replied 'It isn't like I was born both ways.'

For our purposes in this chapter the question that comes to mind is this: if IDKWIDI is a genuine denial of knowledge of reasons/causes of what one did, is it thereby a claim to an original agency in the performance of the action that has led to the interrogation, e.g. a violent attack on someone, an attempt at suicide, an incident of shoplifting and so on? Notice that one is almost never asked 'why' when what one did was entirely ordinary and routine. I have asked people who regularly lunch in college 'Why did you have lunch today?', and if not irritated by the question they are more inclined to express puzzlement as to the point of the query than to answer IDKWIDI. Though, if pressed, they give IDKWIDI in reply.

Unlike non-pathological uses of disclaimers of the existence or efficacy of external or internal 'forces' determining one's actions, the case where we claim an original agency, IDKWIDI, is an epistemic rather than an ontological disclaimer. That is, Crowle's cases of 'It was the last straw', 'I don't know what came over me', and so on, are not ways of denying the existence of whatever it was that brought about the action; they are statements that since it was something of which the speakers were unaware, it is also something over which they had no control. The important point established by Crowle is that it is no good turning to social-psychological research to fill the gap. Statistical methods cannot be bent to this task.

The narrative of akrasia (of doing what I decided I will not do): a discursive strategy

I shall try to show that the best account of the situation of the akratic is not to assume that akratic discourse is a kind of rough sketch of a psychological theory invoking some hidden psychological mechanism that leaves the actor prone and unable to fulfil what he or she believes to be required on some occasion. Rather akratic discourse is best understood as a pathological form of agentive discourse. It is a way of claiming membership of a certain social order and at the same time of repudiating that membership.

The akratic is one who, having declared to others or to himself or herself that he or she is determined on a certain course of action, fails to perform it. The phenomenon is only too well known, and has been variously described. In one particularly pervasive metaphor it is called 'weakness of will'. In 'will' talk, the will is a hypothetical entity existing in different degrees of strength or weakness, invoked to explain the differences in the determination with which people pursue their declared or displayed ends. Thus those who are not distracted by objections or opposition or boredom and so on are described as 'strong-willed', and those who *regularly* fail to carry out their commitments are described as 'weak-willed'.

Are 'will' talk, and other invocations of the same general sort, rough sketches of psychological theories, having something of the same form as a theory in physics, for instance the invocation of strong and weak gravitational fields to account for differences in the distances we can jump on the earth and on the moon? At first sight 'will' talk looks very like such a theory. We would follow it up in the way we do physical theories of this form, by checking its empirical adequacy (does the assumption that the 'will' exists facilitate prediction?), its ontological plausibility (is the 'will' the sort of thing we would expect of a faculty of mind?) and its manipulative efficacy (does the assumption of the existence of the 'will' facilitate designing and planning effective interventions in the (untamed) course of nature?). Before *we* start on this project, following innumerable others, lay and professional, we might heed Wittgenstein's advice: do not take for granted that the obvious grammatical model for understanding the usage in question is the correct guide to understanding it; look closely at what people use this way of speaking to accomplish. What does the discourse of the akratic accomplish and what role does an accusation of weakness of will play?

I shall begin this analysis with a reminder of a point already made: namely that there is fundamental difference in discursive role between those acts in which I, as speaker, take responsibility for my actions and those in which I give reasons for them. Giving reasons for an action may be a way of disclaiming responsibility, of cancelling the illocutionary force of the initial 'I' with which as speaker I index my utterances with properties unique to myself, such as spatio-temporal location and moral standing.

Occasionally I may be prevented from carrying out my declared intentions for one reason or another: a sudden qualm, forgetting what I had promised, an overwhelming physiological response, the obstructiveness of others and so on. This does not make me an akratic, or my failing akrasia. The akratic is a habitual offender. We might express our judgement that he or she is 'like that' by ascribing a permanent psychological property, weakness of will. In just this way we express our judgement that Granny is getting forgetful by ascribing a permanent neurophysiological property such as the state of one who has Alzheimer's disease. In the latter case we could look for the appearance of lots of senile plaques in the old lady's brain. But in the former case there is nothing to answer to the expression 'weak will'. Its reference goes no further than persistently failing to deliver when committed. So let us look back a stage further in the discourse of akrasia. What was the role of the display, usually verbal, of commitment to some course of action? For most people the role of acts of commitment is to give oneself or others some ground for expecting that one will act in accordance with that commitment. It might even be a way of getting oneself to do something which one is a bit disinclined to do. So by agreeing to write a chapter in someone's book, I help myself to do it. But, I submit, the akratic's use of the language of commitment is quite other. It is a pathological use of that form of talk. It serves not to make commitments, but to display the speaker as a person of the right sort, that is someone who belongs in the moral world of his or her companions, colleagues, children, parents, spouse etc. despite habitual failures to live up to the moral order of that world, or rather to have presented as such in some other discursive practices! The akratic has not made a commitment to action when using commitment talk, and so we have no need of a psychological theory to explain why he or she has failed to carry it out. The whole of the psychological phenomenon of akrasia is already there in the discourse for us to see, once we free ourselves from the temptation to use a certain model for all instances of the use of certain forms of talk.

In one or two places Wittgenstein writes of primary and secondary language games, and the distinction is important to him even when implicit. Akratic talk is a secondary language game, since the conditions under which it will serve the function we have brought out include the existence of the ordinary use of commitment talk to lay down a sketch of how we hope the future will be or what we are giving others the right to think it ought to be. Only in the framework of this style of talk, taken as a primary language game, would the akratic's pathetic efforts to claim a place as one of us make any sense. The upshot of the analysis then is the claim that, for the akratic, commitment talk is a secondary language game, the point of which, though different from the point of the ordinary language game of commitment, depends on its existence as a practice amongst the folk to which the akratic belongs.

Conclusion

Faced with the commonplace phenomena of people doing things, we are struck by the differing degrees to which we carry out our declared intentions, implement our decisions, get on with our work when told to, even get up in the morning, wash the dishes after dinner or do our scales to keep up our musical skills. Conversation is awash with excuses and justifications, both informal and formal. There is plenty of talk in courtrooms, parliamentary inquiries and the like where agency is at stake. Do we explain all these things by reference to an inner force, stronger at some times than others, more efficacious in some people than in others? Could we update the ancient idea of 'the will' to reappear as a cognitive mechanism, which brings about or fails to bring about what seems to be promised or required? Just as the existence of the will is a hypothesis, so is the existence of its modern descendant, the cognitive mechanism. Somehow, in all of this, the person as active agent or enfeebled patient has been set aside for some other source of power to act. Suppose there were no inner forces or mechanisms, other than the ebb and flow of private and public conversations. What should we make of the discourses of action then? The discursive turn requires us to follow Wittgenstein's advice, to drop our theories of what might be going on, and to look at what people are doing, in context and in the full concreteness of their situations. It seems overwhelmingly clear that the positions of agent and patient are constructed in the talk. They are the products of strategic acts, existing nowhere else but in those acts. The task for the psychologist is to try to understand the patterns of the practices in and through which persons present themselves as agents and patients. But this move reveals a final paradox. Behind whatever is the presentation, whether of activity or passivity, there must be an active player, the person as strategist. Speaking and hearing, conversing, is something we do. It is not something that happens to us. In the very act of displaying oneself as a patient one demonstrates one's agency!

6 Decision-Making

Donal Carbaugh

Decision-making processes are sometimes conceived as individual activities. One popular version of the process goes like this. One reflects upon a current problem, and explores the various options available for solving the problem. One weighs the advantages and disadvantages of the alternative options, then selects the most desirable from among them. This process results in a decision. Envisioning the process in this way is perhaps to make this process a property of one's unitary self, a way of presenting and evaluating the self's predispositions, a kind of internal dialogue radiating from what Harré (1991) calls the 'self-1'. As Harré discusses, the resources that one uses in order to engage in this process are fundamentally discursive. And further, what is intelligible – what is commonly sensible as a problem and what is coherent as solutions to it – is cultural. Responses to the questions 'What is a "self"?' and 'What, if anything, can (or should) one "say" to one's "self"?' derive from the available discourses in one's cultural communities.

The questions posed here are efforts to suggest that what a person (or 'self') is, that whether a person can and should 'make decisions', that how the person conceives of actions, and similar 'things' or processes, can all be conceived as deriving from particular discursive formations. Indeed, that one even has a 'problem' and 'decision' to make, that there are 'options' or 'solutions' to 'problems', and so on, invoke a particularly distinctive discursive (uniquely American?) heritage – with the words in quotes indicating key terms in this one community's customary ways (Carbaugh, 1988). That one has a shared heritage, or contests one, or creates with some variety of it, that it is constituted discursively, are essential and presumed for the operation of the main processes of concern to us in this chapter – those of decisions, persons, motives and cultures.

Moving the site of one's thinking about decision-making from the inside of the person outwards suggests that one explore the social and cultural dimensions of this discursive process. With this view, decision-making entails the personal, yet moves beyond the personal to larger interactional matters. This implies relocating thought into discursive patterns, and moving these from an internal speech – which one also plays – to a communally based, socio-political conversation. Decision-making, writ this way, is immanently tied into a complex matrix of social interaction and cultural conversations. This suggests perhaps a complex movement, development, and counter-playing between discourses and social identities, through the variety of bids for social and personal standing that are associated with each. For example, in the specific case described below, the process involves personal and political interests, institutionalized resources, sacred ancestors and government intervention, all of which lead eventually to the construction not only of a human socio-political scene, but moreover to newer ways of being and living in a natural environment. My hope is to show the promise of a discursive psychology of decision-making that can span this broad range of personal and cultural territory.

I use the concept of social drama to help organize the variety of discursive and cultural formations activated in the complex decision-making process explored below. The concept derives from Victor Turner (1974; 1980) and largely encompasses Goffman's (1967) idea of ritual disequilibrium. As a whole, it suggests that some processes of decision-making begin with some sense of a rupture, or a breach, or a violation. This realization ignites, then, a large-scale discursive process which has four recognizable phases:

1   The event or incident of a breach or violation occurs.
2   This is followed by a discourse which publicizes the violation, thus ratifying it socially as a crisis, with various social relations being formed in the process.
3   The crisis is responded to in some ways, with the responses involving various types of remedial discourses as efforts to redress the violating incident(s).
4   The redressive actions may or may not suffice, resulting in some sort of social reintegration, or a recycling through of violations, creating continual social division or schism.

For each phase of the form, there is a distinctive rhetoric, style and mode of discursive action, with the redressive phase being crucially important, for it is in this phase, through some kinds of discursive and cultural formations, that attempts are made to repair the violation, and thus to bring contesting factions and interests together. From the vantage point of decision processes, it is here that attempts are made to draw the competing alternatives and options – that arise during the crisis phase – into a conjoint plan.

The following case of decision-making revolves around a land-use controversy. The land-use debates of concern here followed one version of the social-dramatic process outlined above. Through the use of particular discursive patterns, within this larger communicative form, particular configurations of persons, social actions, motives and a natural environment were being played into a larger-scale cultural scene. In the process, particular models, or identities of the person, or 'selves-2' to use Harré's (1991) term, were constructed and subsequently associated with publicly contested actions and motives (see Mills, 1940). The drama thus demonstrates how discursive activities as these carry great psychological consequences, for as the discourse gets produced, so too are various personae, motives and social relations being created. And further, in this case, the consequences are immanent materially in two prominent ways. In one way, the discourses carry inward, as the discursive process subjects persons to bodily anguish, dissonance and considerable consternation. In another way, the discourses are materialized outwardly, as they carry designs for living with the environment, through two contesting ways of inhabiting a natural landscape.

It is thus the conceptual movement of decision processes between the inner and the outer, from the personal outwards and back again, through a drama of cultural discourses, that guides the following analyses. The main objective is to hear, in participants' own words, not only individuals speaking but cultural persons; not only internal thought but communal conversations; not only dyadic dialogue but socially dramatic action. This discursive model of persons, actions, motives and social relations contributes, I hope, to a thoughtful reflection on human and humane living, a sometimes delicate dance *between* the inner and the outer, a conception of life through a dialectic of discourses that creatively constructs the personal and cultural conditions of life. It suggests, at its base, that the psychological process of deciding can be conceived as discursive, as a conversation that penetrates personal and cultural worlds, with persons creating senses of themselves, their motives and their relations by creatively playing the discourses of socio-cultural life.

Participation procedures

Data were collected and analysed from a communicational perspective on discursive psychology (see Carbaugh, 1994; 1996).[1] Intensive field work spanned a nine-month period from March to November 1990, with subsequent periods of data collection occurring through 1994. Primary data collected for the study included eight intensive interviews, averaging about 75 minutes each, all of which were fully transcribed. Participant observations consisted of attending several public meetings, several informal conversations and various social gatherings. Also included, but less central to the present study, were seven and one-half hours of audio-recorded and fully transcribed public hearings about the land. Additional data were collected during a unique set of field observations made while scrambling with 2,000 others up the massif Mt Greylock, to which the disputed land is attached. Other data included newspaper accounts about Greylock, an archive collected by the Appalachian Mountain Club pertaining to Greylock, files and reports of the development group, a book about the mountain and its cultural history (Burns and Stevens, 1988), and two televised broadcasts about this land. Harder to specify as data, but equally important to the above, were the hours I spent wandering about the disputed Greylock land during all four seasons.

Data were analysed largely within a social-dramatic frame, and further refined by attending carefully to a particular communicative form – verbal depictions of the land – which helped 'track' the decision-making process. This focus was chosen because of the potent meanings this kind of discursive expression carried for this community (see Carbaugh, 1992). The analytical procedure involved isolating each reference to the Greylock land (e.g. as 'the mountain') and the terms which naturally concurred in people's speech with that reference (e.g. 'a beautiful natural area'). Eventual interpretations of each reference were constructed by searching the discourse naturally supplied by speakers for terms that contrasted and were substitutable for each reference to the land. The speakers naturally supplied these in their remarks. The verbal depictions I report here thus reflect ways that persons constructed references to this land through their own terms, through their discursive system. The discourse involves the basic terms used to refer to the land, and others with which these concurred, terms which could be substituted for or contrasted with each, as well as the various interactional uses to which each was put. My eventual claim should, if effective, show how – in this case – decision-making involves depictions of the land, and illustrates how each verbal depiction consists in local terms, their meanings and uses. More generally, and with the concerns of the discursive psychologist in mind, my claims should demonstrate how social uses of cultural discourses construct various models of persons as agents, social relations among these agents, and distinctive motives, as well as particular patterns of living with nature. The psychological and practical process of deciding, in this case, involved nothing less.

The scene and historical roots of the discourse: Greylock Glen, Mt Greylock State Reservation, and Adams

Greylock Glen is a 1,040 acre parcel of land in north-western Massachusetts in the north-eastern section of the United States of America. The land consists mainly of wooded mountainside, some rolling pasture land, a series of ponds, hiking trails, and dirt roads. The parcel is immediately to the east of Massachusetts's flagship state park, the Mount Greylock State Reservation. The reservation was formed in 1898 with the state purchase of 400 acres on the summit of Mt Greylock which, at 3,491 feet, is the highest mountain in the state of Massachusetts. The reservation has now grown to over 11,000 acres. On the other side of Greylock Glen, about one mile from its centre, is the town of Adams with a population of about 11,000. The geographic relationship of Greylock Glen to the Mount Greylock State Reservation and the town of Adams is shown in Figure 6.1.

Since the early 1940s, Adams and much of north-western Massachusetts has experienced deep and relentless economic decline including the closing of many manufacturing industries with an attendant loss of employment,

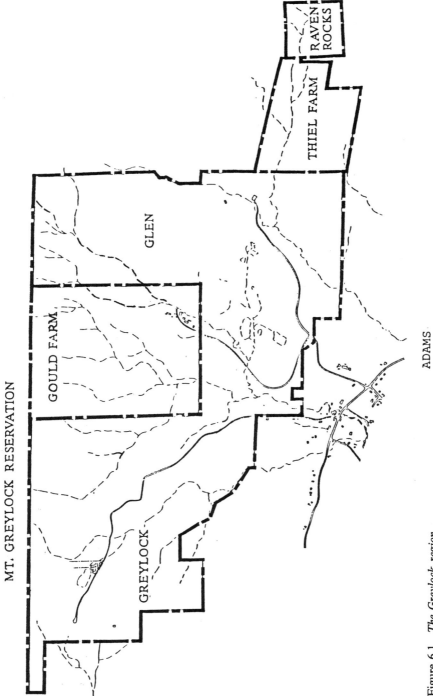

Figure 6.1 *The Greylock region*

population and tax base. Because of these general economic woes, and because the Greylock natural area was and is such an attractive parcel of land, it was sought by many, becoming, it seems, a site of continual struggle. In the 1940s, clear-cutting was begun, yet was protested, then halted. In the early 1960s, the Mount Greylock Tramway Authority was formed, with some state support, to plan a 'highly commercial $5.5 million downhill-ski resort project, including four chair lifts, 11 miles of ski trails (some of them hundreds of feet wide), restaurants, cocktail lounges, a dance terrace, swimming pool, sauna, motels, fountains, riding stables, an amusement park, an international shopping center, and a 1,000 car parking lot. The centrepiece of the resort [was to] be "the world's largest" aerial tramway, transporting passengers to a 100 foot tower on the summit of Mount Greylock' (Burns and Stevens, 1988: 77). After news of the full proposal got public, and this took from two to three years, a public rallying of forces was spearheaded by the Mount Greylock Protective Association. This group was able to raise $18,250 from 1,300 members to delay and finally defeat the proposal.

In the early 1970s, when a private developer began to piece together several private properties totalling 1,040 acres, the area became known as Greylock Glen. This development proposal – more modest than the earlier Tramway idea – involved a condominium complex, convention centre, golf course and ski area. Despite some ground breaking and foundation pouring, financial backing for this resort idea began to fall through. In 1980, as a last-ditch effort to save the project, the developer proposed bringing Las-Vegas-style casino gambling to the area, but the state legislature refused to consider the bill, and the then Governor Dukakis opposed the measure.

An economic breach: unemployment, business failures

In the early 1980s, when much of Massachusetts was experiencing 'a miracle' of economic growth, the north-western corner of the state was not. Companies were leaving the area and unemployment had reached double-digit figures. The northern Berkshire area had earlier seen no money trickle its way, nor had it now been 'saved'.

An attempted redressive act: Massachusetts state legislation

Because of the economic doldrums in the Greylock region, the history of development failures, and the conflict of interests, the state in 1984 decided to intervene and solicit a private developer who would appease the various interests. The general idea was to propose for this land, with the input of state officials, environmental leaders, area residents and business leaders, 'a public–private partnership'. The main objective was to provide – as it is worded in the developer's final environmental impact report – 'a recreational facility of regional economic impact'. Specific goals of the Massachusetts Commonwealth in the legislation were:

1   to ensure continued protection of Mt Greylock State Reservation and the unique scenic, natural and historic resources that it encompasses; and

2   to facilitate the diversification of the northern Berkshire economy through the development of a four-season destination resort/recreation area at Greylock Glen.

By 1985, the 'Massachusetts miracle' had yet to reach the Greylock environs, but with this legislation passed, help seemed on its way.

Back to the future: potential redress

As time passed, the euphoria among many Adams residents about the legislative act could not help but wane. As the specifics of the development 'partnership' became known, some environmental horns sounded, while the state economy began to crumble. By 1988 and 1989, two environmental groups, Massachusetts Audobon and the Mount Greylock Protective Association, had gone public in opposing the project. The main items of dispute included the number of dwellings to be placed on the land (from 1,275 'condos' to 850 'mountain homes'), the size of a pond/lake to be built (from 35 to 25 acres), money issues (how much money should a state put into a partially private development?), to questions about the proposed 'public–private' ownership of the land itself (why is this a public–private partnership, when this land could be annexed to the public reservation?). In mid October 1990, the place hit the headlines again. This time, however, for undisclosed reasons, the Massachusetts Inspector General was 'investigating the proposed construction of a state-backed $220 million vacation home resort on Mount Greylock'. The investigation occurred amidst much political activity: Democratic Governor Dukakis, the original proponent of the plan, was about to leave office, with Democrats and Republicans worried that the project would, respectively, die out or be secretly finalized. So, one group filed a bill prohibiting development on the land, while the other attempted quickly to ratify a land disposition agreement on what parts of the land would be state owned and how profits would be divided between the state and the private developer, so ground breaking could begin. Finally, the land disposition hearings were held, but not until Republican Governor Weld entered office. After the above investigation, and hearings, his early (1991) administration decided to halt the agreement between the state and the developer, and to reassess the fate of Greylock Glen.

Further violations and crises

At this point in the discussion, in the wake of the legislative act, one could hear various alleged violations. One was the attempt to develop the land: 'development' was cast as a violation by the government of the 'Commonwealth's' land and landscape. These allegations were stated through a rhetoric of environmental destruction that motivated certain parties, mainly environmentalists and some who live adjacent to the land, to publicize this fact and form alliances with others whom they could rally. The other alleged violation involved the government's withdrawal of the state plan, which precipitated discourse from many in the town of Adams, especially those in the Chamber of Commerce, who felt that 'the rug was pulled from under us.' On this front, one heard a rhetoric of abandonment. Crises ensued as the earlier attempt at redressing the situation through the state's legislative act, along with an economic decline in the state, resulted in further complications of economic, environmental, political and personal sorts.

Let us enter this conflicted conversation a little closer to the ground, as people discuss the land situation and with it their current lives and livelihood. As a result of listening more closely, we will begin to hear in their discourse their concerns and their motives for decisions they are making, and eventually to identify the relations this discourse creates among the various persons involved, and between them and their natural environment.

Crises and competing factions: two depictions of a natural environment

> Conflict seems to bring fundamental aspects of society, normally overlayed by the customs and habits of daily intercourse, into frightening prominence. People have to take sides in terms of deeply entrenched moral imperatives and constraints. (Turner, 1974: 35)

Simple turns of phrase can get read into ongoing cultural discourses in ways that are puzzling to outsiders. For example, people in western Massachusetts might refer to this land as 'the mountain' or as 'the project', with these phrases implicating larger motivational systems through a communal sense. By using these terms, even if unwittingly, a social stance is forged with regard to decisions that are being (or should be) made. Caught in this discursive process, persons and competing factions are being constituted, with relations among them and their world assuming a dramatic quality. In other words, these two main discursive references to the land are coding this drama – in Turner's terms – according to the 'customs and habits of daily intercourse'. In the process, each creates a rupture between those who 'see' (or speak?) the situation similarly, and those who do not. Each, from the vantage point of the other, carries with it an associated sense of violation, a continuing of the crisis, and different ideas about proper redressive action. Consequently, each way of speaking about the land has associated with it specific beliefs about persons, actions and living with nature. I will call the one discourse a coding of economic needs, and the other a coding of natural ecology – following the issues being foregrounded with each. As each solidifies a particular rhetoric, style and mode of discursive action, it further accentuates its own senses of violation and crisis. As a result of each being played *against* the other, an immediate conjoint decision, an integrative redressive action, is rendered even more divisive, distant and difficult – if not downright impossible – to formulate.

'Up on the project': coding local economic needs

On a hot summer afternoon, in an office suite in downtown Adams, I sat down with 'the developer' (his term for himself) to discuss 'Greylock'. Surrounding us were detailed and attractive diagrams which showed the vision of what 'the Greylock project' would be. After showing aerial photographs of the land, and how certain features of the project (e.g. cluster housing, golf course, ponds, ski trails) would be situated upon it, he described several past projects in Adams which were 'stalled' – housing projects, real estate businesses, a colour photograph laboratory, a furniture store, various attempts with restaurants – and contrasted these with successful ventures further away, both to the north (in Vermont) and south (in 'southern Berkshire'). Against this backdrop, he described 'Greylock' as 'a catalyst' for Adams, an energy boost for the town ('bus loads of people going to Boston to lobby' for it). He described the considerable efforts taken by the town to prepare itself for 'the project' (rewriting zoning ordinances, getting public aid grants to redo Main Street, hiring a town planner). All of this, according to him, showed how eager the Adams people were to 'try to get the economy back on track'. Because the development would bring others to the Adams area, rather than to the outlying areas which are relatively well-to-do, he reasoned, the project would 'provide demand for the businesses that are here, to prosper and grow'. He went on:

> This project is perceived as more a catalyst than anything else . . . The business community is not so much concerned about how many and exactly what kind of jobs we can create up on the project, even though that is clearly an important issue, but they are mostly concerned with whether this project is going to bring *X* number of warm bodies *here* with money to spend and we need that. Our economy desperately needs that . . . We have a thousand acres of land up there that until this project came along, had always been a private ownership and was never public and was never part of the Greylock Reservation, so it's been privately owned. One of the benefits of this project is that it has forced a master plan upon the land, a four season recreation community on a large piece of continuous acreage in a way that's responsive to the land and to the desires of those who use adjacent lands . . . It's a magnificent piece of property. It can be a hugely successful project if done properly.

Others depicted this piece of Greylock land similarly. Each used a discourse – of co-selected symbols and meanings – which depicted the land as an 'up there', thus suggesting symbolically to listeners that they view – or portray, or sense, or feel – the land from down below, as a member of the developmentally minded segment of Adams. The depiction of the land within the physical space of Adams included 'feeling' this town's current dismal climate, as well as its history of failed economic projects. Activated with this discourse is also an explicit contrast to those who are relatively well-to-do in surrounding areas. By using this discourse, the developer has created a symbolic sense of this 'Greylock' land as a 'project' and 'catalyst' that could transform Adams' current dismal conditions into a better place. He also has created a sense of himself, his motives, and relations to others with his words. There is much getting said here. Let us look in a bit more detail at some of the prominent meanings in the discourse constituting this phase of the decision-making drama.

Notice how the developer described the land above the town: 'We have a thousand acres of land *up there* that . . . was never public and was never part of the Greylock Reservation, so it's been privately owned. Anything could happen *up there*.' The use of phrases like 'up there' in the developer's speech carry great symbolic weight in this cultural scene. Uses of the preposition 'up', plus an indexical locator like 'there', 'on the project', 'on the Glen', 'on the site' or 'on the property', create phrases which refer to the land as 'up there', 'up on the Glen' or 'up on the project'. This phrasing – along with the associated terms described below – constructs 'Greylock' as a particular place above, and suggests symbolically that participants view the land from 'down below' in Adams. This spatial dimension of the discourse creates a very specific symbolic and cultural position from which to view the land (and from which to listen to others who so construct the land in this way). Through this discourse, participants are positioned down below, looking 'up'.

This 'locational' coding invites participants into a physical *and* moral space in which the land and its people should be conceived in highly particular ways. In the process, certain ways of thinking, acting and feeling are evoked which are prominent down below in Adams, such as *that* town's particular historical, economic and political concerns. By depicting the land from this particular physical location, speakers invite interlocutors into that town's physical *and* symbolic place. The land, then, rendered as an 'up there' above Adams, is not merely a reference to an external reality, although it is that, but is moreover a socially based moral move within a cultural game, a move which creatively evokes a complex of associations, and invites one's interlocutors into a discursive space from which to see, hear, feel and act upon 'this land' in particular ways.

This symbolic location of one down below looking up at the land, it is important to make clear, is not a simple verbal artefact of a speaker's physical situation when speaking, such as down below the land. While such usage is prominent down below in Adams, I also heard it up higher when I was above the disputed land, on top of the mountain – that is, this usage appeared also above the land where it makes no literal sense – and similarly I heard it away from the base of the mountain (in other nearby towns). As we shall see, this usage does invoke a spatial dimension, but it is more than a simple literal reference to a physical place. It is a socially based moral claim as well.

By positioning 'down below', interlocutors are being invited into a very specific physical *and* cultural space from which to experience the land. The complex of meanings specifically associated with this type of coding are geographic, economic and political.

Cultural geography is being implicated when the parcel of land is symbolized as 'up there', physically above the town centre (e.g. 'a thousand acres of land up there'). Solidifying this view is the hearable claim that 'this land' is also, 'officially', a part of 'the town'. As a prominent resident asserted: 'It's our land. We'll win any law suit if it comes to that.' Speaking 'the land' this way draws it into the town's boundaries, thus drawing a verbal map of a cultural geography which includes Adams and this piece of land within a single geo-cultural space (see Figure 6.1). As such, it becomes a site which is included in the town's boundary, is a part of that town's history, and is the location of its most recent civic 'project'.

Within this geo-symbolic system, the land becomes a distinct part of a town and its activities, thus positioning participants to see/hear this land from the standpoint of that particular town and its concerns. To interpret the full meaning, then, of Greylock within this system, we must have some sense of these concerns, especially the very real economic and political conditions which town members see as their own, and which create further the larger symbolic scene within which this 'land' plays its distinctive role.

The economic climate of Adams in 1990 was avowedly dismal. As several consultants put it: 'The business climate is really suffering'; 'In this month of July in the year of 1990, yesterday it was announced 400 jobs are leaving Adams'; 'Last week they announced that we're beginning the reduction of 22% of the work force: 550 people leaving good paying employment.' This theme of economic deprivation runs deeply into the past: 'We lost 3,000 jobs in the last five years'; 'We never experienced any of the [then President Reagan's] "trickle-down" in the early eighties, or of the [then Governor Dukakis's] "miracle" of the mid eighties.' In fact, the only economic heyday for the region seems to have been short-lived and occurred around 1875 when the Hoosac Tunnel was blasted through the Hoosac Mountains to provide for the cheap and efficient transportation of manufactured goods to Albany and Boston.

It is rather ironic that what has been the main attraction of this area to so many, the scenic geography, has also been a key source of its economic problems. Placed between mountain ranges in a valley, Adams is relatively inaccessible. The remoteness which is created by the geography has had, so town members say, its further economic and political consequences.

The town land is thus symbolized as economically bypassed. When the discourse encompasses the larger cultural map, as the developer mentioned above, Adams is contrasted with its surrounding areas. These contrastive areas provide symbolic counter-spaces, symbolic sites where things and people are better. One such place is 'southern Berkshire county' (a distinction common throughout Massachusetts), which has its associations of wealth, stability and upper class. 'Southern Berkshire' is the location of Stockbridge (a popular tourist destination, former home to the artist Norman Rockwell, summer home to the Boston Symphony, Tanglewood, and several summer theatres) and Sheffield (the place of second homes for many wealthy New York and Connecticut residents). The 'southern Berkshire' space thus connotes – from the vantage point of this economic coding – greater affluence, upward mobility, a different and higher class of people and activity. Similarly, this discourse identifies the area to the immediate north as 'great ski country', which includes the major ski resorts of southern Vermont, Stratton Mountain, Bromley, Haystack and Mount Snow among others. Associated with these places is the wealthy and upper status that Adams' people so desperately seek.

The full discourse of which this code is a part thus positions the land as a place, and the speaker as a vested person within a general geo-cultural scene. It invites one to locate within a historical and current site of economic deprivation (i.e. the town of Adams), and thus to promote its main symbol of economic opportunity (i.e. 'the project up there').

Promoting the land 'up there' counters not just these economic deprivations, but also the image of the town as politically marginal. The larger cultural map introduced above, when extended in another direction, to the east, amplifies this meaning, except that symbolic movement in this direction introduces not just economic but political deprivation. As an informant put it, importing a phrase from another region of the United States commonly portrayed as marginal and deprived: 'The perception of Berkshire County, in particular northern Berkshire in eastern Massachusetts, is very bad. It's like the dreary Berkshire County backwater.' During a public hearing about 'Greylock', an older man from Adams described how 'a Boston newspaper' referred to Adams as 'the boondocks' and 'a cultural nowhere', and to its people as 'millrats' and 'Joe six-pack'. It is the Appalachia of Massachusetts.

A similar symbolic reference to Adams' relative political impotence occurs as 'environmental groups' are mentioned. Although somewhat implicit, when introduced within this coding strategy, the point is made: from the vantage point of this economic code, the people in the east – including some 'environmental groups' like Massachusetts Audobon whose headquarters are close to Boston – are given much more public press, more than the Adams Chamber of Commerce or the project developer, and are thus portrayed, in contrast to Adams, both as 'outsiders' and as sources of political power, like the state officials way over in the capital of Boston. The frustration of being 'marginalized' geographically, economically and politically is shown in this comment, made by a successful native son of Adams: 'let [the head of Massachusetts Audobon] sit in somebody's living room who just lost their job and explain to them why he would oppose something like this [the Greylock project] . . . He wouldn't have the courage to go in and tell them.' The potent symbolic meanings created in this discursive form contrast Adams' people, actions and needs (i.e. as geographically peripheral, economically deprived and politically marginal) with potent distant forces from the east (i.e. as geographically central, economically endowed and politically efficacious). With these words, people are heard not just as personally invested, but as *representative* of the town and its woes, as opposed to others who see (or speak) the situation differently and as one who is motivated to become a champion of the town's 'project', its most important current cause.

The redressive act associated with the economic coding

Because many members of Adams see themselves as deprived of essential political and economic resources (as contrasted with virtually everyone around them), and because they see Greylock Glen as a part of their town and its most valuable resource (e.g. 'the last developable land in the town'), they advocate seeing the land 'up there' as a 'project', as a chance to transform their dismal present and past into a promising future, as a chance to make something more of their community and themselves. 'The project', within this system, takes on what Kenneth Burke would call a God-term quality, a cure-all for past and present social ills.

When 'the project' was mentioned by town members, I would sometimes ask them to describe it to me. Most typically, it was elaborated, as one person put it, by mentioning 'some cross-country skiing, a golf course, and some housing'. This quick coding of 'the project' was elaborated by the developer on a 'fact sheet'. Quoting from that sheet: 'recreation facilities include nordic ski and hiking trails (46 km), a norpine ski area (1 chair lift; 80 acres of trails), an 18 hole golf course, a 1,000 seat outdoor amphitheater, 10 tennis courts, 3 swimming ponds, 2 swimming pools; community facilities include a 150–200 room village inn, a retail commercial center, a fitness center, a golf pro shop and nordic center, a country club, 850 units of cluster housing, and a 150–200 room conference center/health fitness resort.' The developer goes on to explain that all of the project is adjacent to, not on, the state reservation: 'of the 1,040 acres of land, approximately 300 will be utilized for development of the village, country club, conference center and all housing. Approximately 740 acres are devoted to open space and public recreational uses.' The developer predicts that, by the year 2010, the 'cumulative municipal benefit to Adams' will be $45 million.

'The project' is thus seen from, and as inextricably linked to, Adams, and holds one giant ray of light within – what those from the east portray as, and those from Adams sometimes agree is – the 'dreary backwaters' of an economically deprived, politically usurped and geographically bypassed region. Within this larger symbolic system, a parcel of land 'up there' becomes a promising 'project' and presents itself as one giant remedy to the town's considerable, mainly economic, needs.

Understanding this land, through this local cultural discourse, helps one hear some of the meanings creatively evoked when people depict the land 'up there' (and thus invokes a telling from down in the town): with this discourse, the land is (and should be) 'a project' or 'property' which holds great symbolic and material force. Users of this code are heard to claim that this land can (and will) potentially transform this tired and troubled hill town into a greater cultural (economic and political) force.

At the foot of Mt Greylock: coding cultural ecology

An alternative coding of this land positions participants in a very different physical and symbolic place. One prominent environmentalist is leader of a local land trust and conservation fund. When asked about 'Greylock', he began by saying:

> Well, Greylock Glen . . . well Mt Greylock, maybe I'll start with the reservation. It is wonderful. It's a wonderful reservation. It's the oldest [state park], has great dignity, has great character, has great historic presence. And it has a warm and loving constituency who feel strongly that it should be preserved. Greylock Glen, that troublesome property to the east of the Greylock reservation, has been subject to any number of ill-conceived proposals . . . by a succession of scoundrels [he excepts the present developer from this label] . . . It's right beside Mt Greylock. It's an attractive piece of land.

Others depict the area similarly. From a naturalist on the state reservation:

> I'm a naturalist and emotionally attached to the mountain, so seeing anything like this [the Glen project], you look down like now and it's a pretty area. It's open land and lakes . . . and just to think that it's going to be developed into more houses . . . would make me feel sick to my stomach looking down on it.

The land is being symbolized here, literally as part of the Mt Greylock massif. Similarly:

> Greylock is a unique, natural resource, the best one and probably the most famous one in Massachusetts, and we ought to keep it that way . . . I have visited all of the meadows and farms at the foot of Mt Greylock . . . While it [Greylock Glen] is a beautiful spot for a few condominiums, that would virtually destroy the scenic aspect of the lower portions of the Greylock landscape.

These depictions symbolically place participants in a very specific physical place, 'up', on the state reservation, most likely from the summit viewing area, looking down. Note the first speaker above who audibly fluctuated between the two available depictions, deliberately anchoring his position above (starting with 'the mountain' and 'reservation') rather than below (on 'the glen' or in 'Adams'). Greylock, depicted this way, is viewed not from the town below but from a different geographic place, from up above. Coding the land this way draws it into the borders of the state reservation, associating it with an alternative discourse of symbolic meanings, elaborating themes not explicitly of local political economics but of Massachusetts' highest natural environment and its inspirational effect on contemporary Americans and their ancestors.

This depiction of Greylock Glen from above looking down creatively evokes symbols of wildness, a refuge of nature. The depiction is sometimes even elaborated with descriptions of the natural environment: 'It's scenic land . . . There are bears and bobcats and things coming around . . . and an occasional sighting of a mountain lion or cougar.' From a biologist:

> Massachusetts doesn't have much in the way of mountains, compared to other areas of the country, but this one mountain is pretty impressive. It's the one highest mountain. It's unique. It's a monadnock in the geologic sense. It's isolated and it's pretty spectacular . . . It harbors a lot of scarce or rare flora that we ought to be concerned about. One species I know of has only two individual plants growing on the mountain and both of them are very close to foot and vehicular traffic . . . I'm concerned about things like that. Lower down in the area of Greylock Glen, there's unique crayfish, the Appalachian crayfish.

Another described the Glen as 'a marvelously quiet and tranquil area'.

The symbolic sense of Greylock as a pristine natural environment is associated with another that is more historical, an American literary tradition, and as such this land is even considered to be a generative force for some classic American literature and poetry, such as some of the famous writings of William Cullen Bryant, Nathaniel Hawthorne, Henry David Thoreau, Herman Melville and Oliver Wendell Holmes. I did not fully appreciate this symbolic link upon first hearing it. After climbing a rugged ridge to the summit of Greylock, I was more than a little puzzled to discover that regular gatherings were held at the rustic summit lodge for 'tea, poetry, and literature'. I eventually was told by patient others about the great Americans who were associated with Greylock, who had walked and hiked here. Many claimed even today to sense their presence. In fact, appearing in the summit lodge during the summer of 1990 – and periodically since – was a proud display of these great American figures who are linked to Greylock (see the summary in Burns and Stevens, 1988: 42–50, 93–100).

The early American poet, William Cullen Bryant, wrote numerous poems about Greylock's streams, peaks and natural features. Nathaniel Hawthorne was the first to refer to the mountain in print as 'Graylock'. He was reportedly fascinated by the local scenery, especially relations between mountains and clouds. He hiked often on the mountain and wrote of it as 'a most romantic and picturesque country'. In his story 'Ethan Brand', his title character spends his last night on Mt Greylock. In 1844, Henry David Thoreau climbed Mt Greylock, spending the night on its summit with a board as a blanket, and wrote extensively of the experience in *A Week on the Concord and Merrimack Rivers*. Thoreau's mentor, Ralph Waldo Emerson, dubbed Mt Greylock 'a serious mountain'. Herman Melville finished writing *Moby Dick* in the nearby town of Pittsfield, and dedicated his novel *Pierre* 'To Greylock's Most Excellent Majesty'. Oliver Wendell Holmes wrote many poems that mentioned Greylock. Perhaps most salient for present purposes are the following lines penned by Holmes as a tribute to the Berkshire Mountains in the last year of his life (1894).

> Oh how I should love to look on Pittsfield again! And yet I have always dreaded the rush of memories it would bring over me, and dread it still. But there lie buried many of my dearest and sweetest memories of my earlier middle age; and, if I cannot look on Greylock and Pontoosuc with these eyes which are fast growing dim, I can recall them with infinite affection and delight.

Upon being exposed to these well-known American writers, and their association with Greylock, I began feeling, seeing and hearing this land anew, as a most majestic, historically evocative natural environment and culturescape. The literary history integrated into this depiction renders Greylock as a generative force in American literature and lives. Foregrounded in the depiction from 'above' is not just a physical location, a mountain park and forest, but a whole multifaceted tree whose branches span widely over a vast natural refuge, and whose roots run deep into America's past. So informed, one begins to see, hear and feel this natural place through an alternative discursive coding, being placed differently (up above in a heavenly space?) for viewing, highlighting natural features of its environment, and evoking its own natural and cultural past.

The above depiction of this land is activated with local communicative forms such as 'at the foot of Greylock'. Speaking the landscape this way places interlocutors in a very precise physical place, up above on the mountain, and suggests looking down at a natural environment that is linked to this mountain. Verbally portrayed is a place that is (and should be) a part of the state's first park ('the foot of Greylock'). This communicative placing − of interlocutors in space − invokes two additional sets of cultural meanings, with one elaborating the uniqueness of this specific ecological system, and the other identifying a specific literary tradition which is associated with it. So positioned, 'Greylock Glen' assumes status as a part of Mt Greylock, on it or 'at its foot'. This verbal portrait conceives the land as a natural refuge that is public (in the broadest sense of a state and national property) and should *stay that way*, because its particular ecologic and literary meanings would benefit the larger common good, rather than enhancing just one community's economic and political power. Those who portray the land this way thus display an identity (often heard as 'environmentalist'), through a motive of preservation, which contests those more developmentally minded.

Political factions: deeply duelling discursive codes

The two decisions associated with the above codes are to preserve the pristine (the ecological implication) or to promote the project (the economic implication). These are sometimes invoked discursively through a quick mention of 'the mountain' or 'the project', suggesting that 'the land' is (and should be) one thing rather than the other. Here we will explore just how these proposed solutions to a community problem operate interactionally, one with the other, to create antagonistic identities and conflicted relationships between participants. Forging a decision – an efficaciously integrative action and persona – between these contesting codes seems nearly impossible.

Three interactional messages are being foregrounded when these two depictions are brought together into one discursive occasion. One involves the symbolic presentation of social *identities*, or typical personae, which are affiliated with each depiction; a second, introduced above, involves the advocacy of a redressive *action* that is associated with each of these positions or personae; the third entails the *social relationships* that are constructed between the two general personae and their advocated actions. This complex of dynamics is perhaps most pronounced when participants praise one code, thereby asserting one identity, position or action over the other. I call this dynamic a duelling of depictions (see Carbaugh, 1992). Within one forceful version of this process, when one code is in use, the other looks – or is rather said to be – downright preposterous. I write 'said to be' because it is also abundantly clear that whenever one of my friends or consultants used one of the above codes, or a feature of it, they also generally demonstrated an awareness of or familiarity with the other.[2] So, it is not so much that each depiction is unintelligible to the other, but rather that they are treated as such, interactionally, in order to make the moral claim that the one is better than the other. In the discursive process, participants thus engage in deeply coded 'socio-interactional work'.

These dramatic messages are shown here in an excerpt from an interview with a naturalist, who lived in Pittsfield, and brought the codes together as follows:

> When I've talked to the folks in Adams, and I've talked to a lot of them about this project, it's a sense of 'How dare you as an outsider tell me how to run my town. What I'm doing is in Adams, it's for the people in Adams, and why should you who lives in Lennox, Pittsfield, or Williamstown be concerned with this?' It's a real sense of local rule and local entitlement that drives these arguments, and when I say 'Wait a minute, I've got people from across the street who care about this reservation of Mt Greylock', they get mad and say, 'It's always the outsiders. It's the people from the east who are telling us what to do.'

In this instance, the codes are played one against the other in this way: 'this project' is mentioned and associated with 'the people in Adams' and matters of 'local rule and local entitlement'; this cluster of symbols is contrasted with 'the reservation' or 'Mt Greylock' and those 'outsiders' who 'care about' it. By invoking the symbolic meaning systems described above, we can hear the 'Adams people' promoting the 'project' to bolster their economic and political standing, while the 'outsiders' orient to 'the mountain' and its cultural history as a natural preserve. This illustrates a way the codes are played against one another, with the proposed solutions of each being further separated and solidified in the process, just as the motives and identities of each party are also being separated and solidified.

From the standpoint of the economic code, as it is used here, local people have made up their own minds about the project and don't need anyone from the outside meddling in their own affairs. From the standpoint of the ecologic code, the locals are so insular and provincial that they can't hear an alternative view even if just 'from across the street'. The social work getting done by the naturalist here, in his utterances, maligns the local economic code. It is discursively cast as one promoted by a provincial, perhaps even selfish, persona who, by means of a symbolic contrast with the ecologic code, 'cares less' about 'the mountain'. Associated with the ecologic code is a persona who may not live immediately in the town of Adams (although some who code the event this way do), but cares nonetheless deeply about its 'mountain'.

These dynamics sometimes become more intense, leading in some cases to name-calling, with discursive attributions being made about others' personae. Those promoting the ecologic code were called, from the standpoint of the local economic code, 'environmentalists', 'outsiders' and 'intellectually dishonest' (because they seemed first to support, then later to oppose 'the project'). Their actions were said to be 'insulting' (because as outsiders they could not hear local issues) and condescending (who are they to tell us what to do?). As one put it: 'Our view is, you don't live here, we live here. That property and that land is part of a functioning community and that community has, should ultimately have control over it. And I look distastefully at the folks who come in from almost everywhere and tell me what I should and shouldn't do with my property.' The most intense hostility and anger was expressed against 'outsiders' by those promoting the local economic code (see Lange, 1990, 1993).

By playing the depictions in reverse, valuing ecologics over economics, proponents of the natural code portrayed the others, especially the developers, as 'scoundrels' (those from the earlier Tramway gambling era), 'land speculators' and 'rapists of the land'. Their activities, or desired activities, were said to involve 'a commercial enterprise' which was 'evil', a 'real estate misadventure' which would 'destroy the scenic aspect of lower Greylock' and 'sacrifice bird and animal life'.

Constructed through this dynamic of duelling depictions are two sets of personae, each being aligned with a primary motive and strategic action. One set is thus avowed by each party. For example, when a 'town member' says 'I'm for the project', she or he is heard to be motivated by local (primarily economic but also political) needs, and meets those needs through advocating 'the Greylock Glen development'. The 'environmentalist', on the other hand, is heard to be motivated by ecologic problems, and a literary aesthetic, and is heard to act in order to preserve or conserve 'the mountain' for the 'common' good.

During this drama, each such avowal can be used as a basis for attributing to the other a suspect persona, strategic action and motive. From the economic code, the ecologists are portrayed as 'outsiders' who want town land as a site for their playground (their motive) and are condescending and meddling in local affairs which they don't understand; from the ecologic code, the locals are profit-driven economists who are provincial and self-interested (their motive) and don't understand the more general environmental consequences of their 'project'. The social relationships thus created through these duelling depictions derive from these competing personae, while the competing decisions each is heard to have made is creating – through these duelling codes – an antagonistic, intractable and strained social drama.

The above discursive formation has a firm grip on these participants. This is especially evident mainly because the discourse is conducted so often *as if* there are two extreme, mutually exclusive, personae and patterns for action. In other words, features of this 'talk' presume, and re-create, the very dilemma being discussed. When discussing 'the project', it is assumed that development should proceed as planned; or with regard to 'the mountain', the land should be annexed to the state reservation. Generally, in a nutshell, this land-use controversy is spoken simply, as that cut and dried.

Hints of an integrative redress: a community seeks common ground

Rarely, in 1989–91, sometimes in a back room, in quieter moments, with few people listening, one could hear – as some put it – some 'middle ground'. These cautious proposals began to moderate the antagonisms by scaling down the degree of development, suggesting more 'low-level development' or 'limited development'. In the other direction, the hard-line ecological code was being 'scaled up' to include some very modest development. Mentioned here during these times were several rather undeveloped ideas such as fewer housing units, or a small public campsite on the north-east part of the Glen (The Thiel Farm area) which would have minimal impact on 'the foot of Greylock', but would provide modest economic benefits from 'up on the project'. Still other proposals involved channelling economic development towards other parts of the northern Berkshire area, thus abandoning the Greylock Glen project altogether. That these ideas were rarely mentioned, and if mentioned were in private, demonstrates the dramatic grip the economic and ecologic depictions held on this communal conversation, and the difficulty in depicting 'this land' in economic *and* ecologic terms, as the original legislation put it, as a protected preserve which diversifies the local economy.

With the January 1991 change in state government administrations – from the Dukakis Democratic to the Weld Republican – came a period of reassessment. The government plans for this land were being re-evaluated. Creative ways of resolving or mediating between the divisively different proposals needed to be found.

A key move in this reassessment was the eventual formation of a widely representative Advisory Committee by the state of Massachusetts Department of Environmental Management (DEM). This committee consists of

20 members: six from state agencies, six from the town of Adams, four from various environmental groups (i.e. Sierra Club, Mt Greylock Protective Association, Audobon Society, Appalachian Mountain Club) and four from more local governing groups (e.g. community and regional development offices, Berkshire Visitors' Bureau). The essential task of this committee has been to generate a mediating 'concept', a broad-based consensual decision for this land that could meet the ecologic and economic criteria of all involved parties and the original state legislative act.

The formation of this committee was extremely significant for several reasons. First, the government was acting as mediator among the various interests, a position not adopted by others or by the other available institutions in this case. Second, the formation of the advisory committee put into one setting people who had been advocating opposing decisions. As a result, the members of the committee could not simply rely upon the solidified codes outlined above, and be socially productive in this group, given its purposes. The committee, acting as diplomatically as possible, was being charged with generating newer, integrative 'visions' that could weave its various interests into a single cloth. In short, the competing groups were being 'welded' into an official government group, and as members of that group, together, they must create a discourse that represents their own interests while incorporating the interests of the others. The formation of the committee then created a significant shift in motivational exigencies. Speaking simple vested interests would not be sufficient to this task. Movement must be made from the competing codes to a more cooperative discourse. Could this group move itself – and help model for others how to so move – from insular and competitive enclaves to an integrative community?

As a part of the committee's considerable task, they commissioned outside consultants' advice about the land. After receiving the consultants' reports, the committee met in September 1992, and not surprisingly, at that meeting, the proposals made by the consultants largely fell prey to vested interests in terms of the two codes outlined above. The one was being labelled 'an environmental education center' and the other 'a conference center'. The former plan was of a small economic scale, ecologically focused, and largely motivated by 'an educational agenda'. The latter was of a larger economic scale and foregrounded a 'profit motive'. Introducing these plans from 'outside' consultants, however, enabled significant symbolic movement by the committee, if ever so slight. It helped begin weaving the two codes into an integrative 'concept' that could create, possibly, the basis for a decision that the committee sought and the wider public – and the state government – anticipated.

The process of attempting to forge such a vision out of these earlier codes and consultant plans has been a long and tedious one and has produced what the advisory board called the Greylock Center Concept Plan. The committee noted in a recent (1994) document: 'The concept plan is the result of an eighteen month consensus building project.' Neither the language of the document, nor the process that produced it, can be analysed here in any detail, but I can mention that the concept is now referred to as the 'Greylock Center' and has 'three main components'. These are 'a conference center, an environmental education center, and a variety of recreation areas and facilities'. These 'will attempt to creatively integrate recreation, education, and sustainable approaches to development' (p. 16 of the August 1993 final draft). In a 1994 letter to prospective developers (recall this is a 'public–private partnership'), Governor Weld captures the idea in this way:

> The development of the Greylock Center is a public–private venture melding economic and environmental interests. As envisioned, the Greylock Center will contain a full amenity conference center, a residential environmental education center, and a network of year-round recreation areas and facilities, including a championship 18-hole golf course. All development companies are encouraged to utilize state-of-the-art energy saving and environmentally sensitive technology.

The 'concept plan' created by the committee, then, is not so much the invention of a new idea, as it is the bringing together into one 'plan', a 'centered plan', ideas – and identities – that were previously kept farther apart. This is by no means a meagre accomplishment. The plan presents, and subsequently requires, a discourse that affirms historically antagonistic codes, in various degrees, and thus attempts to find in this social and natural scene some common ground. The process – if evolving ever so slowly, and in short – seeks an integration of the traditionally competing factions. Representatives of groups which the community cast as antagonists are now working together in the hope of producing such a joint decision. These current efforts are interesting in their attempts to forge for this public – at least for some period – a community-wide plan. Whether this can be done, and for how long, and whether this social drama has played its last major crisis, or will again rupture into a social schism, all remains to be seen.

Decisions, drama, dialectics and depictions: the work of discursive forms

Decisions undoubtedly involve individual predispositions and judgements. Yet, in order to formulate them, we draw from a complex discursive formation, and as we implement them, we are drawn to some degree into that formation. As I began inhabiting the symbolic world reported here, I soon realized my own initial 'senses' about 'the mountain' were only part of the picture. I was deeply perplexed when I would mention 'Greylock' (thinking, myself, of 'the mountain') yet find others responding directly to me with a sometimes lengthy discussion of Adams' economic or political woes. I wondered: how can a mention of the 'mountain' create a grand discourse about Adams, its history and its political economy? By now, the reasons for this discourse, and the associated proposal for this land, should be clearer. From the one view, I had asked about 'Greylock . . . the town's project' – not about the 'mountain' – and was simply being instructed in a local way to understand it.

This exploration of a large discursive system can help us understand the ways decisions like these are not simply our own, but are perhaps more like evolving ships upon a shifting discursive sea. Given the state of the sea, we select – or realize in retrospect that we have selected – a vessel (or coded discourse) that is to our liking. We ride it along and see how it traverses the terrain through which we are moving. Eventually, we get some sense of our vessel both as we move with it, and as we begin seeing others – in other vessels – travelling along. We may learn, sometimes sooner, sometimes later, more deeply about our vessel, or that another vessel may serve us better, or that this vessel we are on has itself changed (or should change) its shape and its means (or motives) of propulsion. Travelling like this, our decisions are *part* of a shifting discursive terrain, with its own geography, its own history, its own constraints upon what we can (and should) do, upon what indeed we 'are' doing. As we move our lives along, deciding as we go, we realize similarly that our psychological make-up is not simply in our hands, but is more largely a part of shifting seas and terrains that move through and sometimes engulf us. These seas I have called discourses, and they are instrumental in making us what we are, just as we struggle to make what we will of 'them'. Decisions as discourses span the vessels and seas that individuals inhabit, the personal and cultural conditions of life.

Some such geographic metaphor is particularly apt, I hope, for the case examined above. Each proposal that participants advocated earlier responded to its own storm of violation, thus forming both alliances and conflicting factions. Later, the grip of each vessel was loosened, with each moving slightly closer together and into calmer seas, but also into uncharted territory. The more hostile scene had been recrafted with more conjoint – yet still strained – constructions being somewhat in the air. This general process, the movement from violations, crises and factions to attempts at redress and integrative efforts, demonstrates the social-dramatic form of this decision-making process. Each phase of the drama carries with it its own rhetoric, its own plot, its own mode of enactment (Turner, 1974; 1980). The rhetoric of violation and crises would temporarily give way to a rhetoric of redress and integration, only sometimes to precipitate further crises; the plot turned from antagonistic to cooperative actions, with various ebbs and flows between these; the mode of enactments were sometimes official and governmental, including legislative acts and advisory committees, and at other times were more informal. The drama of decision-making is, then, in this case, of a large and particular dramatic form, with its various ships and terrains, its shifting rhetorics, plots and subplots, and its modes of enactment.

The decisional process detailed above – as perhaps many psychological processes – consists of discourses that create nothing less than various ways of being, various ways of living with others, and various ways of inhabiting material worlds (bodies included). Our psychologies, our senses of being, of being related, of how we should act and so on, are being crafted from discursive systems (like these seas) and from discursive codes (like these vessels) that we can individually select from and create with. What discourse is being used is partly a matter of habit, but is also possibly a matter of individual choice. And thus it was for those in this case who consciously decided, for example, to purge 'the project' from their vocabulary, and thus to fight for 'the mountain' as a matter of principle, knowingly re-creating a conflictual and contentious scene. Others made decisions about the issues more privately, unwilling to talk much about them, knowing a few words would say much more than they desired. If people would talk, they often expressed their concerns more in one code than the other, somewhat bewildered when the dramatic contest played out again and again in a seemingly interminable process. As they'd say: 'I wish people could just get along on this.' To 'get along' and bring people together meant, in this case, that one be willing or able not only to understand one's own code, but moreover to speak both codes – and hybrid codes – forcefully, in order to give each its due, and possibly work each together. Indeed, the tide of the debate has been moving this decision mostly between these conflicting vested interests – with little common ground – for at least two decades now.

Understanding how this decisional process is working, and being able to embrace its considerable psychological importance, suggests then that we envision decisions as discourses, and further hear how these discourses are not only locally tailored, socially forceful and individually applied, but are moreover consequential for our senses of identities, social relations, motives and material living. Decisional discourses can thus be understood as being guided partly by our own rudders, with these helping to navigate particular vessels, seas and terrain; that is, our decisions are partly our own to make, yet these inevitably are part of the larger communicative climate and territory of our times. A discursive approach can thus help us understand not only our ruddered wills but also our contemporary worlds; and thus, the approach can enable thinking of our psychologies with the personal and the cultural in mind.

Focusing more upon the discourse, we can see and better understand not only the general forms of these decisional and dramatic processes, but a more specific one as well, in this case, verbal portraits of nature. In concluding, I will briefly elaborate the constituent features of this depictive form of discourse, mention several of its dialectical qualities, and discuss prospects for its use in discursive studies of decisional discourses. The ways these dramatic and depictive discourses create identities of selves, motives for acting and social relations among people may be of some use in our future studies of discursive psychology (see Carbaugh, 1994; 1996).

The references to nature which are made by these people during this land-use drama demonstrate how a small communicative form, the verbal depiction of nature, is sometimes a very powerful symbolic expression. When this form is used, it can ignite a potent complex of socio-cultural messages. First, with regard to a referential function, depictions make reference to a very specific physical place in a very specific way through the selection of (a) particular term(s) of reference (e.g. of 'mountain' or 'project'). To make reference to a place is to suggest to one's contemporaries that some place is worthy of attention (that physical place), that it can (and should) be attended to in this way (through this term of reference), and that it can (and should) be viewed from this physical location (the way the term physically places one for viewing). The communicative act of referencing nature thus invokes a complex of geographic messages: a place at which to look, a way for living with that place, and the optimal place from which to view it; all of this is getting said. The use of (a) depictive term(s), then, generates claims that are both about and from a physical place, positioning one to see from a particular vantage point into that place, and to live with it in a particular way.

Communicating about natural space further invokes a *system* of social personae through particular meanings. For example, the way 'nature' is turned into an expressive means says something about the people who express it in that particular way. As a result, these expressions help construct not only typical personae, but also – when a part of a social drama – political factions, counter-actions, and the disparate motives deriving from each. Put differently, each social-dramatic depiction of nature is heard as an avowal of some identity, while attributing another to others. Developers want a 'project' in order to better the town's civic life; environmentalists want the 'mountain' preserved in order to better the ecological life. Created through this duelling of depictions is a complex of dialectical messages, of how the land (above or below) and people (outside or inside) could be and/or should stay.

Dialectical meanings such as these are perhaps immanent in social-dramatic depictions of nature, as they powerfully integrate, through competing forms, a referencing of a physical world, a complex of cultural associations, and various social identities, political factions, modes and motives for action. This potent communicative process seems a prime candidate for what Basso (1988: 123) has called a 'mini-maxing' phenomenon (the mini form being 'the project' or 'the mountain'), a cultural discourse in which 'a few spoken words . . . accomplish large amounts of communicative work'. Most noteworthy as well, in this case, is the way in which a single depiction within this larger dramatic form can radiate, in a saying, various dialectical messages.

While the symbolic meaning systems of primary concern in this essay are deeply local and conflicted, they are also of a larger cultural field, igniting as they do traditional American dualisms and dialectics. Some of these include the relative weighting and conception given to classic counter-forces, such as the impulse to transform versus the impulse to render permanent and stabilize; the locus of the decision-making process, whether done locally, inside (by the town) or elsewhere, outside (by others); the scope of the decision, whether short term or longer term; the nature of the problem, whether of a community or of a larger natural environment; the role of village or town versus national or state government; the ownership and use of land, whether private or public, conserved or preserved (see Oravec 1981; 1984); the motives for public policies, be they economic or ecologic, and whether these can be simultaneously met. All such large concerns are woven into the fabric of the conversational cloth. With each single thread, one weaves a hearable, potentially robust dialectical design – whether one wants to or not. One's heritage often speaks louder than one's will!

The dialectical complexity of the particular political issues involved here is particularly noteworthy for American audiences. The contemporary two-party political scene is often cast as a drama between the 'liberal Democrats' and the 'conservative Republicans'. Typically, the liberal left is heard to be champions of rights for the disadvantaged, the poor and the environment. The conservative Republicans are heard to be champions of small government and private enterprise. In Adams, the dialectic between the political left and right worked in alliances that do not neatly fit these grand political images. The 'environmental left' argued for preservation of the land as a common good for all people. They antagonized the private business interests in the process. But also in the process, they argued for 'preservation' of a common good (the land) and a national heritage (the literary tradition). A perhaps unintentional consequence of this argument was the further muting of the disadvantaged, the economically deprived townsfolk of Adams. Stepping into this American picture from afar, one cannot help but puzzle over finding the liberal left arguing in favour of preserving tradition at the expense of disadvantaged locals! The conservative right, on the other side, argued for development of the land in order to help the local economy. They antagonized the environmentalists from elsewhere in the process. But in so doing, they argued for change of a local good (the land) and transformation of deprived people (the poor). The conservative Republicans were arguing for the disadvantaged, for change and transformation!

The untypical – to the American public – alliances and arguments shown here demonstrate how general cultural political images can shed very little light on some local circumstances. One wonders further if general abstractions (e.g. 'thinking globally') mitigate against or confuse subsequent local actions and interactions. Some of the most difficult dynamics in the above occurred when 'global thinking' spoke over and above the local scene, making local circumstances almost impossible to hear. Abstract dialectics, untutored by local discourses, at times tower over such debates, and in the process do little to help us understand them.

Running through all of these dualisms and tangles is some version of a nature/culture distinction, some vacillating relation between the order of nature (or wildness) and the order of culture (or cultivation). How can one address and redress this apparently robust bipolar categorization in human thought and action? Here, I think, is where the study of cultural discourses, social dramas, processes of decision-making, and verbal depictions of nature holds great promise.

First of all, to know people – who they are and how they are related – and the places they inhabit in a holistic sense, that is, to know how life is experienced *and* expressed in its place, is to know both a physical place and a cultural space. Knowledge is needed of the emphatically material *and* symbolic 'there', and how each plays its settling role. Not to recognize this is to blindly impose one's own symbolic orientation on to a 'peopled place', where others are currently living. Focusing upon a 'here', though not necessarily staying only 'there', commits one to some degree of local knowledge of people and their place, to knowing both what is indeed there, the local terrain, to knowing the ways that place is currently inhabited by its people or discursively coded by them. It is to know also the people there, how they are related, and what motivates them. This point of departure is crucial not only because indigenous people and places, like the Hopi (Johnson, 1991) and others (Mitchell, 1991), have fallen prey to outsiders' interests, but also because all living is of a place, to a degree unique unto itself and its people. To know, then, is to go 'there' to that peopled place and experience it, and it is also to discover, while there, the psychological space which that place holds for those who inhabit and use it.

To know the local system, one needs a framework for discovering, describing and interpreting it. Through ethnographic field work, one can come to know the ways in which a people inhabit and play out dramas about a place, the space it holds in their lives, what they see in it and seek from it. By listening to the ways that places (including bodies) are depicted, and their geographic positioning through a complex of cultural associations (historical, economic, political and social), one can gain access into local places and lives. Depictions of nature help bring into view the relative weighting and potential antagonisms between the experiencing of nature's space and the cultural expressions of that place, exploring what both permit. Through depictions one can see and hear with an integrative double allegiance, asking of this natural place what it permits, *and* of this people what they have made of it and themselves. Assessments, such as decisions and discursive studies about them, then would be grounded in natural and cultural space, permitting judgements which are in or are seeking balance.

Notes

I am grateful to the Office of Research Affairs, University of Massachusetts, for a grant which enabled me to do the field work for this project. Also, I thank Gary Briere, Stephen Brown and Dennis Regan for making various documents available to me.

1 For related theoretical positions see Denzin (1994) and Much (1994) in *Rethinking Psychology*.

2 Note the audible fluctuation in the environmentalist's comments given earlier. He demonstrated an awareness of the two positions and deliberately anchored his response to the one, from 'above', coding his response into a natural ecological position, rather than building with the other.

PART III
THE LANGUAGE GAME OF LANGUAGE ACQUISITION

---

7 Language Development

Christina Erneling

In this chapter I will show that the two main problems all theories of language acquisition have to solve, namely the problem of linguistic creativity or productivity (i.e. that any competent language user can produce and understand a potentially infinite number of sentences) and the problem that learning presupposes prior knowledge (i.e. the seemingly logical requirement that learning a language presupposes a prior framework of meaning), can be solved by seeing the process of acquisition as a discursive phenomenon. Acquiring one's repertoire of linguistic skills as an individual is a joint venture between children and their care-givers. The joint venture is the creation of an ever enlarging conversation which has a very special quality, namely that in the early stages of this conversation much of the discursive work is done by the senior members for the more junior. The key idea is that there are, in Wittgenstein's terms, language games of language acquisition. Coming to be a competent user of a language does not and could not occur in an isolated individual. It is the shaping of individual skills in a social context. This approach is inspired by, but goes beyond, the ideas expressed by the later Wittgenstein (1953).

The child, according to Wittgenstein, learns language by being domesticated, that is, by having its natural reactions and behaviours shaped in accordance with prevailing socio-linguistic activities. It does not acquire the relevant skills by learning to translate from an innate language of thought into its mother tongue. These claims suggest that the two fundamental problems of learning can be solved without the assumptions of individualism and cognitivism.

According to this general approach, language mastery is not the result of a process internal to the human mind, but is the shaping of such processes, physiological or mental, by the socio-linguistic environment. There is no shadowy language of thought or more general thought processes underlying the acquisition of language. That achievement is the result of the interaction of the child with its care-givers in specific language activities or language games, which in their turn are dependent on the wider language community. Neither the individual child nor the care-giver can provide the necessary framework for learning. To speak meaningfully is not just to utter speech sounds but to do this correctly according to the rules, explicit and implicit, of the language community. This assumes that the framework necessary for language acquisition actually consists of three interacting frameworks, which all in themselves are productive. There are the innate biological skills of the individual; the social contexts within which the right kinds of conversation occur; and finally there is 'language itself'. To show how a model based on this insight would look is the aim of this essay.[1]

I have chosen to call this theory the *domestication model* to emphasize that learning a first language is a matter of social training, where the child's natural behaviours and reactions are shaped by socio-linguistic interaction and training (see Harré, 1984). The framework of learning consists not of innate or acquired cognitive-linguistic mental structures, but of a combination of the child's natural behaviour, socio-linguistic interaction and the language spoken around him or her, that is, the conversation in which it is embedded. The individual's mind develops in its close interpersonal social context as well as the community-wide environment. Following Wittgenstein, I take the child's non-linguistic behaviour to be fundamentally productive as well. It is through training or domestication that this productivity is limited from mere randomness, making room for meaningful language and communication. To show this, one does not need to undertake new empirical studies, but rather one must look at what we already know about children, their behaviour and the socio-linguistic contexts in which they are raised, from a non-cognitivistic and non-individualistic perspective. Children's brains, their perception and production of speech sounds, increasingly complex and structured motor behaviours and activities like imitation and play, all change as a result of maturation, brought about through socio-linguistic interaction and training. It is around the child's first birthday that they come together, resulting in the first displays of linguistic skills. It is at this time that the child's indiscriminate babbling has been narrowed and shaped to include only the sounds of the child's mother tongue. This has been accomplished by domestication of natural behaviours, by the combination and training of different innate and acquired language-like behaviours to approximate those of a competent language user.

From this perspective it is fruitful to look at language acquisition as assembling and modifying two different sets of skills which become interrelated, with one overruling and shaping the other. Both types of skill have their origin in motor routines. Thus, learning a language involves a purely linguistic or phonological and syntactic aspect, the perception and production of speech sounds in accordance with syntactical rules; and a communicative-semantic aspect, the communication of concepts in varying circumstances with different people. A precondition for this interaction is the plasticity and redundancy of the developing brain which only slowly reaches its growth potential.

The behaviours/skills involved in the phonological and syntactic aspects of language are present from an early age, some even from birth (the capacity to discriminate speech sounds). Others come into play when the relevant anatomical structures have developed (in particular the capacity to produce specific sounds), but cannot be successfully used for the production of anything resembling language until the communicative and semantic skills have developed enough complexity. This occurs around the infant's first birthday. The development of both types of language skills, and their subsequent interaction, is best seen as a process of training or domestication rather than of maturation. The developing skills of various kinds are shaped and changed by the socio-linguistic environment, that is, by the conversation activities of adults who function as interlocutors of a special sort, and whose speaking serves as a model to imitate. As interlocutors they direct, encourage and discourage the child's actual behaviours so that they more and more closely resemble those of the speaking community. It is in this way that the child is learning conventional skills. This is done by what I will later describe as symbiotic interaction: that is, the adult encourages or discourages the child not only on the basis of its behaviours but also on the basis of the attributed semantic and communicative intent which the adult reads into them as it 'speaks for the child' in conversation with the adult, himself or herself. Thus, as the child is treated as meaning things, intending to communicate and so forth, its purely natural behaviours are brought in line with and take on meaning and communicative intent. It is then that we can begin to speak about the child's activities as uses of language. Although language is only found in humans, rudiments of related skills and behaviours can be found in non-human primates such as chimpanzees. They can be taught to use signs for simple descriptions and requests resembling those of a two- to three-year-old human child, but do not develop their linguistic skills any further. This shows that, although language is species-specific, the skills involved in it are not confined to human beings but are present to some degree in some phylogenetically close species as well. What is unique to humans is not a specific language capacity but certain skills, for example production of voluntary speech sounds. We have a slowly developing but complex brain which enables greater shaping by the socio-linguistic environment and enables members of our kind to develop their manipulative, cognitive and social skills far beyond those of our closest relatives among the primates. Once language has developed it also enhances these skills, leading to further discrepancies with species lacking language. I thus claim that by a reconceptualization of what we already know about children along the lines that Wittgenstein suggests, we can identify the framework of learning in language-like behaviours and socio-linguistic interactions. The two problems of learning can be solved in non-individualistic and non-cognitivistic terms.

Phonemic and syntactic skills

As already mentioned, the normal human infant is equipped with special anatomical and neural mechanisms for the basic phonemic aspects of language, namely the perception and production of speech sounds. Newborns can sense the loudness and pitch of speech sounds as well as adults (Sinnott et al., 1983), and after a few weeks they can detect discrete phonemes (Eimas, 1985). These early discriminations, which sometimes are better than those of adults, do not seem to be learned, but are increasingly changed and limited by the language activities the child takes part in. Children will acquire the ability to recognize specific sounds of the language spoken around them, but lose the ability to discriminate others. For example, certain sounds of Hindi can be detected by a seven-month-old infant from an English-speaking environment, but not by a 12-month-old infant or an adult raised in an English-speaking setting (Eimas, 1985).

Unlike the ability to perceive speech sounds, which humans share with other mammals, vocalization in humans seems to be the result of our unique and species-specific supralaryngal airway, the 'voice box'. As the voice box matures around three months of age and begins to take on adult-like structure, the first speech-like sounds such as cooing start to occur. This is followed by babbling at around six months. All infants, including deaf children, babble. Up to their first birthday all children produce virtually the sounds of all languages (Lieberman, 1984). As in the case of perception, production of speech sounds seems to be genetically coded and greatly modified by the experience and exercise of a specific language. Children eventually come to produce a narrower range of phonemes, that is, those present in their native language. To use its phonemic skills in anything resembling language the child has to use them in a systematic and rule-like way corresponding to their use in its mother tongue: that is, it acquires syntactic skill. Although these motor routines of language use eventually become very complex and specific, children early on engage in behaviours which, just like speaking a language according to syntactic rules, can be described in terms of following rules. Such a commonplace and seemingly simple behaviour as eating a piece of bread involves complex goal-directed routines performed in a certain order. Lieberman (1984; 1985; 1988) suggests that syntactically constrained speech may be the result of utilizing such non-linguistic motor behaviours in new contexts. Similarly Piaget has suggested that language acquisition is based on sensorimotor non-linguistic behaviour (Sinclair, 1972). Others have pointed to the child's manipulative and perceptual skills as playing a role in the acquisition of syntax (Gentner, 1983; Nelson, 1973). In sum, the claim is that phonemic and syntactical skills, both of which are necessary but not sufficient for language, are a result of the combination of speech production skills and automatized non-linguistic motor skills. These skills seem not to be fundamentally different from other sensorimotor skills. We do not need to assume innate 'knowledge' of syntactical rules or some such device as an inherent 'grammar machine' to explain these aspects of language. But they cannot be acquired by an isolated child. They require active participation in a linguistic community which not only provides models of speech but actively involves the child in linguistic interaction in different contexts.

Semantic skills

There is more to language than uttering phonemes in accordance with syntactical rules: a parrot does not have language, however well it modulates and formulates its sentences. One has to say something meaningful and one has to make these sounds in varying contexts and to different people: that is, adequate language use also requires semantic and communicative skills.

What are the individual skills involved in the acquisition of semantic capabilities? Clearly the skill to speak meaningfully involves two different aspects. First the child has to master the skill to use one thing, an object or a linguistic or other sign, to stand for or represent something else. Secondly the child has to acquire the conventional meanings of the words and other linguistic symbols of his or her language. The first type of skill, I will try to show in this section, is based on two more rudimentary skills which have an innate basis but develop during the first year, namely imitation and play. The second type of skill is a result of combining these with the child's growing social skills which develop on the basis of close and regulated interaction with care-givers. This social interaction is important because it delimits idiosyncratic meanings and constrains the productivity inherent in language. Without social interaction there would be no language.

The two clusters of skills I discuss in this section – those of imitation and of play – can be described as meta-skills. They involve most of the child's sensorimotor skills employed in special ways: one could say they are a skilful way of using other skills, or that they are skills applied to skills. In imitation, sensorimotor skills are matched with external copies of the same behaviour. In the beginning the child's own earlier behaviour serves as the model, while later what other persons do and say, or even the behaviour of inanimate objects, can serve as models. In play sensorimotor skills are used outside their normal context. Both imitation and play in many cases modify the 'original' behaviour: for example a behaviour sequence is not performed in full or is simplified. This requires or involves skills 'over and above' the purely sensorimotor. Furthermore, imitation is a prerequisite for play, especially for pretend play which has a crucial role in developing semantic skills. Both imitation and play are skilful activities that involve displacement. They involve a connection to events, objects and so forth that are not present. Here is the germ of the 'idea' that actions, objects and eventually words can signify or symbolize things other than themselves.

Imitation

Imitation clearly plays a role in the linguistic skills I have discussed. The narrowing of the range of babbling as well as the acquisition of new sound combinations seem to some extent to be the result of the child imitating the speaking activities of an adult. There is evidence that young infants imitate intonation (Lieberman, 1984) and at three to five months they can imitate pitch (Rathus, 1988). Bower (1977) reports that children as young as six days can imitate some of the orofacial movements of adults, that is, stick out the tongue and wiggle it. Later on children also imitate the syntax of the speech of others, such as the grammatical forms of irregular verbs and the construction of the past tense, but most of the child's early syntactical combinations are not straightforward imitations. Children frequently say things such as 'bye-bye shoe' and 'allgone milk' but it is unlikely that the parents, although simplifying their syntax when engaged in so-called baby talk or motherese, have provided these. Kuczaj (1982) points out that children even avoid imitating syntactical forms. In spite of this, imitation of speech sounds and syntactical structures of the child's native language clearly has a central part in explaining why French children speak French, English children speak English and so on. The skill of imitation does not just give the child new specific motor skills, such as the ability to make novel sound combinations required by its socio-linguistic environment; it also, when used in play situations, provides the prerequisite for meaningful language and thought: that is, it is involved in the development of semantic skills. Piaget sees imitation as a forerunner to mental representation. This points to the most important aspect of imitation, namely that in imitation behaviour is related to something different yet similar to itself.

In this section I will only give a short description of Piaget's studies on the emergence of imitation. The point is to show that imitation is a skill that grows out of the child's sensorimotor skills, and neither the ages at which the different stages are supposed to occur, nor the details of each stage as Piaget saw them, are important to the overall claim that the acquisition of meaning is based on skills and not on an innate grammar or an intrinsically meaningful language of thought. Piaget describes the emergence of imitation in stages (Piaget, 1962). During the first three stages up to around eight months, Piaget claims, the child is not able to imitate responses it has not already mastered. Imitation of behaviours not visible is mastered in the fourth stage (eight to 12 months) but the child is restricted to immediate behaviours already in its repertoire. However it is now able to combine or correlate different behaviours in new situations.

At this stage the child can first imitate speech sounds, because it now masters actions not visible to itself. According to Piaget the crucial change occurs between 12 and 18 months when the child has gained the concept of object permanence, specifically the related idea of a permanent object distinct from the child's own action. This means that objects as well as the actions of other persons are distinguished from the child's own manipulations of the object or the child's own actions. The child can now imitate novel actions and incorporate these into existing systems of behaviour. Between 18 and 24 months, the last stage of imitation development according to Piaget, the child becomes capable of deferred imitation, that is, the child can imitate complex new models, objects as well as persons, present as well as absent. This means that behaviours can be taken out of their immediate context and exhibited in novel situations. In a sense the child can use behaviours productively because he or she can relate them to other, different contexts, situations or objects. This is the beginning of displacement and semantic skills. Behavioural patterns that are associated with one context can become symbols of that context. For example, imitation of an action such as lying down, closing the eyes and putting the head on a pillow can stand for the behaviour sequence of going to bed. Soon part of an action system can represent the whole action pattern (metonymy): that is, closing the eyes represents going to sleep (Hattiangadi, 1987). This partial imitation can then be combined with or exchanged for the appropriate word such as 'sleepy', where the word takes the place of or signifies the whole action pattern. It is interesting to note that children often use many of their first words to stand for many different aspects of the whole behaviour sequence associated with the word. For example the word 'sour' was used by a child studied by Lieberman (1984) to stand for the lemon, the act of eating it and its taste.

To sum up, it seems that the child's skill in imitating at early stages involves the practice and combinations of already mastered motor behaviours (e.g. the production of phonemes in babbling), and it is when the child has reached a certain mastery of object manipulation (i.e. object permanence) that this skill can first be combined with other sensorimotor skills. At this stage we have real imitation of speech. The child can now distinguish between its own action and that of another. He or she can distinguish between similar yet different actions and can associate similar behaviours with different contexts: that is, the behaviour is freed from its immediate context and can be exhibited or used in another, or, in other words, deferred imitation enables the child to engage in pretend play. Piaget argues that this is the basis for the distinction between signifier and the signified, that is, between a symbol or sign and what it stands for or refers to (Piaget, 1962).

It is first around this time (12 to 18 months) that we can expect the child to use its first words, or combinations of speech sounds, as signals. Imitation has enabled the child both to 'tailor' its speech sounds, through practising, to the sounds occurring in its socio-linguistic environment, and to master the skill of letting behaviours and words stand for or signal something else. The child now masters signifying. When the child is able to combine the speech sounds with the semantic skill acquired in imitation, the learning of new words really takes off. Up to 18 months the child normally masters 50 words, but around the age of 24 months this has grown to 200 words, and continues to grow rapidly (Rathus, 1988).

As mentioned in passing above, imitation leads to semantic skills first when it is used in so-called pretend or symbolic play, to the acquisition of which I will now turn. It is in play that imitation comes to have a clear representative or semantic function.

Play

Play is found in the activities of all children and in those of many animals. It is not only a way of getting rid of surplus energy. Animals have been observed to play even in cases of extreme food shortage (Lieberman, 1984). Studies of play have yielded a list of at least 30 different functions of play in different animals, for example, muscular development, social skills and exploration of the environment (Lieberman, 1984; Rathus, 1988). Just as diverse as the ideas on the functions of play are ideas on how it should be characterized. For the present purpose I will characterize 'play' as behaviour or a system of behaviour which exhibits a normal patterning, but which is cut loose or liberated from its usual or instrumental situational constraints or consequences. The feedback system inside the behavioural system is, however, unimpaired.

This characterization of play applied both to so-called practice play (i.e. the repetition of patterns of behaviour for their own sake) and to so-called pretend or symbolic play, which involves reference or a relation to something other than itself. Both are exhibited out of their normal instrumental context but with an unimpaired internal feedback system. This is true both of the practice of phonemic combinations in babbling, and of playing with dolls or with a stick as a horse. Play behaviour would be a waste of energy in an organism whose behavioural repertoire functions 'perfectly' and/or could not be modified. If the genes rigidly determine behaviour, play seems redundant. But as we know the child's brain is both plastic and has considerable excess capacity: hence play has an important function. Play, as imitation, is a skilful way of utilizing sensorimotor skills, and as imitation undergoes development from 'pure' practice play in the newborn to symbolic or pretend play in the year-old infant. When the child first masters pretend play, the skill of deferred imitation combined with speech production skills yield meaningful language. The crucial difference between practice play (the exercise of skills for their own sake) and pretend or symbolic play is that the latter includes deferred or delayed imitation and hence presupposes the imitation of new objects and behaviours, both present and absent. Imitation is used in the service of play.

Let me expand on this by recounting, in a condensed form, Piaget's stages of play development (Piaget, 1962). During the first four stages (birth to 12 months) the child is repeating and practising movements already mastered and begins to manipulate objects for the sake of manipulation, without any specific instrumental function: that is, it engages in practice play. In the fifth stage (12 to 18 months) we have true pretence or make-believe: for example, the sight of a pillow triggers part of sleeping behaviour. It is in the last two stages that one can first ascribe to the child the beginning of semantic skills. For example, one of Piaget's children, on seeing her pillow (or a blanket looking like her pillow), laid down her head and closed her eyes, put her thumb in her mouth and the like. Here she is clearly producing an action out of context but the behaviour is only a representation of itself, that is, it is both signifier and the signified. The behaviour is clearly done 'for fun' (it is not instrumental) in a partially different or untypical setting (presence of the pillow but absence of the rest of the bedroom things such as drawn blinds, pyjamas etc.), but the behaviour of going to sleep is much the same as in the real situation. A little later the same child starts to exhibit sleep behaviour but does not finish it, and only closes her eyes. The last aspect of the play situation is, according to Piaget, the beginning of a differentiation between the signifier (the behaviour actually made) and the signified (the whole action pattern of going to sleep). In stage six this is carried further and the behaviours are found not only out of context and incomplete, but also applied to new and inadequate objects. Piaget's daughter, for example, used a piece of cloth and later the tail of a play donkey as a pillow. Another example (Vygotsky, 1976) is that of a child playing with a stick as a horse, which involves deferred imitation of behaviours appropriate to a horse (feeding, riding etc.) to the inappropriate object of a stick. The child reproduces behaviour not directly related to the object at hand, the stick, but to some other object. The stick, in this sense, evokes the absent horse. The stick is quite different from a real horse or wooden horse, but it is more similar than, say, an apple or an envelope. The stick is clearly different from what it signifies but is not yet used only on conventional grounds, as a word would be used. But the basis of a semantic skill is already established and speech will be combined with this skill. According to Vygotsky: 'abstracting the meaning of "horse" from a real horse and transferring it to a stick . . . and really acting with the stick as if it was a horse is a vital transitional stage in operating with meanings' (1976: 548). Behaviour related to one object is transferred or combined with another object. More or less 'real' actions on inadequate objects are carried further in language, where words and sentences are manipulated not as motor behaviours but as representations of these. This enables the child to plan ahead, test behaviours and so forth, without immediate and perhaps disastrous consequences. Play, and later language, liberate the child from external, immediate constraints. Piaget and Inhelder (1969) add that language enables the quick representation of long event chains and simultaneous representation of different structures. But how does all this come about?

Words and sentences are signifiers determined by social conventions. Unlike idiosyncratic signifiers, such as the stick or donkey's tail in the example above, they have a fixity or constancy of meaning and a generality which is broader than individual experience. Using words and later sentences presupposes that the child is capable of deferred imitation and of pretend play, and it is not surprising that the child's acquisition of words speeds up when the newly developed skill of pretend play is combined with speech production skills. But since the meanings of words are conventional the child also has to master interindividual communicative skills. This will be discussed in the next section.

Playing horse with a stick or mother with a doll involves not only symbolism but also rules of how sensorimotor behaviours are to be combined (Vygotsky, 1976): that is, the child is transferring a set of structured behaviours to a new context and an object 'symbolizing' the real object. Hence pretend play also utilizes the child's object manipulation and what I have earlier called the syntactical skills. Speaking syntactically is exhibiting structured speech behaviour and, if my claim in the section on syntactical skills is correct, involves the combination of motor behaviour (e.g. orofacial) and object manipulation skills combined with speech production skills. Speaking a language is just playing in the sense that it involves combining different skills and transferring a set of structured behaviours from one context to another. It seems thus that the skills involved in play also have a role in syntactical development. Again, the child's first syntactical constructions, telegraphic two-word utterances, start when the child masters pretend play. If the skill of playing is necessary for syntactical speech this explains the fact that it is not enough to have orofacial and manipulative control over hands and so forth to have syntactical speech. It explains why syntactical speech, although standardized phoneme combinations occur earlier, is delayed to this stage of the child's development. Not only syntactical skills but also speech production skills are turned from mere sounds into language with the development of play.

Let me now try to explain how speech production develops in a way that is parallel to the development of play sketched above. Babbling, the repetition and combination of phonemes, starts around six months, and can be characterized as a motor skill without a function. It is true that the babbling gets the child more attention from adults, but children seem to babble for the pure pleasure of it, and infants of deaf parents babble just as much as infants of hearing parents, at least in the early stages. Hence, speech sound production seems from the beginning to be freed from instrumental restraints or a particular context: it is an example of pure practice play. Babbling is pure practice play that becomes pretend play. Both types of play are exhibited 'out of context' but the latter has a semantic aspect as well, in that it is related to something other than itself.

Speech sounds become instrumental when the child engages in social interaction and this becomes even more effective when hooked up with the skill of pretend or symbolic play. The fact that speech sounds have minimal instrumental value (as compared with object manipulation and perception), and can be emitted concurrently with other ongoing motor behaviours, facilitates the distinction between signifier and the signified, in that the real thing (behaviour) and simulation (speech sounds) are differentiated by sensory channel. Speech sound seems thus to be an ideal vehicle for symbolic manipulation. Furthermore any speech sound can be combined with any extra-linguistic situation, event or object and hence allows for great flexibility and productivity in its use. This is shown by differences in sound in different languages and by the new use to which old sounds can be put. Actually, it lends itself to too great productivity or flexibility in that any sound can be a representation of anything. To achieve the 'fixation' or limiting of possibilities which is necessary for communication or information gathering and planning, the child's semantic skills of using speech sounds have to be restricted by intersubjective and socially shared conventions or ways of behaving. Without social training we would have idiosyncratic and inconsistent use of speech.

Deaf children and chimpanzees obviously master manual signs earlier and quicker than speaking children, but I think that this can be explained by the fact that speech motor control is more complex than manual manipulation, and hence it takes longer to develop sounds and syntactical combinations. Thus, to acquire language, the child also has to master communicative and social skills, to which I will now turn.

In this section I have only dealt with speech production. Something similar takes place in speech understanding, only here the development occurs earlier because auditory discriminations are developed earlier.

Communicative-social skills

In the section on semantic skills I have tried to show what skills underlie the child's grasp of the semantic function, that is, that an object, event, action or word can stand for, symbolize or represent something other than itself. I have only discussed the conditions for the acquisition of a general semantic skill, not how children learn specific meanings. I have said nothing of how it is possible for a child to acquire specific meanings or mean the same thing or use a symbol in the same way as other people do: that is, to use conventional symbols in speaking to different people in different contexts. To have language-using capacity is not only to be able to speak in well-formed sentences or to be able to use words that have idiosyncratic meanings, but to be able to use language or speech in a way that meets the requirements of the socio-linguistic environment. The child has somehow to acquire signs or symbols which are fixed enough to allow communication and information gathering, and are general in that they 'embody' experiences that go beyond individual experience. The child has to learn to mean the same thing with its words and sentences as the rest of the socio-linguistic community. This is a communicative or social skill. One must be able to adjust what one says to the person to whom one is speaking, to be sensitive to the discursive contexts, to speak with a purpose and so forth. These social skills presuppose or build on the skills I have discussed above but also on some specifically social skills. It is when all these skills converge or are combined around the child's first birthday that we have the beginning of language capability. Before I turn to the discussion and illustration of the social skills necessary for the ability to use language appositely and correctly, the character of the linguistic input the child encounters has to be discussed. Considered as a data base for making inductions about the rules of language use, it is incomplete and underdetermines what we know can be learned. According to the discursive theory, without the structuring the socio-linguistic community provides, the child could not utilize this input. Thus, the child needs basic social skills to be able to utilize the language or rather speech that she or he overhears as a set of models or exemplars for talk. The child's ability to engage in social interaction is necessary not only to acquire the conventional skills involved in language, but also to make sense of the socio-linguistic input.

Let me explain. Chomsky (1959), in his criticism of Skinner, pointed out that the language the child hears is incomplete and faulty as a data base, which is apparent from listening to any normal conversation in a family. But the situation is even worse in that the child only encounters a limited set of examples of any particular language usage. Add to this the indeterminacy of all uses of language, and the task of learning from experience seems impossible. If language and thought are inherently underdetermined or open-ended (that is, if any lexical item can be used in an indefinite number of ways), just overhearing examples (often faulty) of speech cannot by itself be the ground from which a child acquires the full repertoire of linguistic skills and capacities. How, then, can the incomplete experience be structured to reveal norms, and how are the capacities for communication acquired, depending as they do on objectivity and constancy of meaning? Following Wittgenstein, I will try to show that the structuring or limiting framework is found in the child's social interactions. We do not need to assume an innate language of thought to explain how the child learns from experience. Furthermore the 'learning mechanism' involved is not a rational process of hypothesis formation and testing, but a process of training, which combines social and non-social skills, all taking place in the daily conversational encounters of ordinary life.

Social interaction and the acquisition of social skills have two functions: they help the child to utilize and learn from experience and to acquire the conventions of language. The necessary structure, limitation or interpretation of examples overheard is not provided by explanation by the adults (which presupposes what is to be learned, namely a range of basic language-using skills) but through social constraints and interventions. What the child's mind is not providing, and the adults cannot provide by explanations, is provided by supplementations and complementations of a child's performances, by corrections, encouragements and other social or interpersonal techniques for getting a child to conform to the standards of the local socio-linguistic environment.

Symbiosis

Wittgenstein suggests that the acquisition of language is a matter of training: that is, the child learns language in the same way as a dog is trained to hunt. In training the dog, horse or circus animal the trainer is rearranging, recombining or shaping the innate and natural behavioural systems of the animal according to standards external to the original or innate behaviour. The elephant's innate motor behaviour is used to get it to stand on two legs, sit on a drum and the like. Something similar is taking place when the child is learning language: that is, its innate motor behaviour (phonemic and syntactical skills, object manipulation, imitation, play etc.) are combined to meet the standards of the local socio-linguistic environment. Although language acquisition in this respect is training or domestication, it is better understood in terms of symbiosis (Shotter, 1974; 1976). By this I mean that the child and its care-giver stand in a symbiotic relationship, where the child is dependent on the adult not only for the satisfaction of its physical needs (i.e. the adult is a physical extension of the child) but also for its social, linguistic and mental activity. Not only does the adult provide examples of use, for example in baby talk, and correct the child's own attempts to speak; but adults engage in conversation with children in such a way as to ascribe to the child meanings and thoughts that the child would have were it a fully developed member of the linguistic community. These supplementations are based on the child's natural expressions and behaviours and later on its limited repertoire of linguistic utterances.[2] Parents speak for the children, as in 'Is baby tired?', 'Oh, we're so tired', 'Does baby want to go sleepies?', 'We want to take our nap now, don't we?' and so on. Parents thus pretend to have a two-way conversation with the child. In this way parents seem to be trying to help their children express themselves by offering supplements to what the children can currently offer for themselves. *Inter alia* these offerings come to serve as models of sentences that the children can first imitate and so can learn to use later on (Rathus, 1988: 276).

Furthermore the adult not only ascribes meaning and thoughts to the child, but also reacts towards the child as if he or she had actually thought or meant something specific. The adult treats the child as a unity but this unity is synthetic, since it consists of the child's actual behaviours together with the supplementations and interpretations the adult gives to the child's behaviour. In this way the child's innate expressions of pain and other behaviours, and its (often idiosyncratic) imitations of linguistic usage, are incorporated into a social and communicative context. The child becomes a rational being by being treated as such.

The dyad of the mother (or other care-giver) and the child can be viewed as one psychological or linguistic being, where the mother gives social, intersubjective or conventional meaning to what the child does naturally and instinctively without concern for others. The mother, by interpreting the child's behaviour and reactions and then acting on them accordingly, coordinates her own behaviour to the child's. The child's behaviour and reactions are from the beginning made part of a social system which is both more stable and wider than the child's individual reactions. In the beginning the child does not make a distinction between its own actions and that of the mother (Piaget, 1954), but sees them as a continuation of its own behaviour. The interaction is one-sided and not really social in that the child is not an actor but a recipient. As the child grows and acquires skills such as manipulating objects, true imitation and so on, he or she starts to play an active role, performing for himself or herself those meaningful actions performed first as supplementations by the care-givers. Around 15 months (Shotter, 1976) the child begins to say 'No!' to the mother and is able to resist the mother's interpretation of its behaviour, wishes and so on. The symbiotic relationship is breaking up and the child becomes a social actor in its own right.

The symbiosis has trained the child first by combining its actions with another's, then coordinating its behaviour with that of others in a patterned and reciprocal way, and eventually, in social play, doing this according to shared conventional rules. By participating in forms of life the child becomes prepared to participate in language games and to acquire the management of meaning, syntax and the pragmatics of the language spoken around it.

The child is pre-adapted for social interaction[3] by such automatic responses as reflexive crying, smiling and selective attention to speech sounds and the human face. Much of the child's early reflexive behaviour is patterned, which enables the mother to relate her own actions in a systematic way to the child's, for example by smiling and talking to the infant only in pauses between sucking. There is evidence that these early interactions are patterned and stereotyped in most mother–child dyads (Richards, 1974; Bower, 1977; Rogoff, 1990), but it should be noted that although the child's behaviour is innate and reflexive the mother's interpretation (and subsequent reaction) involves cultural assumptions. There is no inevitable labelling of universal behaviours. In Western cultures crying is often seen as a sign of hunger, but for mothers among !Kung speaking Bushmen, where the infant is carried on the mother's back most of the time, certain movements are the usual sign for hunger (Konner, 1972). The same undoubtedly holds true for other things, as for example pain or discomfort. The ascription of meaning to different behaviours cannot, though, be completely arbitrary because the child would never be satisfied or would not even survive (see also Lock, 1978;

Gray, 1978). However there seems to be enough variation and diversity of natural expressions to allow for enormous cultural and contextual variation. Hence, children's behaviours are from the beginning combined and coordinated with others based on social conventions. The very meaning and significance of the child's reactions are thus restricted by social conventions and so are the stimuli or input, both linguistic and non-linguistic, that the child encounters.

Peekaboo

Let me now illustrate the emergence of social play with an example from Bruner (1976) of the emergence of the game 'peekaboo'.[4] He studied six infants from 10 to 17 months of age and he describes the developmental changes as an example of 'gut play' turned into play with conventions (1976: 284).

In the beginning the game utilizes strong pre-adapted response tendencies in young infants. The mothers studied by Bruner reported that 'looming', in which the mother approaches or looms towards the child's face from approximately one metre and says 'Boo!', precedes the peekaboo game. If the 'loom' is directly towards the face there is a reflexive avoidance reaction which seems to be innate. Hence, one of the important aspects of peekaboo, that is, disappearance or avoidance, builds on the child's reflexive responses. Furthermore, appearance and disappearance, the main aspects of the game, are aspects of object manipulation, and are also innately based (Piaget, 1954). So, in the beginning and also as it becomes more structured and two-sided, the game is governed not by conventional (i.e. arbitrary) rules but by strong pre-adapted responses in the infant. These are used by the mother in the structuring of her interactions with the infant.

All peekaboo games have the same basic structure: (1) initial contact, (2) disappearance, (3) reappearance and (4) re-established contact. In the 'looming' stage this is only present in an incomplete form but it soon characterizes all peekaboo games. Initially the game involves a limited set of hiding tools, time variations, vocalizations and so forth, but as the child matures and becomes more skilful in the game, which presupposes the concept of object permanence, modifications in for example the hiding tool occur: for example, a rag, a hand, even a chair can function as the hiding tool depending on the context. Having reached this stage in playing the game the child seems to master not only the rules for turn-taking, that is, appearance and disappearance, but also a wide range of variations inside a set of relatively fixed rules, 'patterned variations within constraining rules' (Bruner, 1976: 283). As the rules become more arbitrary they also become more conventional in that anything that is agreed upon can function as a hiding tool, and so on. Before 10 to 12 months the mother controls the unmasking, timing and so on, but after this age the child begins to take control. A few months later (15 months in one of the children Bruner studied) the child invents and controls variations in the game, for example hides behind a chair. The child has now become an actor and the mother a recipient and the symbiosis is breaking up.

Bruner also points out that vocalizations play a role in peekaboo. In the beginning they help the child localize the mother's face but soon become parts of the game, occurring concurrently with specific behaviours and responses. This and other vocalizations by the mother help the child make the transition from initially non-linguistic games to language games (Newson, 1978).

To sum up: the child, by combining different skills in interaction with the care-giver, has developed the skill of taking turns, coordinating its own action with others, following intersubjective or conventional rules and mastering variation inside a set of relatively determined rules. The child has now, around 12 to 15 months, the skills required for participating in language games, which are just other systems of conventional rules which vary to fit the context and can be changed if the change is socially accepted. The child has acquired the skill of communication and of productive use of conventional rules. This is a result of combining what I have called linguistic and semantic skills with communicative skills.

Another example of symbiotic learning can be seen if we consider how the child learns a word like 'pain'. The child naturally exhibits both bodily signs of harm (e.g. bleeding) and typical expressions of pain such as crying. The care-giver not only attends to the child, that is, stops the bleeding and feels the sore leg, but also treats and talks to the child as if it felt pain, and in this way language is attached to the natural signs such as crying. The child comes to imitate the use of the word and use it as part of the natural expression (i.e. as in play when one thing is used to stand for something else). Eventually, and this is the crucial step, the child uses it instead of the natural expression. 'Pain' does not refer to the pain behaviour; nor, to make a subtle Wittgensteinian point, is it used to describe the bad feeling. Rather it expresses the state of the child. It gets attached, just as crying is, to the inner sensations, as one of their proper modes of expression. The symbiotic relationship has thus helped the child to acquire a new skill and to relate it to something naturally present in the mind. As a result the child eventually can express its own subjective feelings in speech. All this is possible only because the child, first, can imitate something not present, and then can engage in pretend play and manage to handle conventional rules at around 12 to 15 months.

Although the symbiotic interaction seems to be breaking up around the time the child begins to speak, traces of it are important in the acquisition of language even at later stages. Many of the child's first utterances are difficult if not impossible to understand, and later idiosyncratic use of words or grammatical constructions, even when correctly pronounced, leads to difficulties. Ryan (1974) and others report that mothers often respond to children's utterances by expanding on them, adding to or changing them. They make interpretations of what the child is saying on the basis of such things as the child's intonation pattern, accompanying actions (e.g. pointing) and the circumstances (e.g. absence of an object), and delimit the meaning more exactly. This is illustrated by the example of baby talk in the section on symbiosis.

Hence, by participating in such language games, the child becomes more and more proficient in its native language by acquiring social skills such as turn-taking. A similar, but more complicated, account can be given for the acquisition of the concept of 'self'. With 'self' I am referring to the unifying and organizing principle of perception, action and emotion. The adult treats the child and speaks to it as if it already 'had a self'. Certain behaviours are reacted to and described as if they originated from a self. The self as an organizing principle originates from these public descriptions and reactions and the adult helps the child to connect language and concepts with its natural behaviours.[5] The child has become able to coordinate its own actions with those of others. Exposed to a limited and underdetermined set of examples of particular linguistic usage, the child is able to combine its speech production skills and imitative abilities with its social skills so as to use the language in a systematic yet varied way. The child can communicate concepts in varying circumstances to different people.

The communicative and social skills illustrated above build on the linguistic and semantic skills, yet come to control these. By this I mean that the child's aim in communicating or gathering information controls the skills used to accomplish this. In this sense the communicative or social skills are higher-order skills or skills applied to skills.

The child's acquired language is a result of a social construction utilizing many different skills which have some aspects that are isomorphic with language, but could not, by themselves, be sufficient to permit a mastery of language. The skills are productive, as are the underlying neural structures.

Later learning

My account of the acquisition of language and the process of learning have been limited to very early learning, but of course much important learning takes place after this. It is both similar and in important respects different from the early training. For example, imitation skills help the child to continue to learn new words and syntactical constructions. Through practice, speech production improves and becomes adult-like around the child's 10th birthday (Lieberman, 1984), when the child's increasing skill in the manipulation of objects results in the use and understanding of words such as 'cause', 'time' and so on. The child's increasing social network, in play with peers and adults, increases its mastery of the pragmatics of language. In addition to these continuations of skills developed before the acquisition of language, language itself adds a new and powerful skill to the child's repertoire of skills. Language can be applied to, or combined with, other skills and with itself. It sharpens the child's capabilities in manipulating objects[6] and enables quick representation of long chains of events as well as simultaneous representation of different structures (Piaget and Inhelder, 1969). With language the child can plan ahead and 'test' actions before doing them. It makes the child radically more independent from adults. It can also influence other persons in a new way. The continued acquisition of language, and cognitive knowledge, is also language based in that the child can now benefit from explanations, especially when its metalinguistic awareness develops in a few years' time. This makes later learning quite different from the early training I have discussed above.

The same processes or mechanisms are, though, still part of learning later in life. For example, symbiotic learning is found at universities. One frequently observes how undergraduates ask questions with words they do not fully understand. Very often the teacher reformulates the question in an appropriate way and answers it on the basis of the reformulation. Although the subject matter is very different, the situation is not far from a mother interacting with her young child.

Concluding remarks

The domestication model of language learning sees learning as a process of social construction, in a symbiotic relationship with a discursive partner. The learning of language is based on the child's innate behaviours and skills which are shaped by social-discursive interaction. There are two main types of skill involved in the learning of language. The first is linguistic skills, which can be further divided into speech and syntactic skills. Speech skills are based in the innate ability to perceive and produce speech, and syntactic skills are based in different kinds of motor behaviour, such as orofacial and object manipulation skills. As they develop, the linguistic skills are combined with the second type of skill, namely communicative-semantic skills. Examples of semantic skills are imitation and play. The communicative skills are based in the child's natural and patterned social interactions (e.g. turn-taking). But these skills are not sufficient for the acquisition of language. The child has to use them in the context of a linguistic community in close contact with a care-giver in what I have called symbiosis. The last is crucial because it is in this interaction that the natural linguistic and communicative-semantic skills are shaped, or domesticated, to the expectations of the linguistic community. Learning is thus the training of specific innate skills to conform to social standards. It is not a 'triggering' of an innate language of thought, or the result of a quasi-scientific process where the child forms and tests hypotheses.

This social training, shaping and combining of skills is made possible by the plasticity and redundancy of the developing brain, the unique human ability to form speech sounds and the long childhood of humans. These may well be some of the factors responsible for the fact that only humans can learn language. The domestication model of learning could also be described as a transactional or tripolar model of learning, in that it sees the acquisition of language as the combination and coming together of many different biologically grounded skills in accordance with the demands of the socio-linguistic environment. Language ability is the result of a nexus of interacting skills adapted to the linguistic environment. The details of this model are of course extremely complex, even if the underlying principles are simple, and it is bound to be added to and changed by further empirical as well as *a priori* research. At this stage the domestication model should be understood as an outline for a future research programme that needs to be filled out and tested on both a theoretical and an empirical level.

Notes

1 For a more comprehensive description of this model see Erneling (1993).

2 This is the basis of our anthropomorphic attitude to children: we are teaching them what we must take them already to know if we are to teach them by symbiosis!

3 Its physical dependence makes social dependence a necessity.

4 Peekaboo seems to be a universal game: *Eckergiek* (German), *tittut* (Swedish), *kurkistus-lekki* (Finnish), *coucou* (French), *cucu* (Spanish) and *nascondino* (Italian).

5 For a detailed account of the discursive development of the self see Harré (1984).

6 See for example Vygotsky's (1962) discussion of children engaging in so-called 'egocentric speech', that is talking aloud to themselves.

PART IV
SOME USES OF
TRADITIONAL METHODS

8 Emotions and Discursive Norms

Muriel Egerton

Recently, social psychologists doing discourse analysis have concentrated on the exegesis of written or spoken texts, and this practice has been put forward as a definition of discourse analysis (Potter and Wetherell, 1987). This type of analysis emphasizes pragmatics. Texts are analysed in terms of the goals of the speaker, whether as a member of a social group, employing traditional rhetorical stratagems to oppress members of another group, or when following a personal agenda in an interactional context.

However, discourse analysis may engage with any social practice, or aspect of social practice, which has a signifying function (Van Dijk, 1985). In this chapter I discuss the use of quantitative methodology to identify semantic regularities, or discursive norms, which develop to fulfil specific social functions at particular times.

The meaning of discourse elements depends on their placing in a network of semantic similarities and contrasts (Harré et al., 1985, chapter 5). Conceptual analysis, or ordinary language analysis (Ryle, 1949; Heider, 1958; Kenny, 1963), uncovers the complex structures of implication, differentiation or association which frame the construction of meaning and discourse. However, this type of analysis is abstract and normative and cannot address semantic configurations which are employed or constructed to serve particular ends in particular social contexts.

Culler (1982) points out that language users are for the most part unconscious of the semantic infrastructure underlying their use of language. Because of this opaqueness the form and structure of discursive norms often cannot be seen through the qualitative methods used for text analysis. But these semantic configurations can be explored using quantitative methods which identify and represent relationships, e.g. correlation, factor analysis, multi-dimensional scaling.

Before discussing the advantages and disadvantages of these methods, I would like to describe in detail their use in identifying norms in emotion discourse.

Emotions and discourse

Feelings and emotions play multiple roles in discourse. Emotion displays and statements are communicative in themselves. They may be used to promise, threaten, reassure. The automaticity of emotional responses may be exploited in social life: in conventional forms such as mutual polite smiling, in less conventional forms such as political or professional rhetoric, in idiosyncratic forms such as teasing. At a more reflective level, explanations of, or in terms of, emotions may be used to justify, persuade, malign.

As interpretative constructs, emotion terms have complex structures of implication. Emotion concepts link context, action and character. The objects and therefore contexts of emotions partly constitute the meaning of emotion terms. Prototypically, emotion concepts embed causal schemata, with the object of the emotion being perceived as its cause (Kenny, 1963; Harré, 1986a). However, emotions also involve motives, values, commitments and therefore character (Kenny, 1963; Armon-Jones, 1986). Appropriate actions are also constitutive of emotions, and are perceived as being caused by the emotion sensation. It can be seen that both inner and outer aspects of emotions are profoundly involved in the construction of personality and in social order, and emotions are themselves socially constructed (Berger and Luckman, 1966; Harré, 1986a).

Part of the Western representation of emotions is that they are sincere, authentic, natural. Therefore, in many interesting cases, the social formation and function of emotion expression or discourse is hidden. It is not visible through the normal methods of discourse analysis, being opaque to both research participants and researcher. However, appropriate quantitative analysis may uncover hidden structure.

Description of studies and methodology used

Study 1: discursive norms for Northern Ireland 'troubles' victims

This study was carried out in Northern Ireland during the last (1982) IRA hunger strike. The news media were dominated by the hunger strike and the accompanying grief and violence. As a member of the community, I felt that my emotional responses were constrained and believed that during the course of the 'troubles' Northern Irish people had developed strategies to cope with the emotional pain and threat posed in news broadcasting about 'troubles' victims. On the basis of Lazarus et al.'s (1964) work, I expected to find several different strategies.

I asked a well-known local news broadcaster to make a fictional news broadcast tape which described, among other items, two 16-year-old innocent victims, one who had been shot as a bystander at a post-office robbery and one who had contracted cancer. There were two variants of the tape, one with female victims and one with male victims. One hundred and fifteen first-year university students listened to the tape and filled in a questionnaire on the news items about victims. The questionnaire started with a 28-item scale of emotion and mood words including adjectives around the poles of grief, fear, anger, sympathy, indifference and relaxation. The questionnaire continued with a number of open-ended questions about perceptions of the victim, responses to the victim, experiences of similar incidents, responses to news broadcasts, and ratings of local and national news consumption. In this way I elicited discourse apropos the described events.

Factor analysis was carried out on the emotion scale, in order to identify emotion descriptions which clustered together. Factor analysis can identify underlying semantic dimensions in which disparate items cohere. For instance, respondents are likely to give similar scores to items with similar meanings, e.g. relaxed and calm. This identifies a simpler structure of underlying meaning. Factor scores can then be extracted from these dimensions to explore patterns of meaning (for more detail on factor analysis see Clarke and Crossland, 1985). For the cancer victim, seven semantic dimensions were found, reflecting clusters of semantically similar emotion words (see Table 8.1 for factor loadings, i.e. the weights of the individual items on each factor). However, for the violence victim, only two dimensions were found. On one dimension all the negative and compassionate emotions were scored similarly; the other semantic dimension was one of indifference and relaxation (see Table 8.2). The factors for the violence victims were extremely clear and cohesive, indicating a high degree of consensus among research participants. Analysis of individuals' scoring on these dimensions showed that they could be used to express varying degrees of concern, modified by varying degrees of indifference. Scores were grouped according to whether approximately equal concern and indifference were shown, more concern than indifference was shown, or more indifference was shown. Figure 8.1 shows the percentage distribution of grouped scores for the female and male violence victims. Scores could be related to the qualitative data collected, but the real interest of this study was in showing the existence of a powerful and unsuspected discursive norm constraining statements about emotions for 'troubles' victims.

I came to believe that the political importance of responses to violence and victimization had brought about the development of this convention, which is clear and unambiguous, and can be used to make statements of different degrees of involvement by different people. The convention casts responses in a 'rational' (i.e. emotionally balanced) form, with expressions for emotions such as 'anger' and 'fear' being balanced by 'pity' and

Table 8.1   *Summary of factor loadings on emotion scores for the cancer victim (salients only)*

Emotion	\ I	\ II	Factor III	\ IV	\ V	\ VI	\ VII
Relaxed	0.82						
Content	0.66						
Comfortable	0.65						
Calm	0.63						
Indifferent		−0.68					
Sympathetic		0.67					
Pitying		0.66					
Concerned		0.65					
Detached		−0.60					
Sorry			0.79				
Sad			0.79				
Bored			−0.35		0.32		
Depressed			0.32	0.68			
Nervous				0.65			
Worried				0.61			
High-strung				0.53			
Irritated				0.46			
Over-excited				0.43			
Disgusted				0.37			
Remote					0.69		
Uninterested					0.57		
Uninvolved					0.53		
Powerless						0.80	
Helpless						0.62	
Pleasant							0.47
Angry							0.44
Jittery							0.30
Eigenvalue	2.41	2.52	2.15	1.84	1.70	1.33	1.08

'compassion'. This discourse is probably modelled by, among other people, newsreaders themselves.

Study 2: discursive norms in interpretations of anger

The second series of studies explored the implications of Averill's (1979; 1982) analysis of anger. As stated above, in emotion terms a conceptual connection is made between the object of the emotion, i.e. the instigation, and the actions which characterize the emotion, such as, in the case of anger, actions that are intimidatory, aggressive, coercive. A causal hypothesis is embedded in the term which links the angry action to the instigation and the agent may be perceived as acting involuntarily. The anger is glossed as a passion. Averill suggests that the notion of anger as a passion developed in order to resolve a normative conflict between social proscription of aggression and rightful retribution. The notion of just

Table 8.2 *Summary of factor loadings of emotions for the violence victim (salients only)*

Emotion	Factor	
	I	II
Sad	1.06	
Pitying	1.02	
Sorry	0.97	
Depressed	0.95	
Sympathetic	0.93	
Angry	0.89	
Worried	0.89	
Concerned	0.88	
Disgusted	0.79	
Detached		1.08
Indifferent		0.99
Uninvolved		0.97
Uninterested		0.95
Relaxed		0.95
Bored		0.89
Calm		0.86
Content		0.85
Remote		0.84
Eigenvalue	11.47	9.46

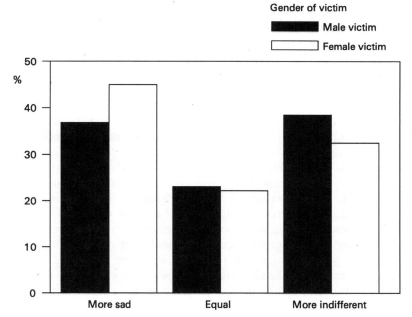

Figure 8.1 *Percentage scoring more, same or less on factors I and II for violence victim*

anger, anger which is caused by the situation, exculpates the agent from responsibility for aggression. Anger serves as a 'personal judiciary', thus further involving notions of rights and responsibilities. Angry displays become part of moral discourse, and reflect the social distribution of rights and power (see Bailey, 1983 for further discussion).

Averill's analysis suggests that it is only when the angry display is counter-normative that it is interpreted as a passion, that is, situationally caused and uncontrollable. It was decided to explore interpretations of an angry display in a bureaucratic setting. Two social workers disagree about whether to take a child into care. Research participants were asked to interpret this episode, in a set of retrospective judgements, as if they were the social worker who had wished to take the child into care and had become angry when prevented.

If Averill's analysis was correct, only those participants who judged the angry display to be counter-normative would give passion interpretations of the episode. A further discursive dimension is involved in that women have fewer rights to coerce through angry displays (Frodi et al., 1977; Egerton and Lalljee, 1992). It was decided to explore the interpretations of men and women separately.

The method used, which was based on Cornelius (1984), was an adaptation and simplification of Pearce and Cronen's (1980) techniques for exploring the construction of the meaning of communicative acts. Pearce and Cronen suggest that the meaning of communicative acts is dependent on and nested in various layers of contextualization: features of the actual episode, relationships between participants, life scripts of participants, overarching cultural scripts. This contextualization has both past (or reactive) and future (or proactive) aspects. Pearce and Cronen's basic questionnaire could be adapted to examine the relationship between judged counter-normativeness of angry displays and passion interpretations.

A passion interpretation was considered to be one in which an attribution of causation to a feature of the episode covaried with judgements of the uncontrollability of the anger. That is, the more uncontrollable the anger was judged to be, the more it was attributed to the situation. It was found that this relationship only existed for men who judged the angry display to be counter-normative. It did not exist for men who judged the angry display to be acceptable or creditable. This was identified initially as a statistical interaction between judgements of external causation (situation attributions) and judgements of counter-normativeness (relationship and life-script costs) in regression equations predicting judgements of the uncontrollability of the anger (see Table 8.3), and then explored further by graphing the results for the two subgroups (see Figures 8.2 and 8.3). This relationship was not found in the judgements of women respondents, although, on average, they judged the angry display as more counter-normative than men did. It is not acceptable for women to suggest that uncontrollable anger is a 'natural' response to this situation.

Table 8.3   *Men: correlation matrix and regression equation for uncontrollability of anger*

	Uncontrollability	Norms			External attribution		
		RC	LC	UNA	SIT	ANT	COL
Controllability	1						
Norms:							
RC	0.632‡						
LC	0.360*	0.604‡					
UNA	0.354	0.283	0.227				
External attributes:							
SIT	0.575†	0.283	−0.159	−0.017			
ANT	0.536†	0.389*	0.029	0.314	0.665‡		
COL	0.405*	0.476*	−0.288	−0.040	0.616‡	0.545†	

* $p < 0.05$; † $p < 0.01$; ‡ $p < 0.001$.

Variable	B	SE B	t	σ	$R^2\chi$	$F\chi$	σ
LC	0.416	0.118	3.505	0.001	0.1300	2.989	0.099
UNA	0.264	0.116	2.269	0.018	0.0782	1.876	0.186
SIT	0.574	0.114	5.034	0.000	0.4047	18.823	0.000
LC × SIT	0.116	0.040	2.873	0.005	0.1265	8.256	0.010
Constant	4.279						

Adjusted $R^2 = 0.6782$ $F = 12.065$ (d.f. 4, 17) $p < 0.000$

RC   relationship cost
LC   life-script cost
UNA   unacceptability of behaviour
SIT   situation attribution
ANT   antecedent act attribution
COL   colleague attribution

The passion interpretation explained a considerable amount of variance, sufficient to suggest that this was an established convention or discursive norm. Other emotion judgements had also been requested and other interpretative patterns could be identified for the episode through examining regression equations for these judgements (for details see Egerton, 1988; 1991). The experiment was repeated a number of times with alterations to episode or display, and further discursive conventions were identified which could be related to gender roles. However in a final part replication men did not use a passion interpretation, but interpreted the angry display as something which was inevitable given their characters, obligatory in terms of their life scripts.

Over the period during which the studies were carried out, the meaning of the episode had changed. The first study was carried out at a time when public opinion was strongly in favour of more intervention on the part of

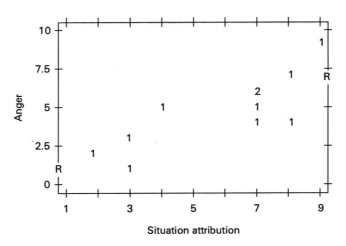

Figure 8.2 *Plot of uncontrollability of anger with situation attribution: men scoring above 0 on life-script cost*

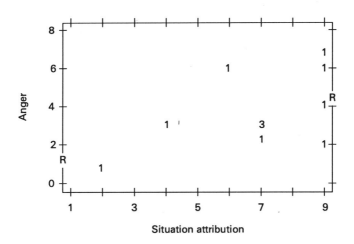

Figure 8.3 *Plot of uncontrollability of anger with situation attribution: men scoring at or below 0 on life-script cost*

social workers. The second study was carried out at the time of the Cleveland child abuse scandal, when it was widely believed that social workers had acted wrongly in removing children from their homes. The change in public opinion meant that a passion interpretation was not acceptable even from men. The warrant of social workers to remove children from their homes was questioned, and their right to attribute just anger to the situation was no longer unequivocal. This short and simple questionnaire, when analysed using methods which examine relations between discursive elements, was able to throw light on the interpretative resources of respondents, to identify systematic gender differences in the parameters of discourse about such episodes, and to demonstrate sensitivity to changes in public opinion.

Discussion

The first study described showed a convention or discursive norm held within one political community. The semantic elements (emotion adjectives) examined were not on the face of it related to each other, except in terms of similarity or dissimilarity. They were configured by the convention so that people could indicate varying degrees of involvement in the community, within a common paradigm of political rationality and emotional balance. The second set of studies capitalized on semantic relations within emotion concepts, and showed that these were differently configured according to gender and context. These studies also underline the linking of discursive norms to public opinion.

The methodology of these studies will be discussed, first, in terms of translatability and convenience; and second, in terms of their utility in exposing hidden semantic relationships and generating unexpected results.

Translatability and convenience

An objection which could be raised to the rating scale measures used in these studies (which were necessary to the relational analyses carried out) is that people do not normally say, 'I feel four points disgusted on a four-point (or nine-point) scale anchored in: not at all, somewhat, moderately, very much so.' However, the anchor points do show how scores can be translated into verbal statements. A more serious point is that it is relatively infrequent for people to make direct statements about their own emotions. Emotions are more frequently conveyed by non-verbal means. The emotional gloss in discussions of 'troubles' incidents is likely to be conveyed by bodily expression combined with indirect verbal indications. However, in the case of these repeated incidents of physical injury and violence, which are most threatening to this age group, participants were easily able to make direct verbal judgements of their emotions and welcomed the opportunity to do so. It would be cumbersome, time-consuming, perhaps impossible, to elicit the same discourse using qualitative methods.

Because the anger studies asked respondents to give retrospective judgements, it is easier to see how the interpretations elicited can be translated into speech-like statements. A passion interpretation might be expressed as 'I felt ashamed of losing control of myself, but the behaviour of my colleague (the parlous state of the child) made me uncontrollably angry.' Other speech-like translations can easily be found for other interpretative schemata identified. Again it seems that, for descriptive purposes, this is a more convenient method.

Hidden semantic configurations

It can be argued that these methods do not examine actual occasioned discourse. The ecological validity of the translations suggested above may be questioned. However, this is not a loss if the objective is to identify discursive norms which constrain the interpretations which people may give, as was the case in the anger studies. In the Northern Ireland study, a good deal of discourse about 'troubles' victims and the 'troubles' generally was elicited. Although this discourse was interesting and sometimes moving, it gave no indication of the *unexpected* discursive norm which underlies responses to 'troubles' victims. Similarly, unexpected conventions were found in some of the anger studies. Where the underlying convention is opaque to both researcher and research participants, it will not be found through qualitative analysis. Yet these conventions which constrain our interpretations, but are outside conscious awareness, are of considerable psychological interest, and reflect directly on the construction of meaning and discourse.

Using quantitative methods to analyse discourse

As the previous discussion should have made clear, quantitative methods are of use when it is possible that conventions constrain discourse in a way which is not accessible to ordinary linguistic or scholarly competence. There are two aspects to using quantitative methods to analyse discourse: the quantitative methods used, and the salience of the questionnaire or other method of data collection.

There are a variety of quantitative techniques which identify patterns in data: multi-dimensional scaling, cluster analysis, network analysis, repertory grids, methods such as factor analysis and multiple regression which are based on correlation. These techniques have been used to explore structures of attitudes or perceptions of causation (see for instance, Lunt, 1988), but have not so far been used with methods of data collection which allow the emergence of discursive, as opposed to semantic, norms. These techniques are suitable for exploring static norms but are not suitable for examining extended patterns of discourse.

A more difficult question is the design of appropriate questionnaires. The researcher has to rely on her/his intuitions as a member of the community, supplemented by knowledge of relevant previous analyses of the discourse. It is of particular importance to be aware of relevant semantic analyses. It is necessary that the questionnaire is sufficiently open and flexible to find any patterns which are there. It is likely that very clear patterns are only found in discursive issues which are a focus of public interest. In general, these patterns are likely to be found in issues in which there is social conflict or conflicts of interest, particularly conflicts which are concealed. Where several discourses may exist, larger samples than are usual in psychology must be used. When concealed discursive norms are found, it would be desirable, if feasible, to continue research by discussing the norms and their function with research participants. This should throw light on how the norm translates into discourse outside the experimental setting, and should also elicit discourse which is of interest in itself.

There is a risk that no norm or no discursive pattern of any interest will be found. This is always a risk in research, particularly if the research is exploratory. It may be advisable to structure the study so that other questions can be addressed simultaneously.

Although this approach involves some risk, the rewards are considerable. The identification and description of discursive norms is of intrinsic interest and can be used to guide further exploration of the particular discourse. In addition this approach opens up questions about the modes of social influence which are involved in constructing (or changing) these norms, and so helps ground discourse analysis in social process research.

9 Pictorial Discourse and Learning

Sandra L. Calvert

The focus of most methodology, including the chapters presented in this book thus far, has been upon verbal, discursive approaches. When one examines children's memory, however, studies using verbal inquiries alone are insufficient to tap into their stores of knowledge. Researchers in this area must develop methods of enquiry that adequately reflect the quality of children's initial comprehension as well as the extent of their subsequent memory, the tools for which are predominantly iconic. Language, a key skill that is required for there to be any point in asking another person what they know, is relatively undeveloped in the repertoire of abilities mastered by young children. Thus, we have often underestimated children's knowledge because we were not sensitive to the competencies that children actually have.

The purpose of this chapter is to describe a range of discursive skills that children have other than the purely verbal, and then to build upon that repertoire of skills to develop methods to tap into their 'stores' of knowledge. To illustrate the conceptual and methodological issues involved in broadening the range of discursive skills drawn on in developmental inquiries, linguistic and non-linguistic interactions can be constructed within television and video contexts. I shall illustrate these methods with some examples.

The development of communicative skills

As children develop, their ways of displaying their knowledge shift from relatively concrete forms of expression to more abstract ones. Both Vygotsky (1962) and Piaget (Flavell, 1963) assumed that thought was prelinguistic. According to Vygotsky (1962), speech and thought began their development independently. As capacities for speech are acquired, language and thought coalesce, the former shaping the latter. Other skills contribute to the structuring of thought, particularly those involved in the manipulation of material objects.

For Piaget, too, thought is grounded in action (Flavell, 1963). Children first use tactile and kinetic body representations of what they know, then visual ones, and finally they come to use linguistic expressions. Thought is aetiologically prior to language, since it is, as one might say, a 'secretion' of the active brain and nervous system. The acquisition of symbol systems, including language, brings about a major transformation in possibilities for developing patterns of thought through the manipulation of the symbols themselves.

One of the early behavioural manifestations of symbolic thought can be observed in children's play. Symbolic play is literally thought in action. By enacting the roles of others, such as 'mommy' and 'daddy', children actively demonstrate a certain level of understanding of those people. Symbolic play has both an imitative element, as manifested in attempts to 'copy' the activities of others, and an imaginative element, as manifested in attempts to integrate what is known within their pre-existing knowledge structure. Language is also an integral aspect of play episodes, as children participate actively in re-creating patterns of discourse typical of the kinds of episodes they encounter in play. Hence, symbolic play combines physical and linguistic forms of representations in a mode that is easily rehearsed and understood by young children. Imitation, in this instance, becomes an active symbolic, behavioural representation of another's actions.

There are at least two major kinds of knowledge that a person can acquire. There is 'knowledge how', one's repertoire of skills. Piaget's discussion of symbolic play is an instance of 'knowledge how', for children display their practical capacities in their use of symbolic activity. Then there is 'knowledge that', one's store of what we could loosely and non-technically call 'information'. Bruner et al. (1968) described three levels or ways in which information, in this sense, can be represented: enactive (e.g. with the body), iconic (e.g. with pictures) and symbolic (e.g. with words). These three ways parallel Piaget's indices, symbols and signs as representational devices. During development, children begin by using enactive forms of representation (indices), then change to iconic ones (symbols), and finally adopt symbolic devices (signs). Elements can also be combined. For example, for Bruner et al. (1968) symbolic play could be considered a combination of enactive and symbolic representational forms.

Bruner's icons and Piaget's symbols are concrete and easily used by young children. Icons include both pictorial and echoic forms. The comparatively abstract language system is called a symbol by Bruner and is a sign for Piaget. Language systems, by nature, are arbitrary in their use of representational forms, a characteristic that allows users to represent abstract thoughts, but which also requires more competence by a child than the use of more primitive icons.

At this point, a subtle and important point must be made. Adopting the term 'representation' for what a child does with an action (an icon or a symbol), we may seem to imply that knowledge exists independently of the action, icon or symbol which merely 'represents' it. That is not so. When we talk of a senator 'representing' his constituents in Congress, there are two existents, the senator and the constituents, the former representing or standing in for the latter. But in the matter of thought, there is no knowledge in the absence of some sort of representation. For this reason, some psychologists prefer the term 'expression' to describe the relation between a sign and what it conveys (Budd, 1989).

The premise upon which a great deal of empirical research is based is that young children tend to think in visual, echoic forms that are relatively concrete (Huston and Wright, 1983). When language is used, it too reflects concrete rather than abstract qualities of what is known. Therefore, the focus of this chapter will be on the use of icons as devices that children use to express concrete information they have acquired about specific things.

In the concept of discursive representation of knowledge, 'discursive' must refer to something broader than just language use. There are many non-verbal ways that knowledge is represented. It follows that icons are a particularly appropriate means to tap very young children's conceptual capacities, their pre-linguistic cognitive skills. Because television is an audiovisual medium that relies upon the representational competencies of viewers and listeners for comprehension and memory, research in that area will be used to explore how information presented in visual and musical forms can be used to elicit children's verbal comments, thereby providing a window into their thoughts, by utilizing iconic, echoic and verbal discursive capacities.

Comprehension and memory

When researchers ask what children understand, they are examining the realm of comprehension. Comprehension refers to 'online' processing of information; it refers to what children understand as they deal with information at a specific moment.

If a piece of information is to remain available to someone, it must be remembered. It is in the realm of memory that representational forms or modes of expression are particularly relevant. Researchers assess the retention of information immediately after exposure to a task (short-term memory), after a delay (long-term memory) and after extended delays (very long-term memory). Tasks that require delayed memory are usually administered a few days, weeks or months after exposure to some stimulus. Very long-term memory tasks are administered years later (Calvert and Tart, 1993). In the latter case, we may be interested in knowing what an adult remembers from childhood.

Active constructions of one's memories, based on what one has done, can be observed in linguistic interactions (Harré, 1992). The discursive presentation of a memory reflects not just what happened, but how what happened is interpreted by the person who remembers it. Thus, what children remember, and what they forget, tells us something about what is important, and thus memorable, to them. Children, like everyone else, distort information and remember events differently from how they really happened, perhaps to preserve their own concepts of how the world should operate (Martin and Halverson, 1981). This activity is called schematic processing, whereby a child's expectations guide perception, memory and even inferences about content (Fiske and Taylor, 1984). This phenomenon has been shown to be widespread even amongst the most sophisticated scientific researchers (Gilbert and Mulkay, 1982).

Two lines of research have emerged that share overlapping methodologies, but which target either comprehension or memory as the issue of concern. Initial comprehension of information is necessary, but not sufficient, for subsequent accurate recollections. However, all information is filtered through a person's knowledge base, and all knowledge reflects active constructions of that content, be it at the exact moment that information is encountered or at a later time.

Assessments of comprehension: how much does a child know?

Active engagement

Individual attention   Consider a child who is watching television in their living-room. That child actively 'processes' that television programme, based on the schemata brought to the viewing situation (Anderson and Lorch, 1983; Huston and Wright, 1983). One way to tell that children are actively engaged in televiewing is to observe their visual attention to the dynamic audiovisual images that pervade their homes. From the early years, children selectively attend to information-bearing aspects of the presentation, based on programme comprehensibility and personal interests (Anderson and Lorch, 1983). Young children, for example, rarely watch the news, a format that presents abstract dialogue with content that has little perceived relevance to children's worlds. However, they will look up from their play when they hear a peculiar voice or a theme song from a children's programme like 'Sesame Street'. Auditory features can serve as signals to children that comprehensible content is coming, and they guide their attention accordingly (Huston and Wright, 1983).

Drawing another's attention   One activity that children engage in while viewing television is playing with siblings and friends. When an interesting visual event appears on the screen, children will sometimes talk about it (Rice, 1981). They point at the screen and tell their friends to look. Sometimes they let their viewing partner know that something funny is about to happen. A simple example of a 'sign of comprehension' is when children laugh at televised events that are meant to be funny, or even at incidents that amuse only them. We know that they are comprehending some of the meaning of those events – even if what's funny to them is not the same as what amuses adults.

Methodological illustration: verbal and non-verbal discursive modes

'Barney and Friends' is a recently developed television programme that attempts to elicit active participation from young children. In this series, a small group of children join Barney, an imaginary dinosaur, at the school playground.

'Barney' embeds cognitive concepts relevant to education, such as the A,B,C, and social concepts, such as different kinds of families, within stories and songs. To assess the effect of this programme on children, we need to find out: (1) what they understand of the story as they are watching it; and (2) what they understand of the concept that the programme makers are trying to teach. 'Online' observations of Barney's viewers can tap into both areas by examining: (1) what children say or ask as they view the programme; (2) the songs that children spontaneously sing with Barney; and (3) activities, such as dancing, that children in the viewing audience do with Barney. The observational basis for exploring the initial content that children selectively attend to and attempt to comprehend should include singing and dancing as forms of discursive presentation. By the same technique, we can gain information about how that content may initially be stored in memory. Children who are dancing are using enactive body movements to express the content. Those who sing the words are using a combination of echoic and symbolic forms to understand the content. Those who use words only, such as asking questions, are actively attempting to understand the programme story, the educationally relevant messages, or both, using verbal discourse alone.

The discursive modes employed seem to be related to the mode by which matters of interest are presented to them. If children talk about the actions of programme characters, then visual events may be most interesting to them. If, by contrast, they ask about character motivations, then they are going beyond the information given and thinking about abstract programme events. Children may also integrate programme content with their own life when they tell others that similar events have happened to them. By studying the spontaneous activities of child viewers, observers can gain a wealth of information about initial comprehension of programme content.

Movies, too, are dynamic visual presentations that elicit talk from children. Children actively attempt to understand the complex stories that they view. How do we know? Go to an early evening showing of any children's movie and listen. Young viewers, who have not yet learned the rules of etiquette for movie attendance, ask streams of questions: 'Who is that man? What is he doing? Why did he jump out of the window?' Parents, in reply, whisper answers to these many questions and add 'Shhh' to the verbal exchange. The stream of questions tells us many things about the young viewer. First, the programme is difficult to understand. Even character names and their actions are hard to follow. The motivations of characters are unknown. Hence, the reasons for their actions, which set the stage of the story, are a mystery. Second, the child is actively asking relevant questions which should aid story comprehension. Although the child doesn't know the answers, the child does know what to ask. Children's questions tell us what they do and do not understand. Comprehension, or the lack thereof, reveals itself when one listens to what children want to know.

Children's memory of content

Assessments of how much is remembered are typically used in television research because experimenters want to know what children take away from a viewing situation. Hence, a common research strategy is to show the entire television programme and then assess how much of the content the children remember after viewing. Because remembering is a cognitive and constructive activity, we tend to remember information that is in keeping with our prior knowledge and with our expectations (Collins, 1983). Among the fully linguistically competent, conversation about alleged remembered events is crucial in confirming or disconfirming memories (Middleton and Edwards, 1993), and this interactive skill must have its beginnings in less overtly linguistic practices.

The form of information presentation also interacts with how children will represent and later retrieve a memory. In general, visual information is best remembered in a visual form and verbal information is best remembered in a verbal form (Calvert et al., 1987). The implication is that both visual and auditory retrieval tasks are necessary to find out what children remember after viewing a television programme. Thus, it is methodologically vital to match the sensory mode of the retrieval task to the mode in which the programme content is presented.

Free recall: the verbatim verbal narrative form

In free recall tasks, often used as an initial assessment of what is remembered, visual prompts are rarely used. In free recall tasks, an experimenter may ask a child to *tell* them what they can remember from the programme, a wholly verbal test. Sometimes the experimenter asks a child to pretend to tell the story to a friend who hasn't seen the television programme. When transcribing the thoughts of nine- or ten-year-old children, this approach often produces writer's cramp on the part of the experimenter, so voluble are they. For three- or four-year-old children, however, heavy breathing is often the extent of their auditory responses. Thus, we can be misled about how much children remember if the only discursive mode employed is verbal.

When asked to retell a story, children may tell you everything that they can remember (quantity), or they may focus on the important aspects of the story (quality). How much one can recall and the quality of that recall are related but not equivalent assessments. If a child says nothing, for example, memory for both quantity and quality of story content is scored low. Obviously, the quantity and quality of recall in the verbal discursive mode tends to be better for older than for younger children.

By middle childhood, most children are capable of describing a story in words. Some of these children tell you virtually everything that happened in a story, but do not discriminate between the important and irrelevant aspects of the story line as adults interpret the narrative (but see Adams, 1979 for a comparison between adult assessments of what is important, and a four-year-old's compared with a two-year-old's). Some children remember much of the programme content, but the quality of that recall is not so good. We all, for example, have spoken to someone who talks and talks, but who actually says very little. By contrast, other children tell you the important aspects of the programme, the content that is essential in understanding the story as we understand it. These children do not mince words. For instance, a ten-year-old boy once told me 'You can't judge a book by its cover.' He conveyed the abstract point of the story without having to relate any story details. Children like him may say less than their peers in terms of total word output, but may say more in terms of the quality of that output as assessed by adult standards.

Singing: the verbatim, musical narrative form

Generally, young children's verbatim recall of verbal information is relatively poor. Verbatim memories of songs appear to be the exception to this rule, perhaps because both verbal and musical forms are used to present and to retrieve the linguistic content. The musical structure of a familiar song has been shown to improve recall of the exact words for very long periods. For instance, young adults who repeatedly heard a song about the 'Preamble to the Constitution' when they were children recalled the text much better than did those who had heard the song infrequently (Calvert and Tart, 1993).

The integration of musical and linguistic narrative structures can facilitate memory of content. Although tunes can be remembered independently of the words, words are almost always integrated with a tune when remembering takes place. For instance, children can hum or whistle a tune, but rarely do children speak the words of a song: they sing them. Moreover, adults report that they 'hear' a song play repeatedly in their heads, an echoic form of representation (Calvert and Tart, 1993).

Even so, verbatim recall does not ensure comprehension of the message. For instance, pre-school children were shown a video depiction of the song 'Frère Jacques' (Calvert et al., 1993). On the visual track, a friar was initially in bed asleep, then church bells ring, then he opens his eyes with the ringing bells in the background, and finally he stretches his arms as he wakes up. The song was played at the same time. After viewing the vignette, children were asked to sing the song and then to tell the story, using pictures as guides. One young boy sang the French lyrics perfectly. His verbatim recall was exactly right. But his story focused on the man singing (which was not the case) and revealed no awareness that this was a wake-up song. His verbal discourse illustrates that verbatim recall is not necessarily a good measure of degree of comprehension.

Picture sequencing: the pictorial narrative form

Pictorial events, extracted from the visual track of a television story, can be used to explore how much children remember of the sequence of programme events and how well they remember the meaning of events in the frame of the story. Understanding how events in a sequence are linked is crucial for an accurate memory of what happened, since stories involve both cause–effect and reason–result sequences (Collins, 1983).

Visual sequencing formats are similar to those used in comic strips (Calvert, 1992). The child's ordering of pictures tells us about the sequential structure of a particular visual narrative as the child conceives it to be. Once sequenced, this visual structure can then be used to elicit verbal retellings of the story. However, picture sequencing can be treated as an autonomous discursive mode and can provide an index of purely visual memories.

Picture sequencing tasks can also provide qualitative assessments of children's memory skills. By middle childhood, some children are capable of describing 'how they know' the correct order. For instance, a ten-year-old boy told me that he could 'rewatch the pictures in his head'. His verbal gloss indicated not only the visual form of this memory, but the dynamic nature of that form. His description tells of his meta-memory skills: that is, he knew 'how' he remembered (i.e. by rewatching moving pictures), not just 'what' he remembered (i.e. the story content).

Multiple-choice recognition: the verbal narrative form

Children remember more of the important story information, particularly the implied content, when televised events are presented in verbal action sequences than in verbal non-action sequences (Calvert et al., 1982). This finding suggests that memory of implicit content is facilitated by visual, moving forms of presentation.

By contrast, when verbal information is presented via a televised song, neither children nor adults remembered factual content well, as indexed by a multiple-choice task (Calvert et al., 1991; 1993). One explanation for these findings is that songs lead to superficial processing of information (Calvert et al., 1993). More specifically, Craik and Lockhart (1972) developed a levels-of-processing approach in which they argued that information could be processed at either superficial or deeper levels. Applied to the area of songs, children may focus on the superficial phonic level (sound) rather than on the deeper semantic level (meaning) of the lyrics. In this view, children and adults may sing the words of a song mindlessly with little thought to the message embedded within the song. The earlier example from 'Frère Jacques' illustrates this point.

Many third-grade children (eight or nine years of age) could sing parts of the song from a presentation 'I'm Just a Bill', and even sequence some of the steps by which a bill becomes a law (Calvert and Pfordresher, 1994). However, when asked 'What is a bill?', a common response was that a bill was something that you pay. This illustrates that the type of memory measure employed yields different answers to the question of what children understand and that children sometimes process songs without thinking about the information.

Superficial processing of songs is not the rule, however. Consider, for example, the following responses from a third-grade boy who clearly understood much of the conceptual information presented in the song. 'I' represents the interviewer, and 'C' represents the child.

> *I*: OK. Can you remember how we watched the TV show? Do you remember anything they said or sang exactly? Do you remember any of the words?
> *C*: I'm just a bill. I'm only a bill.
> I'm sitting here on the Hill.
> Well it's a long long journey
> to the Capital City.
> A long long wait sitting in committee.
> If the President doesn't sign me that's a veto.
> Very unlikely I'll become a law.
> President signs him and then he's a law.
> *I*: OK. Can you tell me what a bill is?
> *C*: It's a thing, a law people vote on.
> *I*: OK. Can you tell me how a bill becomes a law?
> *C*: People think of an idea. Their Congressman takes the idea to Washington where they vote on it. If the President signs it, it becomes a law.

The verbal responses of this child reveal that he is thinking about the televised song that he has been watching. He remembers quite a bit of the song that he has heard. He has a concept of what a bill is. And he can sequence the basic steps that are required for a bill to become a law. From this basic structure, he can later elaborate and add details that he already 'knows'. For example, his verbatim recall of the song indicates knowledge that the President can veto a bill, but he does not remember the information that Congress can override the veto. Such additional information can be added as he views the vignette in the future, or when he encounters this information in a class at his school. An interesting question for future consideration is: why do some children, like this boy, think about the meaning of a song while others sing the same song mindlessly?

Symbolic play: the verbal enactive narrative form

A final way that researchers can tap into young children's stores of knowledge is through their symbolic play. In symbolic play, children can re-create television stories by imitating the actions and interactions of the characters. Many times these displays of knowledge are spontaneous, occurring after children have viewed an interesting television programme. By rehearsing the story in their play, children are bringing their own knowledge to bear on the content that they viewed. Distortions of the story occur, reflecting the gap between a child's knowledge base and the content that was presented. Note, however, that children are displaying what is important to them, even if it is not exactly what the producer of the programme intended. Researchers can study children's enactive modes of story representation by observing their symbolic play in settings like day care or pre-school. For example, in the mid 1990s many young children in the US were displaying karate moves in their imaginative play, an outcome reflecting their viewing and imitation of the character actions on the popular American television programme, 'Mighty Morphin Power Rangers'.

Another way that researchers can tap into children's story representations is by having children play with toys that are similar to those that have been viewed on television. The researcher attempts to have the child re-create the story by enacting the plot with these toys (Smith et al., 1985). Children talk as they play, thereby providing an enactive and verbal symbolic re-creation of their thoughts. These methods are particularly useful with children who are two to five years of age, the age at which symbolic play is a dominant form of thought (Flavell, 1963).

Conclusion

The purpose of this chapter was to show the methodological enrichment that is achieved by making use of discursive modes other than the purely verbal. I have illustrated this with some examples of visual, echoic and enactive retrieval methods in relation to children's modes for expressing how much they understand and remember of the content of a television programme. The fact that children display their initial comprehension of story content through their verbal exchanges and non-verbal spontaneous activities strongly suggests that methodology should take this up as part of investigative techniques.

Children's memories reflect how information was initially understood and expressed in relation to the specific demands of a particular retrieval task. Because initial storage may predetermine the form in which recollection will be displayed, what children 'know' and 'remember' depends upon the discursive mode employed and the particular method used to tap into that knowledge base. The study of televised songs highlights the importance of using several techniques to understand children's initial comprehension and later recollection of what they have experienced.

As researchers, we make inferences about what children do and do not know. If these inferences are based on verbal methods of inquiry, as they often are, we are in danger of missing a large segment of what has been remembered and understood. We must remember that our conclusions about children's knowledge are only as good as the research methods that we employ. The fact that children spontaneously use a wide range of discursive modes, including singing, dancing, imaginative play and picture play of various sorts, ought to have a profound influence on our choice of investigative methods.

Note

I would like to thank Ben Titus for his verbal comments.

References

Abraham, C. (1988) 'Seeing the connection in lay causal comprehension: a return to Heider', in D.J. Hilton (ed.), *Contemporary Science and Natural Explanation: Commonsense Conceptions of Causality*. Brighton: Harvester, pp. 145–74.

Adams, J. (1979) *The Conspiracy of the Text: the Place of Narrative in the Development of Thought*. London: Routledge.

Anderson, D.R. and Lorch, E.P. (1983) 'Looking at television: action or reaction', in D.R. Anderson and J. Bryant (eds), *Children's Understanding of Television: Research on Attention and Comprehension*. New York: Academic Press.

Antaki, C. (1985) 'Attribution and evaluation in ordinary explanations of voting intention', *British Journal of Social Psychology*, 24: 141–51.

Antaki, C. (1988) 'Structures of belief and justification', in C. Antaki (ed.), *Analysing Lay Explanation: a Casebook of Methods*. London: Sage, pp. 60–73.

Antaki, C. and Naji, S. (1987) 'Events explained in conversational "because" statements', *British Journal of Social Psychology*, 26: 119–26.

Ariès, Phillipe (1981) *The Hour of our Death*. New York: Knopf.

Armon-Jones, C. (1986) 'The social function of emotion', in R. Harré (ed.), *The Social Construction of Emotion*. Oxford: Basil Blackwell, pp. 57–82.

Atkinson, J.M. (1978) *Discovering Suicide: Studies in the Social Organization of Sudden Death*. London: Macmillan.

Atkinson, J.M. and Drew, P. (1979) *Order in Court: the Organization of Verbal Interaction in Judicial Settings*. London: Macmillan.

Atkinson, J.M. and Heritage, J. (eds) (1984) *Structures of Social Action: Studies in Conversation Analysis*. Cambridge: Cambridge University Press.

Au, T.K. (1986) 'A verb is worth a thousand words: the causes and consequences of interpersonal events implicit in language', *Journal of Memory and Language*, 25: 104–22.

Austin, J.L. (1962) *How to Do Things with Words*. Oxford: Clarendon Press.

Austin, J.L. (1970) 'A plea for excuses', in J.O. Urmson (ed.), *Philosophical Papers*. Oxford: Clarendon Press.

Averill, J.R. (1979) 'Anger', in R. Dienstbier (ed.), *Nebraska Symposium on Motivation*, vol. 26, pp. 1–81.

Averill, J.R. (1980) 'A constructionist view of emotion', in R. Plutchik and H. Kellerman (eds), *Emotion: Theory, Research and Experience. Vol. 1: Theories of Emotion*. Boston: Academic Press.

Averill, J.R. (1982) *Anger and Aggression: an Essay on Emotion*, New York: Springer.

Averill, J.R. (1985) 'The social construction of emotion, with special reference to love', in K.J. Gergen and K.E. Davis (eds), *The Social Construction of the Person*. New York: Springer.

Backmann, C. (1977) 'Explorations in psychoethics: the warranting of judgements', in R. Harré (ed.), *Life Sentences*. Chichester: Wiley.

Bailey, F.G. (1983) *The Tactical Uses of Passion*. Ithaca, NY: Cornell University Press.

Barsalou, L.W. (1988) 'The content and organization of autobiographical memories', in U. Neisser and E. Winograd (eds), *Remembering Reconsidered: Ecological and Traditional Approaches*. Cambridge: Cambridge University Press.

Bartlett, F.C. (1932) *Remembering: a Study in Experimental and Social Psychology*. Cambridge: Cambridge University Press.

Basso, K. (1988) '"Speaking with names": language and landscape among the western Apache', *Cultural Anthropology*, 3: 99–130.

Berger, P. and Luckman, T. (1966) *The Social Construction of Reality*. Harmondsworth: Penguin.

Billig, M. (1982) *Ideology and Social Psychology*. Oxford: Blackwell.

Billig, M. (1985) 'Prejudice, categorization and particularization: from a perceptual to a rhetorical approach', *European Journal of Social Psychology*, 15: 79–103.

Billig, M. (1987) *Arguing and Thinking: a Rhetorical Approach to Social Psychology*. Cambridge: Cambridge University Press.

Bogen, D. and Lynch, M. (1989) 'Taking account of the hostile native: plausible deniability and the production of conventional history in the Iran–Contra hearings', *Social Problems*, 36: 197–224.

Bower, T.G.R. (1977) *A Primer of Infant Development*. San Francisco: W.H. Freeman.

Bransford, J.D. and Johnson, M.K. (1972) 'Contextual prerequisites for understanding: some investigations of comprehension and recall', *Journal of Verbal Learning and Verbal Behaviour*, 11: 717–26.

Briggs, Jean (1970) *Never in Anger: Portrait of an Eskimo Family*. Cambridge, MA: Harvard University Press.

Brown, R. (1986) *Social Psychology* (2nd edn). New York: Free Press.

Brown, R. and Fish, D. (1983) 'The psychological causality implicit in language', *Cognition*, 14: 237–73.

Bruner, J.S. (1976) 'Peekaboo and the learning of rule structures', in J.S. Bruner, A. Jolly and K. Sylva (eds), *Play: its Role in Development and Evolution*. Harmondsworth: Penguin.

Bruner, J.S., Olver, R.R. and Greenfield, P.M. (1968) *Studies in Cognitive Growth*. New York: Wiley.

Budd, M. (1989) *Wittgenstein's Philosophy of Psychology*. New York: Routledge.

Burleson, B.R. (1986) 'Attribution schemas and causal inference in natural conversation', in D.G. Ellis and W.A. Donohue (eds), *Contemporary Issues in Language and Discourse Processes*. Hillsdale, NJ: Erlbaum, pp. 63–85.

Burns, L. and Stevens, R. (1988) *Most Excellent Majesty*. Pittsfield, MA: Berkshire Land Trust and Conservation Fund.

Button, G. and Lee, J.R.E. (eds) (1987) *Talk and Social Organization*. Clevedon: Multilingual Matters.

Calvert, S.L. (1992) 'Pictorial prompts for discursive analyses: developmental considerations and methodological innovations', *American Behavioral Scientist*, 36: 39–51.

Calvert, S.L., Huston, A.C., Watkins, B.A. and Wright, J.C. (1982) 'The relation between selective attention to television forms and children's comprehension of content', *Child Development*, 53: 601–10.

Calvert, S.L., Huston, A.C. and Wright, J.C. (1987) 'The effects of television preplay formats on children's attention and story comprehension', *Journal of Applied Developmental Psychology*, 8: 329–42.

Calvert, S.L., Jarmain, N. and Gomes, A. (1993) 'Preschoolers' recitation versus understanding of a televised song', poster session presented at the biennial meeting of the Society for Research in Child Development, New Orleans, Louisiana.

Calvert, S.L. and Pfordresher, P.Q. (1994) 'Impact of a televised song on students' memory of information', poster session presented at the annual meeting of the American Psychological Association, Los Angeles, CA.

Calvert, S.L., Rigaud, E. and Mazzulla, J. (1991) 'Presentational features for students' recall of televised educational content', poster session presented at the biennial meeting of the Society for Research in Child Development, Seattle, Washington.

Calvert, S.L. and Tart, M. (1993) 'Song versus prose forms for students' very long-term, long-term, and short-term verbatim recall', *Journal of Applied Developmental Psychology*, 14: 245–60.

Carbaugh, D. (1988) *Talking American*. Norwood, NJ: Ablex.

Carbaugh, D. (1992) '"The mountain" and "the project": dueling depictions of a natural environment', in J. Cantrill and C. Oravec (eds), *Conference on the Discourse of Environmental Advocacy*. Salt Lake City: University of Utah Humanities Center, pp. 360–76.

Carbaugh, D. (1994) 'Personhood, positioning, and cultural pragmatics: American dignity in cross-cultural perspective', in S. Deetz (ed.), *Communication Yearbook 17*. Newbury Park, CA: Sage, pp. 159–86.

Carbaugh, D. (1996) *Situating Selves: The Communication of Social Identities in American Scenes*. Albany, NY: State University of New York Press.

Carbaugh, D. (in press) 'The ethnography of communication', in D. Cushman (ed.), *Watershed Theories of Human Communication*. Albany, NY: State University of New York Press.

Carbaugh, D. (forthcoming) 'Naturalizing communication and culture', in J. Cantrill and C. Oravec (eds), *Environmental Discourse*. Lexington, KY: University of Kentucky Press.

Chomsky, N. (1959) 'Review of B.F. Skinner's "Verbal Behavior"', *Language*, 35: 26–58.

Clanton, G. (1989) 'Jealousy in American culture 1945–1985: reflections from popular literature', in D.D. Franks and E.D. McCarthy (eds), *The Sociology of Emotions: Original Essays and Research Papers*. Greenwich, CT: JAI Press.

Clark, H.H. (1985) 'Language and language users', in G. Lindzey and E. Aronson (eds), *Handbook of Social Psychology* (3rd edn). Vol. 2. New York: Random House, pp. 179–231.

Clarke, D.D. and Crossland, J. (1985) *Action Systems*. London: Methuen.

Cody, M.J. and McLaughlin, M.L. (1988) 'Accounts on trial: oral arguments in traffic court', in C. Antaki (ed.), *Analysing Everyday Explanation: a Casebook of Methods*. London: Sage, pp. 113–26.

Cole, M. (1975) 'Ethnographic psychology of cognition', in R.W. Brislin, S. Bochner and W.J. Lonner (eds), *Cross-Cultural Perspectives on Learning*. New York: Wiley. Reprinted in *The Making of Psychological Anthropology* and in P.N. Johnson-Laird and P.C. Wason (eds), *Thinking: Readings in Cognitive Science*. New York: Cambridge University Press, 1977.

Cole, M. and Means, B. (1981) *Comparative Studies in How People Think: a Introduction*. Cambridge, MA: Harvard University Press.

Cole, M. and Scribner, S. (1976) 'Theorizing about the socialization of cognition', in Theodore Schwartz (ed.), *Socialization as Cultural Communication*. Berkeley: University of California Press.

Collins, W.A. (1983) 'Interpretation and inference in children's television viewing', in D.R. Anderson and J. Bryant (eds), *Children's Understanding of Television: Research on Attention and Comprehension*. New York: Academic Press.

Cook, G. (1990) 'Transcribing infinity: problems of context presentation', *Journal of Pragmatics*, 14: 1–24.

Corbin, Alain (1986) *The Foul and the Fragrant: Odor and French Social Imagination*. Cambridge, MA: Harvard University Press.

Cornelius, R.R. (1984) 'A rule model of adult emotional expression', in C.Z. Malatesta and C.E. Izard (eds), *Emotion in Adult Development*. Beverley Hills, CA: Sage.

Costall, A. and Still, A. (1987) *Cognitive Psychology in Question*. Brighton: Harvester Press.

Craik, F.I. and Lockhart, R.S. (1972) 'Levels of processing: a framework for memory research', *Journal of Learning and Verbal Behavior*, 11: 671–84.

Crowle, A.J. (1990) 'IDKWIDI' in R. Bhaskar (ed.) *Harré and his Critics*, Oxford: Blackwell.

Culler, J. (1982) *Saussure*. London: Fontana.

Davidson, J. (1984) 'Subsequent versions of invitations, offers, requests and proposals dealing with potential or actual rejection', in J.M. Atkinson and J.C. Heritage (eds), *Structures of Social Action: Studies in Conversation Analysis*. Cambridge: Cambridge University Press, pp. 102–28.

Drew, P. (1984) 'Speakers' reportings of invitation sequences', in J.M. Atkinson and J.C. Heritage (eds), *Structures of Social Action: Studies in Conversation Analysis*. Cambridge: Cambridge University Press, pp. 129–51.

Drew, P. (1990) 'Strategies in the contest between lawyers and witnesses', in J.N. Levi and A.G. Walker (eds), *Language in the Judicial Process*. New York: Plenum, pp. 39–64.

Drew, P. and Holt, E. (1988) 'Complainable matters: the use of idiomatic expressions in making complaints', *Social Problems*, 35: 398–417.

Edwards, D. and Mercer, N.M. (1987) *Common Knowledge: the Development of Understanding in the Classroom*. London: Methuen.

Edwards, D. and Mercer, N.M. (1989) 'Reconstructing context: the conventionalization of classroom knowledge', *Discourse Processes*, 12: 91–104.

Edwards, D. and Middleton, D. (1986) 'Joint remembering: constructing an account of shared experience through conversational discourse', *Discourse Processes*, 9 (4): 423–59.

Edwards, D. and Middleton, D. (1987) 'Conversation and remembering: Bartlett revisited', *Applied Cognitive Psychology*, 1, 77–92.

Edwards, D. and Potter, J. (1992) *Discursive Psychology*. London: Sage.

Egerton, M. (1988) 'Passionate women and passionate men: sex differences in accounting for angry and weeping episodes', *British Journal of Social Psychology*, 27: 51–66.

Egerton, M. (1991) 'Sex differences in interpretations of emotions: a constructionist approach'. Thesis submitted for DPhil, Oxford University.

Egerton, M. and Lalljee, M. (1992) 'Gender and emotions: a critical review', under review.

Eimas, P.D. (1985) 'The perception of speech in early infancy', *Scientific American*, January: 46–52.

Emmison, M. (1989) 'A conversation on trial? The case of the Ananda Marga conspiracy tapes', *Journal of Pragmatics*, 13, 363–80.

Erneling, C. (1993) *Understanding Language Acquisition: the Framework of Learning*. Albany, NY: SUNY Press.

Fiedler, K., Semin, G.R. and Bolten, S. (1989) 'Language use and reification of social information: top-down and bottom-up processing in person cognition', *European Journal of Social Psychology*, 19: 271–95.

Fillmore, C.J. (1971) 'Types of lexical information', in D.D. Steinberg and L.A. Jakobovits (eds), *Semantics*. Cambridge: Cambridge University Press, pp. 370–92.

Fiske, S.T. and Taylor, S.E. (1984) *Social Cognition*. Reading, MA: Addison-Wesley.

Flavell, J. (1963) *The Developmental Psychology of Jean Piaget*. New York: Van Nostrand.

Frodi, A., Macauley, J. and Thome, P.R. (1977) 'Are women always less aggressive than men? A review of the experimental literature', *Psychological Bulletin*, 49: 634–60.

Garfinkel, H. (1967) *Studies in Ethnomethodology*. Englewood Cliffs, NJ: Prentice-Hall.

Garvey, C. and Caramazza, A. (1974) 'Implicit causality in verbs', *Linguistic Inquiry*, 5: 459–64.

Geertz, C. (1973) *The Interpretation of Cultures*. New York: Basic Books.

Gentner, D. (1983) 'Why nouns are learned before words: linguistic relativity vs. natural partitioning', in C. Kuczaj (ed.), *Language, Thought and Culture*. Hillsdale, NJ: Lawrence Erlbaum.

Gergen, K. (1985) 'The social constructionist movement in modern psychology', *American Psychologist*, 40: 266–75.

Gergen, M. (1988) 'Narrative structures in social explanation', in C. Antaki (ed.), *Analysing Lay Explanation: a Casebook of Methods*. London: Sage, pp. 94–112.

Gibson, J.J. (1966) *The Senses Considered as Perceptual Systems*. Boston: Houghton Mifflin.

Gibson, J.J. (1979) *The Ecological Approach to Visual Perception*. Boston: Houghton Mifflin.

Gilbert, G.N. and Mulkay, M. (1982) 'Warranting scientific beliefs', *Social Studies of Science*, 12: 383–408.

Gilbert, G.N. and Mulkay, M. (1984) *Opening Pandora's Box: a Sociological Analysis of Scientists' Discourse*. Cambridge: Cambridge University Press.

Goffman, E. (1967) *Interaction Ritual*. New York: Anchor Books.

Goffman, E. (1979) 'Footing', *Semiotica*, 25: 1–29.

Goode, W.J. (1975) 'The theoretical importance of love', in *The Practice of Love*. Englewood Cliffs, NJ: Prentice Hall.

Gray, H. (1978) 'Learning to take an object from the mother', in A. Lock (ed.), *Action, Gesture and Symbol: the Emergence of Language*. New York: Academic Press.

Greatbatch, D. (1986) 'Aspects of topical organization in news interviews: the use of agenda-shifting procedures by interviewees', *Media, Culture and Society*, 8: 44–56.

Grice, H.P. (1975) 'Logic and conversation', in P. Cole and J. Morgan (eds), *Syntax and Semantics 3: Speech Acts*. New York: Academic Press, pp. 41–58.

Griswold, Robert L. (1986) 'The evolution of the doctrine of mental cruelty in Victorian American divorce, 1790–1900', *Journal of Social History*, 20: 127–8.

Harré, R. (1984) *Personal Being: a Theory for Individual Psychology*. Cambridge, MA: Harvard University Press.

Harré, R. (1986a) 'An outline of the social constructionist viewpoint', in R. Harré (ed.), *The Social Construction of Emotion*. Oxford, Blackwell.

Harré, R. (ed.) (1986b) *The Social Construction of Emotion*. London: Blackwell.

Harré, R. (1991) 'The discursive production of selves', *Theory and Psychology*, L: 51–63.

Harré, R. (1992) 'Introduction: the second cognitive revolution', *American Behavioral Scientist*, 36: 5–7.

Harré, R., Clarke, D. and De Carlo, N. (1985) *Motives and Mechanisms*. London: Methuen.

Harvey, J.H., Turnquist, D.C. and Agostinelli, G. (1988) 'Identifying attributions in oral and written explanations', in C. Antaki (ed.), *Analysing Everyday Explanation: a Casebook of Methods*. London: Sage, pp. 32–42.

Harvey, J.H. and Weary, G. (1984) 'Current issues in attribution theory and research', *Annual Review of Psychology*, 35: 427–59.

Hatfield, Elaine, Cacioppo, J.T. and Rapson, R.C. (1992) 'Primitive emotional contagion', *Review of Personality*, 151–77.

Hattiangadi, J.N. (1987) *How is Language Possible?* LaSalle, IL: Open Court.

Haviland, S. and Clark, H.H. (1974) 'What's new? Acquiring new information as a process in comprehension', *Journal of Verbal Learning and Verbal Behavior*, 13: 512–21.

Heelas, P. and Lock, A. (eds) (1981) *Indigenous Psychologies*. New York: Academic Press.

Heider, F. (1958) *The Psychology of Interpersonal Relations*. New York: Wiley.

Herdt, G. (1982) 'Sambia nosebleeding and male proximity to women', *Ethos*, 10:3. Reprinted in J. Stigler, R.A. Shweder and G. Herdt (eds), *Cultural Psychology: Essays on Comparative Human Development*. New York: Cambridge University Press, 1990.

Herdt, G. (1987) *Guardians of the Flute: Idioms of Masculinity*. New York: Columbia University Press.

Heritage, J. (1984) *Garfinkel and Ethnomethodology*. Cambridge: Polity.

Heritage, J. and Watson, D.R. (1979) 'Formulations as conversational objects', in G. Psathas (ed.), *Everyday Language: Studies in Ethnomethodology*. New York: Irvington.

Hewstone, M. (1989) *Causal Attribution: from Cognitive Process to Collective Beliefs*. Oxford: Blackwell.

Hilton, D.J. (1990) 'Conversational processes and causal attribution', *Psychological Bulletin*, 107: 65–81.

Hilton, D.J. and Slugoski, B.R. (1986) 'Knowledge-based causal Attribution: the abnormal conditions focus model', *Psychological Review*, 93: 75–88.

Hochschild, Arlie Russel (1983) *The Managed Heart: Commercialization of Human Feeling*. Berkeley.

Hoffman, C. and Tchir, M.A. (1990) 'Interpersonal verbs and dispositional adjectives: the psychology of causality embodied in language', *Journal of Personality and Social Psychology*, 58: 765–78.

Howard, J.A. and Allen, C. (1989) 'Making meaning: revealing attributions through analyses of readers' responses', *Social Psychology Quarterly*, 52 (4): 280–98.

Huston, A.C. and Wright, J.C. (1983) 'Children's processing of television: the informative functions of formal features', in D.R. Anderson and J. Bryant (eds), *Children's Understanding of Television: Research on Attention and Comprehension*. New York: Academic Press.

Jackson, B.S. (1988) *Law, Fact and Narrative Coherence*. Merseyside: Deborah Charles.

Jacob, Herbert (1988) *Silent Revolution: the Transformation of Divorce Law in the United States*. Chicago.

Jayyusi, L. (1984) *Categories and the Moral Order*. London: Routledge.

Johnson, M. (1987) *The Body in the Mind*. Chicago: University of Chicago Press.

Johnson, T. (1991) 'Caring for the Earth: new activism among Hopi traditionals', *The Amicus Journal*, 13 (Winter): 22–7.

Kakar, S. (1981) *The Inner World: a Psycho-Analytic Study of Childhood and Society in India*. Delhi: Oxford University Press.

Kakar, S. (1982) *Shamans, Mystics and Doctors: a Psychological Inquiry into India and its Healing Traditions*. Boston: Boston Press.

Kakar, S. (1985) 'Psychoanalysis and non-Western cultures', *International Review of Psychoanalysis*, 12: 441–8.

Kakar, S. (1990) 'Stories from Indian psychoanalysis', in J.W. Stigler, R.A. Shweder and G. Herdt (eds), *Cultural Psychology: Essays on Comparative Human Development*. New York: Cambridge University Press.

Kakar, S. (1992) *The Analyst and the Mystic: Psychoanalytic Reflections on Religion and Mysticism*. Chicago: University of Chicago Press.

Kelley, H.H. (1967) 'Attribution theory in social psychology', in D. Levine (ed.), *Nebraska Symposium on Motivation*. Lincoln: University of Nebraska Press. Vol. 15, pp. 192–238.

Kemper, Theodore D. (1981) 'Social constructionist and positivist approaches to the sociology of emotions', *American Journal of Sociology*, 87: 336–62.

Kemper, Theodore D. (1987) 'How many emotions are there? Wedding the social and autonomic components', *American Journal of Sociology*, 93: 263–89.

Kenny, A. (1963) *Action, Emotion and Will*. London: Routledge and Kegan Paul.

Kilborne, B. and Langess, L.L. (1987) *Culture and Human Nature: Theoretical Papers of Melford E. Spiro*. Chicago: University of Chicago Press.

Kintsch, W. and Van Dijk, T.A. (1978) 'Toward a model of text comprehension and production', *Psychological Review*, 85 (5): 363–94.

Klein, D.F. (1981) 'Anxiety reconceptualized', in D.F. Klein and J.G. Rabkin (eds), *Anxiety, New Research and Changing Concepts*. New York: Raven Press.

Klein, D.F. (1988) 'Cybernetics, activation and drug effects', in R.H. Van den Hoofdakker (ed.), *Biological Measures: their Theoretical and Diagnostic Value in Psychiatry. Acta Psychiatrica Scandinavica*, 77, suppl. 341: 126–37.

Klein, D.F. and Rabkin, J.G. (eds) (1981) *Anxiety: New Research and Changing Concepts*. New York: Raven Press.

Konner, M.J. (1972) 'Aspects of the developmental ethology of a foraging people', in N.J. Blurton Jones (ed.), *Ethnological Studies of Child Behavior*. London: Cambridge University Press.

Kramer, P.D. (1993) *Listening to Prozac*. New York: Viking.

Kuczaj II, S.A. (1982) 'On the nature of syntactic development', in S.A. Kuczaj (ed.), *Language Development. Vol. 1: Syntax and Semantics*. Hillsdale, NJ: Erlbaum.

LaBarre, Weston (1987) 'The cultural basis of emotion and gestures', *Journal of Personality*, 16: 48–68.

Lalljee, M. (1981) 'Attribution theory and the analysis of explanations', in C. Antaki (ed.), *The Psychology of Ordinary Explanations*. New York: Academic Press, pp. 119–38.

Lange, J. (1990) 'Refusal to compromise: the case of Earth First!', *Western Journal of Speech Communication*, 54: 473–94. *Communication Monographs*, 60, 239–57.

Lange, J. (1993) 'The logic of competing information campaigns: conflict over old growth and the spotted owl', *Communication Monographs*, 60: 239–57.

Latour, B. (1987) *Science in Action*. Milton Keynes: Open University Press.

Lazarus, R.S., Speisman, J.C. and Mordkoff, A.M. (1964) 'Experimental analysis of a film used as a threatening stimulus', *Journal of Consulting Psychology*, 28: 23–33.

LeVine, R.A. (1973) *Culture, Behavior and Personality*, Chicago: Aldine.

LeVine, R.A. (1990) 'Infant environments in psychoanalysis', in J.W. Stigler, R.A. Shweder and G. Herdt (eds), *Cultural Psychology: Essays on Comparative Human Development*. New York: Cambridge University Press.

LeVine, R.A., Miller, P.M. and West, M.M. (eds) (1988) *Parental Behavior in Diverse Societies: New Directions For Child Development*. San Francisco: Jossey-Bass.

Levinson, S.C. (1983) *Pragmatics*. Cambridge: Cambridge University Press.

Levinson, S.C. (1988) 'Putting linguistics on a proper footing: explorations in Goffman's concepts of participation', in P. Drew and A. Wootton (eds), *Erving Goffman: Studies in the Interaction Order*. Cambridge: Polity, pp. 161–289.

Levy, R.I. (1973) *Tahitians: Mind and Experience in the Society Islands*. Chicago: University of Chicago Press.

Levy, R.I. (1984) 'Emotion, knowing and culture', in R.A. Shweder and R.A. LeVine (eds), *Culture Theory: Essays on Mind, Self and Emotion*. New York: Cambridge University Press, pp. 214–38.

Lieberman, P. (1984) *The Biology and Evolution of Language*. Cambridge, MA: Harvard University Press.

Lieberman, P. (1985) 'On the evolution of human syntacticability. Its pre-adaptive bases – motor control and speech', *Journal of Human Evolution*, 14: 657–68.

Lieberman, P. (1988) 'Voice in the wilderness: how humans acquired the power of speech', *The Sciences*, July/August: 23–9.

Lock, A. (ed.) (1978) *Action, Gesture and Symbol: the Emergence of Language*. New York: Academic Press.

Lofland, Lyn H. (1985) 'The social shaping of emotion: the case of grief', *Symbolic Interaction*, 8: 171–90.

Luff, P., Frohlich, D. and Gilbert, G.N. (eds) (1990) *Computers and Conversation*. New York: Academic Press.

Lunt, P.K. (1988) 'The perceived causal structure of examination failure', *British Journal of Social Psychology*, 27: 171–80.

Lutz, C. (1988) *Unnatural Emotions: Everyday Sentiments on a Micronesian Atoll and their Challenge to Western Theory*. Chicago: University of Chicago Press.

Lutz, C. and White, G. (1986) 'The anthropology of emotions', *Annual Review of Anthropology*, 15: 405–36.

Malatesta, C.Z. and Izard, C.E. (1984) *Emotion in Adult Development*, Beverley Hills: Sage.

Marriott, M. (ed.) (1990) *India through Hindu Categories*. Contributions to Indian Sociology, Occasional Studies 5. New Delhi: Sage.

Martin, C.L. and Halverson, C.F. (1981) 'A schematic processing model of sex typing and stereotyping in children', *Child Development*, 52: 1119–34.

McArthur, L.Z. (1972) 'The how and what of why: some determinants and consequences of causal attributions', *Journal of Personality and Social Psychology*, 22: 171–88.

Middleton, D.J. and Edwards, D. (1993) *Collective Remembering*. London and Los Angeles: Sage.

Middleton, D.J. and Edwards, D. (1990) 'Conversational remembering: a social psychological approach', in D.J. Middleton and D. Edwards (eds), *Collective Remembering*. London: Sage.

Miller, Jean Baker (1983) 'The construction of anger in women and men', Stone Center for Developmental Services and Studies, Work in Progress no. 83-01. Wellesley, MA.

Mills, C.W. (1940) 'Situated actions and vocabularies of motive', *American Sociological Review*, 5: 904–13.

Mischel, W. (1968) *Personality and Assessment*. Stanford: Stanford University Press.

Mitchell, J. (1991) 'Sour times in Sweet Home', *Audobon*, March: 86–97.

Molotch, H.L. and Boden, D. (1985) 'Talking social structure: discourse, domination and the Watergate hearings', *American Sociological Review*, 50: 273–88.

Moore, Barrington, Jr (1978) *Injustice: the Social Bases of Obedience and Revolt*. New York.

Morsbach, H. and Tyler, W.J. (1986) 'A Japanese emotion: *amae*', in Rom Harré (ed.), *The Social Construction of Emotions*. New York: Basil Blackwell.

Much, N. (1995) 'Cultural psychology', in J. Smith, R. Harré and L. Van Langenhove (eds), *Rethinking Psychology*. London: Sage.

Muhlhäusler, P. and Harré, R (1991) *Pronouns and People*. Oxford: Blackwell.

Mumford, S.R. (1989) *Himalayan Dialogue: Tibetan Lamas and Gurung Shamans in Nepal*. Madison, WI: University of Wisconsin Press.

Neisser, U. (1967) *Cognitive Psychology*. New York: Appleton-Century-Crofts.

Neisser, U. (1976) *Cognition and Reality*. San Francisco: W.H. Freeman.

Neisser, U. (1981) 'John Dean's memory: a case study', *Cognition*, 9: 1–22.

Neisser, U. (1982) *Memory Observed: Remembering in Natural Contexts*. Oxford: W.H. Freeman.

Neisser, U. (1985) 'Toward an ecologically orientated cognitive science', in T.M. Schlechter and M.P. Toglia (eds), *New Directions in Cognitive Science*. Norwood, NJ: Ablex.

Nelson, K. (1973) 'Structure and strategy in learning to talk', *Monographs of the Society of Research in Child Development*, 149.

Nelson, K. (1981) 'Social cognition in a script framework', in J.H. Flavell and J. Ross (eds), *Social Cognitive Development: Frontiers and Possible Futures*. Cambridge: Cambridge University Press.

Neuman, D.M. (1990) *The Life of Music in North India: the Organization of an Artistic Tradition*. Chicago: University of Chicago Press.

Newson, J. (1978) 'Dialogue and development', in A. Lock (ed.), *Action, Gesture and Symbol: the Emergence of Language*. New York: Academic Press.

Obeyesekere, G. (1981) *Medusa's Hair*. Chicago: University of Chicago Press.

Obeyesekere, G. (1991) *The Work of Culture: Symbolic Transformation on Psychoanalysis and Anthropology*. Chicago: University of Chicago Press.

Oravec, C. (1981) 'John Muir, Yosemite, and the sublime response: a study in the rhetoric of preservationism', *Quarterly Journal of Speech*, 67: 245–58.

Oravec, C. (1984) 'Conservationism vs. preservationism: the public interest in the Hetchy–Hetchy controversy', *Quarterly Journal of Speech*, 70: 444–58.

Pearce, W.B. and Cronen, V.E. (1980) *Communication, Action and Meaning: the Creation of Social Realities*, New York: Praeger.

Piaget, J. (1954) *The Child's Construction of Reality* (trans M. Cook). New York: Basic Books.

Piaget, J. (1962) *Play, Dreams and Imagination in Childhood* (trans C. Gattengo and F.M. Hodgson). New York: W.W. Norton.

Piaget, P. and Inhelder, B. (1969) *The Psychology of the Child*. London: Routledge & Kegan Paul.

Pines, Ayala and Aronson, Eliot (1983) 'Antecedents, correlations and consequences of sexual jealousy', *Journal of Personality*, 51: 126–40.

Pollner, M. (1987) *Mundane Reason*. Cambridge: Cambridge University Press.

Pomerantz, A. (1978) 'Attributions of responsibility: blamings', *Sociology*, 12: 115–21.

Pomerantz, A. (1980) 'Telling my side: "limited access" as a fishing device', *Sociological Inquiry*, 50: 186–98.

Pomerantz, A. (1984) 'Giving a source or basis: the practice in conversation of telling "how I know"', *Journal of Pragmatics*, 8: 607–25.

Pomerantz, A. (1986) 'Extreme case formulations: a new way of legitimating claims', *Human Studies*, 9: 219–30.

Pomerantz, A. (1989) 'Constructing skepticism: four devices used to engender the audience's skepticism', *Research on Language and Social Interaction*, 22: 293–314.

Potter, J. (1984) 'Testability, flexibility: Kuhnian values in psychologists' discourse concerning theory choice', *Philosophy of the Social Sciences*, 14: 303–30.

Potter, J. and Edwards, D. (1990) 'Nigel Lawson's tent: discourse analysis, attribution theory and the social psychology of fact', *European Journal of Social Psychology*, 20: 24–40.

Potter, J. and Mulkay, M. (1985) 'Scientists' interview talk: interviews as a technique for revealing participants' interpretative practices', in M. Brenner, J. Brown and D. Canter (eds), *The Research Interview: Uses and Approaches*. London: Academic Press.

Potter, J., Stringer, P. and Wetherell, M. (1984) *Social Texts and Context: Literature and Social Psychology*. London: Routledge.

Potter, J. and Wetherell, M. (1987) *Discourse and Social Psychology: Beyond Attitudes and Behaviour*, London: Sage.

Potter, J. and Wetherell, M. (1988) 'Accomplishing attitudes: fact and evaluation in racist discourse', *Text*, 8: 51–68.

Potter, J., Wetherell, M., Gill, R. and Edwards, D. (1990) 'Discourse – noun, verb or social practice?', *Philosophical Psychology*, 3: 205–17.

Rathus, S.A. (1976) *Evolution*. Harmondsworth, Penguin.

Rathus, S.A. (1988) *Understanding Child Development*. New York: Holt, Rinehart and Winston.

Ratner, C. (1989) 'A social constructionist critique of the naturalist theory of emotion', *Journal of Mind and Behavior*, 10: 211–31.

Rawson, P. (1978) *The Art of Tantra*. London: Thames and Hudson.

Rice, M.L. (1981) 'The language of television', unpublished manuscript, University of Kansas, Center for Research on the Influences of Television on Children.

Richards, M. (1974) 'First steps in becoming social', in M. Richards (ed.), *The Integration of a Child into a Social World*. Cambridge: Cambridge University Press.

Robinson, D.N. (1994) 'Wild beasts and idle humours: legal insanity and the finding of fault' in A. Phillips Griffiths (ed.) *Philosophy, Psychology and Psychiatry*. Cambridge: Cambridge University Press, pp. 159–77.

Rogoff, B. (1990) *Apprenticeship in Thinking*. New York: Oxford University Press.

Roland, A. (1988) *In Search of Self in India and Japan*. Princeton, NJ: Princeton University Press.

Rosaldo, M. (1980) *Knowledge and Passion: Ilongot Notions of Self and Social Life*. New York: Cambridge University Press.

Rosaldo, M. (1984) 'Toward an anthropology of self and feeling', in R.A. Shweder and R.A. Levine (eds), *Culture Theory: Essays on Mind, Self and Emotion*. New York: Cambridge University Press.

Rumelhart, D.E. (1975) 'Notes on a schema for stories', in D.G. Bobrow and A.M. Collins (eds), *Representation and Understanding: Studies in Cognitive Science*. New York: Academic Press.

Ryan, J. (1974) 'Early language development: towards a communicational analysis', in M. Richards (ed.), *The Integration of a Child into a Social World*. Cambridge: Cambridge University Press.

Ryle, G. (1949) *The Concept of Mind*. London: Hutchinson.

Sacks, H. (1992) *Lectures on Conversation*. 2 vols. Oxford: Blackwell.

Salovey, Peter (1991) *The Psychology of Jealousy and Envy*. New York: Guilford Press.

Sampson, E.E. (1988) 'The deconstruction of self', in J. Shotter and K. Gergen (eds), *Texts of Identity*. London: Sage.

Sapir, Edward (1986) *Selected Writings of Edward Sapir in Language, Culture and Personality* (1949).

Sartre, J.-P. (1957) *Being and Nothingness*.

Schank, R.C. (1982) *Dynamic Memory: a Theory of Reminding and Learning in Computers and People*. Cambridge: Cambridge University Press.

Schank, R.C. and Abelson, R. (1977) *Scripts, Plans, Goals and Understanding*. Hillsdale, NJ: Lawrence Erlbaum Associates.

Schegloff, E.A. (1972) 'Notes on a conversational practice: formulating place', in D. Sudnow (ed.), *Studies in Social Interaction*. Glencoe: Free Press.

Schegloff, E.A. (1988) 'Presequences and indirection: applying speech act theory to ordinary conversation', *Journal of Pragmatics*, 12: 55–62.

Schegloff, E.A. and Sacks, H. (1973) 'Opening up closings', *Semiotica*, 7: 289–327.

Schwartz, T.G.M., White, G.M. and Lutz, C. (1992) *New Directions in Psychological Anthropology*. Cambridge: Cambridge University Press.

Seidman, Steven (1991) *Romantic Longings: Love in America, 1830–1980*. New York: Routledge.

Semin, G. and Fiedler, K. (1988) 'The cognitive functions of linguistic categories in describing persons: social cognition and language. *Journal of Personality and Social Psychology*, 54: 558–68.

Semin, G. and Fiedler, K. (1989) 'Relocating attributional phenomena within a language–

cognition interface: the case of actors' and observers' perspectives', *European Journal of Social Psychology*, 19: 491–508.

Shotter, J. (1971) 'The acquisition of syntax', in E. Ingram and R. Huxley (eds), *Language Acquisition: Models and Methods*. New York: Academic Press.

Shotter, J. (1974) 'The development of personal powers', in M. Richards (ed.), *The Integration of a Child into a Social World*. Cambridge: Cambridge University Press.

Shotter, J. (1976) 'Acquired powers: the transformation of natural into social powers', in R. Harré (ed.), *Personality*. Totowa, NJ: Rowman and Littlefield.

Shweder, R.A. (1977) 'Likeness and likelihood in everyday thought', *Current Anthropology*, 18: 637–58. Reprinted in P.N. Johnson-Laird and P.C. Wason (eds), *Thinking: Readings in Cognitive Science*. New York: Cambridge University Press, 1978.

Shweder, R.A. (1979) 'Rethinking culture and personality theory. Part I: A critical examination of two classical postulates', *Ethos*, 7: 255–78. Part II, *Ethos*, 7: 279–311. Part III, *Ethos*, 8: 60–94.

Shweder, R.A. (1991) *Thinking through Cultures*. Chicago: Chicago University Press.

Shweder, R.A. and Bourne, E.J. (1982) 'Does the concept of the person vary cross-culturally?', in A.J. Marsella and G.M. White (eds), *Cultural Conceptions of Mental Health and Therapy*. Dordrecht and Boston: D. Reidel. Also in R.A. Shweder and D. Fiske (eds), *Pluralisms and Subjectivities in the Social Sciences*.

Shweder, R.A. and Miller, J.G. (1985) 'The social construction of the person: how is it possible?', in Kenneth J. Gergen and Keith E. Davis (eds), *The Social Construction of the Person*. New York: Springer, pp. 41–69.

Sinclair, H. (1972) 'A study in developmental linguistics', *Journal of Child Psychology*, 14: 328–48.

Singer, M. (1972) *When a Great Tradition Modernizes*. Chicago: University of Chicago Press.

Sinnott, J.M., Pison, B.D. and Askin, R.N. (1983) 'A comparison of pure auditory thresholds in human infants and adults', *Infant Behavior and Development*, 6: 3–18.

Slugoski, B.R. (1983) 'Attribution and conversational context', paper presented to the Annual Social Psychology Section Conference of the British Psychological Society, Sheffield, UK.

Slugoski, B.R., Lalljee, M. and Lamb, R. (1985) 'Conversational constraints on the production and interpretation of explanations', paper presented to the Annual Social Psychology Section Conference of the British Psychological Society, Cambridge, UK.

Smith, D. (1990) *Texts, Facts and Femininity*. London: Routledge.

Smith, R., Anderson, D.R. and Fischer, C. (1985) 'Young children's comprehension of montage', *Child Development*, 56: 962–71.

Spiro, M. (1984) 'Some reflections on cultural determinism and relativism with special reference to emotion and reason', in R.A. Shweder and R.A. LeVine (eds), *Culture Theory: Essays on Mind, Self and Emotion*. New York: Cambridge University Press.

Stearns, Carol Zisowitz (1993) 'Sadness', in Jeanette Haviland and Michael Lewis (eds), *Handbook of Emotion*. New York: Guilford Press.

Stearns, Carol Zisowitz and Stearns, Peter N. (1986) *Anger: the Struggle for Emotional Control in America's History*. Chicago: University of Chicago Press.

Stearns, Peter N. (1989) *Jealousy: the Evolution of an Emotion in American History*. New York: New York University Press.

Stearns, Peter N. (1994) *American Cool: Developing a Twentieth-Century Emotional Style*. New York: University Press.

Stearns, Peter N. and Haggerty, Timothy (1991) 'The role of fear: transitions in American emotional standards for children, 1850–1950', *American Historical Review*, 96: 63–94.

Stern, Daniel N. (1985) *The Interpersonal World of the Infant: a View from Psychoanalysis and Developmental Psychology*. New York: Basic Books.

Stroebe, Margaret, Gergen, Mary, Gergen, Kenneth and Stroebe, Wolfgang (1992) 'Broken hearts in broken bonds', *American Psychologist*, 47: 1205–12.

Suchman, L. (1987) *Plans and Situated Actions: the Problem of Human–Machine Interaction*. Cambridge: Cambridge University Press.

Tambiah, S.J. (1985) *Culture, Thought and Social Action: an Anthropological Perspective.* Cambridge, MA: Harvard University Press.

Tetlock, P.E. (1985) 'Accountability: a social check on the fundamental attribution error', *Social Psychology Quarterly*, 48: 227–36.

Thorndyke, P.W. (1977) 'Cognitive structures in comprehension and memory of narrative discourse', *Cognitive Psychology*, 9: 77–110.

Turnbull, W. and Slugoski, B.R. (1988) 'Conversational and linguistic processes in causal attribution', in D.J. Hilton (ed.), *Contemporary Science and Natural Explanation: Commonsense Conceptions of Causality.* Brighton: Harvester, pp. 66–93.

Turner, V. (1974) *Dramas, Fields, and Metaphors.* Ithaca, NY: Cornell University Press.

Turner, V. (1980) 'Social dramas and stories about them', *Critical Inquiry*, 7: 141–68.

Van Dijk, T.A. (ed.) (1985) *Handbook of Discourse Analysis.* London: Academic Press.

Van Kleeck, M.H., Hillger, L.A. and Brown, R. (1988) 'Pitting verbal schemas against information variables in attribution', *Social Cognition*, 6: 89–106.

Vygotsky, L. (1962) *Thought and Language* (trans E. Hofmann and G. Vakar). Cambridge, MA: MIT Press.

Vygotsky, L.S. (1976) 'Play and its role in mental development of the child', in J.S. Bruner, A. Jolly and K. Sylva (eds), *Play: its Role in Development and Evolution.* Harmondsworth: Penguin.

Watson, R. (1983) 'The presentation of victim and motive in discourse: the case of police interrogations and interviews', *Victimology*, 8: 31–52.

Westcott, M. (1988) *The Psychology of Human Freedom.* New York: Springer.

Westcott, M. (1992) 'The discursive production of human freedom', *American Behavioral Scientist*, 36: 73–87.

Wetherell, M. and Potter, J. (1989) 'Narrative characters and accounting for violence', in J. Shotter and K. Gergen (eds), *Texts of Identity.* London: Sage, pp. 206–19.

Wetherell, M. and Potter, J. (1992) *Mapping the Language of Racism: Discourse and the Legitimation of Exploitation.* Brighton: Harvester/Wheatsheaf, New York: Columbia University Press.

Whiting, B. (1980) 'Culture and social behavior: a model for the development of social behavior', *Ethos*, 2: 95–116.

Whiting, B. and Edwards, C. (1988) *Children of Different Worlds.* Cambridge, MA: Harvard University Press.

Whiting, B. and Whiting, J.W.M. (1975) *Children of Six Cultures: a Psycho-Cultural Analysis.* Cambridge, MA: Harvard University Press.

Whiting, J.W.M. (1977) 'A model for psychocultural research', in P.H. Leiderman, S.R. Tulkin and A. Rosenfeld (eds), *Culture and Infancy: Variations in Human Experience.* New York: Academic Press.

Whiting, J.W.M. (1990) 'Adolescent rituals and identity conflicts', in J.W. Stigler, R.A. Shweder and G. Herdt (eds), *Cultural Psychology: Essays on Comparative Human Development.* New York: Cambridge University Press.

Whiting, J.W.M. (1992) *Culture and Human Development: the Whiting Model.* New York: Cambridge University Press.

Whiting, J.W.M. and Child, Irwin L. (1953) *Child Training and Personality.* New Haven, CT.

Winograd, T. (1972) *Understanding Natural Language.* New York: Academic Press.

Winograd, T. (1980) 'What does it mean to understand language?' *Cognitive Science*, 4, 209–41.

Wittgenstein, L. (1953) *Philosophical Investigations.* Oxford: Blackwell.

Wolf, E. (1988) *Treating the Self: Elements of Clinical Self Psychology.* New York: Guilford.

Wooffitt, R. (1990) 'On the analysis of interaction: an introduction to conversation analysis', in P. Luff, D. Frohlich and G.N. Gilbert (eds), *Computers and Conversation.* New York: Academic Press, pp. 7–38.

Wooffitt, R. (1992) *Telling Tales of the Unexpected: the Organization of Factual Discourse.* Hemel Hempstead, UK: Harvester Wheatsheaf.

Woolgar, S. (1980) 'Discovery: logic and sequence in a scientific text', in R. Krohn, K. Knorr and R.D. Whitley (eds), *The Social Process of Scientific Investigation*. Dordrecht: Reidel, pp. 239–68.

Woolgar, S. (1988) *Science: the Very Idea*. London: Tavistock.

Wowk, M. (1984) 'Blame allocation, sex and gender in a murder interrogation', *Women's Studies International Forum*, 7: 75–82.

Yearley, S. (1985) 'Vocabularies of freedom and resentment: a Strawsonian perspective on the nature of argumentation in science and the law', *Social Studies of Science*, 15: 99–126.

Yearley, S. (1986) 'Interactive-orientation and argumentation in scientific texts', in J. Law (ed.), *Power, Action and Belief: a New Sociology of Knowledge*. London: Routledge.

Yearley, S. (1987) 'Demotic logic: causal discourse and the structure of explanations', *Text*, 7: 181–203.

Yearley, S. (1988) 'Settling accounts: action, accounts and sociological explanation', *British Journal of Sociology*, 39: 579–99.

Index